Carlos A. Segovia

**The Quranic Noah and the Making of the Islamic Prophet**

# Judaism, Christianity, and Islam – Tension, Transmission, Transformation

Edited by Patrice Brodeur, Carlos Fraenkel, Assaad Elias Kattan, and Georges Tamer

## Volume 4

Carlos A. Segovia

# The Quranic Noah and the Making of the Islamic Prophet

A Study of Intertextuality and Religious Identity Formation in Late Antiquity

DE GRUYTER

ISBN 978-3-11-053343-9
e-ISBN (PDF) 978-3-11-040589-7
e-ISBN (EPUB) 978-3-11-040605-4
ISSN 2196-405X

**Library of Congress Cataloging-in-Publication Data**
A CIP catalog record for this book has been applied for at the Library of Congress.

**Bibliographic information published by the Deutsche Nationalbibliothek**
The Deutsche Nationalbibliothek lists this publication in the Deutsche Nationalbibliografie; detailed bibliographic data are available on the Internet at http://dnb.dnb.de.


Typesetting: Dörlemann Satz GmbH & Co. KG, Lemförde
Printing and binding: CPI books GmbH, Leck
∞ Printed on acid-free paper
Printed in Germany

www.degruyter.com

To Olga

# Table of Contents


Abbreviations —— XI
List of Tables —— XIII
Foreword and Acknowledgements —— XV
Chapter 1 / Introduction: The Quranic Noah and the Re-mapping of Early Islamic Studies —— 1
Chapter 2 / Tracing the Apocalyptic Noah in Pre-Islamic Jewish and Christian Literature —— 21
Excursus. A Lost Apocalypse of Noah? —— 26
Chapter 3 / Noah in the Qur'ān: An Overview —— 28
*Excursus A.* Full text and translation of the quranic Noah narratives —— 35
*Excursus B.* Quranic allusions to Noah outside the quranic Noah narratives —— 51
Chapter 4 / The Quranic Noah Narratives: Form, Content, Context, and Primary Meaning —— 56
*Quranic Noah narrative no. I* (Q 7:59–64 / *Sūrat al-A'rāf*): —— 57
*Quranic Noah narrative no. II* (Q 10:71–4 / *Sūrat Yūnus*): —— 58
*Quranic Noah narrative no. III* (Q 11:25–49 / *Sūrat Hūd*): —— 59
*Quranic Noah narrative no. IV* (Q 23:23–30 / *Sūrat al Mu'minūn*): —— 59
*Quranic Noah narrative no. V* (Q 26:105–22 / *Sūrat aš-Šu'arā*): —— 60
*Quranic Noah narrative no. VI* (Q 54:9–17 / *Sūrat al-Qamar*): —— 60
*Quranic Noah narrative no. VII* (Q 71 / *Sūrat Nūḥ*): —— 61
*Excursus.* Reworked texts in the quranic Noah narratives —— 63
Chapter 5 / Reading Between the Lines: The Quranic Noah Narratives as Witnesses to the Life of the Quranic Prophet? —— 65
*Excursus A.* The original story behind the Noah narratives in Q 11 and 71 —— 72
*Excursus B.* Q 11:35,49 and the redactional scribal background of the Qur'ān —— 87
Chapter 6 / Reading Backwards: Sources and Precedents of the Quranic Noah —— 89
*Excursus.* A Syriac source behind the blessing of Noah in Q 37.78–81? —— 94
Chapter 7 / Reading Forward: From the Quranic Noah to the Muhammadan *Evangelium* —— 104
*Excursus A.* Ibn Isḥāq's original Noah narrative —— 110
*Excursus B.* Re-imagining ancient messianic roles: Prophets, messiahs and charismatic leaders in the literature of Second Temple Judaism and earliest Christianity —— 112
Afterword: Reading Otherwise, or Re-imagining Muḥammad as a New Messiah —— 116

# Abbreviations

| | |
|---|---|
| ALD | Aramaic Levi Document |
| ApAb | Apocalypse of Abraham |
| Ar. | Aramaic |
| Arab. | Arabic |
| BCE | Before the common era |
| BCR | Biblioteca di Cultura Religiosa |
| BG | Berolinensis Gnosticus |
| BO | Biblica et Orientalia |
| BOT | Biblica: Old Testament |
| *BSOAS* | *Bulletin of the School of Oriental and African Studies* |
| BTS | Beiruter Texte und Studien |
| c. | Around (Latin: *circa*) |
| CD | Damascus Document |
| CE | Culture on the Edge |
| CE | Common era |
| CEJL | Commentaries on Early Jewish Literature |
| cf. | Compare (Latin: *confer*) |
| COP | Cambridge Oriental Publications |
| CSQ | Curzon Studies in the Qur'ān |
| d. | Died |
| Dan | Daniel |
| *DSD* | *Dead Sea Discoveries* |
| ed(s). | Edited by, editor(s) |
| e.g. | For example (Latin: *exemplum gratia*) |
| EJL | Early Judaism and Its Literature |
| EM | Études Musulmanes |
| 1En | 1 (Ethiopic) Enoch |
| 2En | 2 (Slavonic) Enoch |
| fol(s). | Leaf(/ves) (Latin: *folium/folia*) |
| frag(s). | Fragment(s) |
| Gen | Genesis |
| *IOS* | *Israel Oriental Studies* |
| HFS | Historisk-filosofiske Skrifter |
| HTS | Harvard Theological Studies |
| ID | L'Islam en débats |
| i.e. | That is (Latin: *id est*) |
| IPTSTS | Islamic Philosophy, Theology and Science – Texts and Studies |
| Isa | Isaiah |

| | |
|---|---|
| *JAOS* | *Journal of the American Oriental Society* |
| *JBL* | *Journal of Biblical Literature* |
| Jer | Jeremiah |
| *JLARC* | *Journal for Late Antique Religion and Culture* |
| *JMEOS* | *Journal of the Manchester Egyptian and Oriental Society* |
| *JNES* | *Journal of Near Eastern Studies* |
| JosAsen | Joseph and Aseneth |
| *JSAI* | *Jerusalem Studies in Arabic and Islam* |
| *JSP* | *Journal for the Study of the Pseudepigrapha* |
| l(l). | Line(s) |
| LAHR | Late Antique History and Religion |
| Lit. | Literarily |
| LSIS | Leiden Studies in Islam and Society |
| MAIBL | Memoires de l'Académie des Inscriptions et des Belles-Lettres |
| Matt | Matthew |
| MMW | Makers of the Muslim World |
| *MO* | *Manuscripta Orientalia* |
| ms(s). | Manuscript(s) |
| n(n). | Note(s) |
| NHC | Nag Hammadi Codex |
| NHMS | Nag Hammadi and Manichaean Studies |
| No(s). | Number(s) |
| NT | New Testament |
| NTT | *Nederlands Teologisch Tijdschrift* |
| Num | Numbers |
| OJC | Orientalia Judaica Christiana |
| PSITLH | Palgrave Series in Islamic Theology, Law, and History |
| Q | Qur'ān |
| 1QapGen | Genesis Apocryphon |
| 1QM | War Scroll |
| QNN(s) | Quranic Noah narrative(s) |
| QNN I | Quranic Noah narrative no. I |
| QNN II | Quranic Noah narrative no. II |
| QNN III | Quranic Noah narrative no. III |
| QNN IV | Quranic Noah narrative no. IV |
| QNN V | Quranic Noah narrative no. V |
| QNN VI | Quranic Noah narrative no. VI |
| QNN VII | Quranic Noah narrative no. VII |
| QP | Quranic prophet |
| 1QpHab | 1Q Commentary on Habakuk |

| | |
|---|---|
| 1QS | Rule of the Community |
| 4QpIsa | 4Q Commentary on Isaiah |
| 4QTanḥ | 4QTanḥûmîm |
| REB | Revised English Bible |
| Rev | Revelation |
| *RO* | *Res orientales* |
| RSQ | Routledge Studies in the Qur'ān |
| S | Ibn Hišām, *Sīra* |
| SHCNE | Studies in the History and Culture of the Near East |
| STDJ | Studies on the Texts of the Desert of Judah |
| SVT | Supplements to Vetus Testamentum |
| Syr. | Syriac |
| TBN | Themes in Biblical Narrative |
| TEG | Traditio Exegetica Graeca |
| TSQ | Texts and Studies on the Qur'ān |
| TLevi | Testament of Levi |
| VCSS | Variorum Collected Studies |
| vol(s). | Volume(s) |
| v(s). | Verse(s) |
| Zech | Zechariah |

# List of Tables

**Table 1.** The rhetorical scheme in the quranic Noah narratives — **30**
**Table 2.** Noah's distinctive traits in the Qur'ān — **31**
**Table 3.** The quranic Noah narratives — **35**
**Table 4.** Comparative length of the quranic Noah narratives — **57**
**Table 5.** Explicit (and implicit) alusions to the quranic prophet within the quranic Noah narratives — **62**
**Table 6.** Verses containing formulaic duplications and repetitions inside the quranic Noah narratives — **63**
**Table 7.** Intertwining between Noah and the quranic prophet in the quranic Noah narratives, major themes in these, and episodes in the life of the quranic Prophet thus hinted at — **71**

# Foreword and Acknowledgements

Over the past decades the field of early Jewish and Christian studies has been witness to a fascinating number of new, challenging proposals, hypotheses, methods, and insights. Almost everything previously believed about, say, the development of Jewish sectarianism in the Second Temple Period, the emergence and variety of the earliest Christian groups, the gradual formation of rabbinic Judaism, and/or the partings of the ways between Christianity and Judaism has been carefully re-examined and explained by putting forward diverse yet innovative scholarly approaches.

Unfortunately, the same cannot be said of the field of early Islamic studies, although some undeniable progress has been made in recent years. Still in its infancy because of the overly conservative views and methods assumed by most scholars working in it since the mid-19th century, this is a field in which the very basic questions must now be addressed with decision.

We still lack, for example, a critical edition of the Qur'ān. We do not know when exactly its *textus receptus* was established, even though a few new suggestions have been made in recent years. Nor have we been able to locate with accuracy the beginnings of Islam as a new, independent religion. The discovery of two South-Arabic inscriptions from the mid-6th century in Ma'rib (present-day Yemen) and Muraygān (Saudi Arabia) that invoke God as "the Merciful" and Jesus as "his Messiah" instead of "his Son," thus displaying the very same Christological formula contained in the Qur'ān, is certainly astonishing in this respect. So too is the fact that the first non-quranic mention of the word "Islam" occurs in the inscriptions of the Dome of the Rock in Jerusalem, which dates to the last decade of the 7th century. Likewise, it is difficult to say anything about the historical Muḥammad if we move beyond the traditional account of Islam's origins, and we definitely need to do so, given the overly literary nature of the earliest Islamic sources and the very late date when they were composed. To neglect these and other related issues would be like explaining the emergence of the earliest Christ-believing groups by exclusively relying on the author of Luke-Acts, who offers a rather monochrome picture of Christian beginnings centred upon what s/he retrospectively imagined as Paul's mission; or like accepting the Mishnaic and Talmudic legends about Yavneh as the actual birthplace of rabbinic Judaism.

In short, the dawn and early history of Islam must be studied afresh as part and parcel of the complex process of religious identity formation in late antiquity. But in order to achieve some success in this appealing task, we must go all the way and make use of the theoretical notions and the methodological tools provided by the new social-science and literary methods (critical discourse analysis, narrative theory, semiotics of religion, deconstructionist historiography, etc.) set forth in the study of Second Temple Judaism as well as the study of Christian and rabbinic origins. And to re-examine both the quranic narratives on prophecy and the early Muslim representation of Muḥammad as the Prophet of Islam seems to me a good place to start.

Accordingly, the present book is an attempt to explore Muḥammad's early representation from the perspective of quranic intertextuality. That is, my purpose is not to reconstruct the historical Muḥammad. My concern is rather to understand how Muḥammad's image was fabricated and how it eventually matched that of other prophets and/or charismatic figures distinctive to the sectarian milieu out of which Islam arose. But to understand this, one must first critically analyse what the Qur'ān tells us, either explicitly or implicitly, about the anonymous prophet often alluded to in its pages in the second person singular – who is, in my view, too easily identified with Muḥammad in spite of the scarce and possibly late mentions of the latter in the quranic text – and about one of his most salient, though heretofore neglected, intertextual models: Noah. Hopefully the reason for labelling him an "intertextual" model for the quranic prophet will become apparent in the pages that follow.

I would wish to thank Gabriel Said Reynolds (University of Notre Dame), Tommaso Tesei (Van Leer Jerusalem Institute), and especially Guillaume Dye (Free University of Brussels [ULB]) for their comments and critical insights on several sections of this book; the editors of the JCIT book series at De Gruyter, Patrice Brodeur, Carlos Fraenkel, Assaad Elias Kattan, and Georges Tamer, for agreeing to publish it; Alissa Jones Nelson, Albrecht Doehnert, Sophie Wagenhofer, Katrin Mittmann and Sabina Dabrowski, also at De Gruyter, for their kind encouragement and assistance; and above all my wife Olga for her wise advice and tender support. It is with much love and affection that I dedicate this book to her.

# Chapter 1 / Introduction: The Quranic Noah and the Re-mapping of Early Islamic Studies

The connections between formative Islam and late antique Judaism and Christianity have long deserved the attention of scholars of Islamic origins. Since the 19th century, Muḥammad's early Christian background, his complex attitude – and that of his immediate followers – towards Jews and Christians, and the presence of Jewish and Christian religious motifs in the quranic text and in the *Ḥadīṯ* corpus have been widely studied in the West. Yet from the 1970s onwards, a seemingly major shift has taken place in the study of Islam's origins. Whereas the grand narratives on the rise of Islam contained in at least some of the earliest Muslim writings have usually been taken to describe with some accuracy the hypothetical emergence of Islam in the Arabian Peninsula of the mid-7th-century, they are nowadays increasingly regarded as too late and ideologically biased – too eulogical, that is – to provide a reliable picture of Islam's origins. Accordingly, new timeframes ranging from the late-7th to the mid-8th century and a number of alternative geographies are currently being explored (see e.g., Ohlig and Puin 2010).

On the other hand, renewed attention is now also being paid to the once very plausible redactional and editorial stages of the Qur'ān and, thereby, to its presumed pre-canonical *Grundschirften*, in which a number of encrypted passages from the Old Testament Pseudepigrapha, the New Testament Apocrypha, and other writings of Jewish, Christian, and Manichaean provenance can likely be found (see e.g. Wansbrough 2004; Kropp 2007; Segovia and Lourié 2012). Likewise, the earliest Islamic community is presently regarded by a growing number of scholars as a somewhat undetermined monotheistic group that evolved from an original Jewish-Christian milieu into a distinct Muslim group perhaps much later than is commonly assumed and in a rather unclear way (cf. Hawting 1999; Nevo and Koren 2000; Donner 2010), or else as being originally a Christian movement (cf. Van Reeth 2011b; Segovia 2015a, 2015c, 2016). Finally, the biography of Muḥammad has also been recently challenged due to the paucity and, once more, the late date and literary nature of his earliest "biographies" (see e.g. Rubin 1998).

In sum, three major trends of thought define the field of early Islamic studies today: (*a*) the traditional Islamic view, which many non-Muslim scholars still uphold as well; (*b*) a number of revisionist views, which have contributed to reshaping afresh the contents, boundaries, and themes of the field itself by reframing the methodological and hermeneutical categories required in the academic study of Islamic origins; and (*c*) several still conservative but at the same time more cautious views that stand halfway between the traditional point of view and the revisionist views. Surveying the history of these three different approaches to the manner in which Islam irrupted in the late-antique Near East should provide the reader an introductory overview of the way in which this particular field of research has changed in the past decades.

The founding of the École Spéciale des Langues Orientales Vivantes in Paris in 1795 marked the beginnings of modern Islamic studies, for it was under the school's second director, Antoine Isaac Silvestre de Sacy, that the first systematic curriculum for the teaching of Islamic languages, culture and civilisation was established in Europe. Yet the modern study of the Qur'ān began with Gustav Flügel, Gustav Weil, and Theodor Nöldeke in mid-19th-century Germany. Flügel published the first modern edition of the Qur'ān in 1834 (which was largely used until the official Cairo edition appeared in 1923) and a *Concordance* to its Arabic text in 1842, while Weil and Nöldeke each published, in 1844 and 1860 respectively, a critical introduction to the quranic *textus receptus*. Weil's appeared in a second edition in 1878, and Nöldeke's, later completed by Friedrich Schwally (in 1909 and 1919) and Gotthelf Bergsträsser and Otto Pretzl (in 1938), soon became the seminal work in the field, gaining wide, even uncontested prestige until the present day (see Nöldeke, Schwally, Bergsträsser, and Pretzl 2013).

As to Muḥammad, the first modern studies were those published by Abraham Geiger in 1833, Gustav Weil in 1843, Aloys Sprenger between 1861 and 1869, William Muir between 1858 and 1894, and again Nöldeke in 1863. Geiger's pioneering essay on Muḥammad's life and Weil's study of the biblical legends known to the early Muslims (1845) were also the first books to explore a number of possible early Islamic borrowings from Judaism, while apparent Christian influences – on which a few authors such as Ignaz Goldziher and Henry Preserved Smith had already provided some useful insights – were first systematically explored by Carl Heinrich Becker in 1907. Yet modern scholarship on the beginnings of Islam is likewise indebted to the groundbreaking works of Goldziher, whose *Muhammedanische Studien*, published between 1889 and 1890, represented a first, successful, and in many ways still valid attempt to examine the making and early development of Islamic identity against its complex, in fact liminal religious setting.

For the most part, however, and notwithstanding their intrinsic value, these early studies – save those of Geiger and especially Goldziher, which were unconventional in both their approach and conclusions – tended to subscribe to, and thus validate, the traditional master narrative of Islam's origins. This is particularly noticeable in the case of Nöldeke, whose chronology of the quranic text largely follows the traditional Muslim chronology, and whose approach to the Qur'ān as a single-authored unitary document is anything but convincing to a postmodern mentality. Yet as Stephen Shoemaker rightly recalls (2012: 124–6),

Nöldeke had studied with, and was indeed the foremost disciple of, Heinrich Ewald, a conservative German theologian and orientalist who opposed the new critical methods essayed by Ferdinand-Christian Baur and the Tübingen School in the neighbouring field of early Christian studies. In Ewald's view, all that a scholar of early Islam was expected to do was to learn as much Arabic as s/he could and willingly accept the traditional account of the rise of Islam, whose veracity, therefore, ought not to be questioned. Supported by Nöldeke and his followers, this view rapidly became mainstream and has been prevalent in the field—with only a very few exceptions— ever since.

Other likewise prominent works published in the late-19th century and the first half of the 20th century (up to the late 1950s) include those of Hartwig Hirschfeld (1878, 1886, 1902), William Muir (1878, 1896), Charles Cutler Torrey (1892), William St Clair Tisdall (1905), Leone Caetani (1905–26), Israel Schapiro (1907), Paul Casanova (1911–24), Lazarus Goldschmidt (1916), Goldziher (1920), Wilhelm Rudolph (1922), Josef Horovitz (1926), Heinrich Speyer (1931), David Sidersky (1933), Anton Spitaler (1935), Richard Bell (1937–9), Arthur Jeffery (1937, 1938 [see now Jeffery 2007]), Régis Blachère (1947, 1949–50, 1957), and Thomas O'Shaughnessy (1948) on the Qur'ān; Karl Vollers (1906) and Alphonse Mingana (1933–9) on ancient Arabic language and manuscripts; David Samuel Margoliouth (1905, 1914), Arent Jan Wensinck (1908, 1928, 1932), Caetani (1910), Henri Lammens (1912, 1914, 1924, 1928), Bell (1926), Tor Andrae (1926, 1932), Blachère (1952), and William Montgomery Watt (1953, 1956) on Muḥammad, the early history of Islam, and early Muslim dogma; Alfred Guillaume (1924) and Wensinck (1927) on the early Islamic traditions; Joseph Schacht (1950) on the making of Islamic law; and Samuel Marinus Zwemer (1012), Wilhelm Rudolph (1922), Margoliouth (1924), Heinrich Speyer (1931), Torrey (1933), Haim Zeev (Joachim Wilhelm) Hirschberg (1939), Abraham Katsch (1954), Solomon Goiten (1955), and Denise Masson (1958) on early Jewish-Christian-Muslim relations. Among the major arguments, discussions, and controversies put forward in this period, the interpretation of emergent Islam as an heretical offshoot of Christianity (Lammens), the textual discrepancies between the old codices of the Qur'ān and its foreign vocabulary (Jeffery), and the representation of Muḥammad as either a statesman (Watt) or an apocalyptic prophet (Casanova) deserve special mention.

In the second half of the 20th century, growing attention was paid to the situation of the Arabian Peninsula on the eve of Islam and the archaeological witnesses available to us; the information supposedly gathered together by the early Muslim authors regarding the dawn of Islam and the different types of literature that they produced; the biography of Muḥammad and his polemics against both Jews and Christians; the language, structure, contents, message, and apparent Jewish and Christian subtexts of the Qur'ān, as well as its competing interpretative traditions; the formation of the Islamic state and the clash between different Muslim groups in the first centuries of Islamic rule; and both the non-Muslim views of Islam and the relation between Jews, Christians, and Muslims in the first Islamic centuries. Especially noteworthy were the works by François Déroche and Sergio Noja (1998–2001) on the early quranic manuscripts; Günter Lüling (1974), John Burton (1977), John Wansbrough (1977), Neal Robinson (1996), Stefan Wild (1996), and Andrew Rippin (1999) on the quranic corpus, its collection, function, style, contents, and presumably encrypted texts; Cornelis Versteegh (1993) on Arabic grammar and early quranic exegesis; Andrew Rippin (1988), Claude Gilliot (1990), and Marjo Buitelaar and Harald Motzki (1993) on the latter; Toshihiko Izutsu (1959) on quranic semantics; Helmut Gätjie (1971), Fazlur Rahman (1980), O'Shaughnessy (1969, 1985), and Jacques Berque (1993) on the teachings of the Qur'ān; Jacques Jomier (1959), Heikki Räisänen (1972), and Roberto Tottoli (1999) on the analogies and differences between several themes in the Bible and the Qur'ān; Youakim Moubarac (1998) and Reuven Firestone (1990) on the evolution of the Abraham-Ishmael legends in early Islam; David Thomas (1992), Steven Wasserstrom (1995), Camila Adang (1996), Michael Lecker (1998), and Uri Rubin (1999) on early Jewish-Christian-Muslim relations; Räisänen (1971) and Jane Dammen McAuliffe (1991) on the quranic image of Jesus and Christianity; Maxime Rodinson (1961), Watt (1961), Roger Arnaldez (1970), Noja (1974), Michael Cook (1983), Martin Lings (1983), Gordon Newby (1989), Francis Peters (1994), Rubin (1995, 1998), Marco Schöller (1998), and David Marshall (1999) on Muḥammad and his early biographies; Meir Kister (1980, 1990), and Shmuel Ahituv and Eliezer Oren (1998) on pre-Islamic Arabia and the rise of Islam; Schacht (1964), Albrecht Noth (1973), Wansbrough (1978), Gautier Juynboll (1983, 1996), Motzki (1991), and Fred Donner (1998) on the early Islamic traditions and literature; Watt (1973), Cook (1981), and Mohammad Ali Amir-Moezzi (1992) on the formative period of Islamic thought and early Islamic sectarianism; Patricia Crone (with Michael Cook and Martin Hinds, 1977, 1980, 1986, 1987a, 1987b), Donner (1981), Suliman Bashear (1984), Gerald Hawting (1986, 1999), Hamid Dabashi (1989), Garth Fowden (1993), Wilferd Madelung (1997), and Firestone (1999) on the rise of Islam and early Islamic history; and Bashear (1997) and Robert Hoyland (1997) on the early non-Muslim views of Islam.

A number of these studies (e.g., those of Schacht, Lüling, Wansbrough, Crone, Cook, Bashear, Hawting, Rippin, and Rubin) nonetheless adopted a highly critical view of the 'data' transmitted in the early Islamic sources about the economy and politics of 7th-century Arabia, the rise and early development of Islam, the alleged biography of Muḥammad, and the elaboration, collection, and later canonisation of the Qur'ān. Drawing partly on Goldziher, Schacht questioned the historicity of the *Ḥadīṯ* collections. Lüling attempted to reconstruct the textual materials later reworked into the Qur'ān and suggested that they were Christian liturgical texts. Wansbrough analysed both the Qur'ān and the earliest Islamic writings about the rise of Islam with the tools of biblical criticism and concluded that if the former ought to be regarded as a collection of originally independent texts, which were later unified by means of certain rhetorical conventions, about whose origin and function we know almost nothing, then the earliest Islamic sources should likewise be envisaged as elaborated literary reports that tell us more about their authors' concerns than about how things really took place – a point of view shared by Rubin in spite of his more traditional curriculum. For their part, Crone and Cook analysed the way in which such purely literary sources re-presented the rise of Islam and its historical and geographic background by reviewing the non-Muslim documents contemporary with the emergence and early expansion of Islam, in addition to which they also studied the plausibly limited role played by the Arabian Peninsula along the trade routes of the late-antique Near East, which led them to cast doubts on the apparent causes that coalesced to make possible the rise of Islam. Bashear also rejected the traditional account of Islam's origins and ventured a new interpretation, according to which Islam gradually arose from within a Jewish-Christian context – a thesis that was independently developed by Hawting, a pupil of Wansbrough, who later focused his research on the first centuries of Islamic rule. Another of Wansbrough's disciples, Rippin, undertook the task of scrutinising the beginnings of quranic exegesis.

Accustomed to looking at things through the lens of the Muslim tradition, many scholars were not convinced by these revisionist approaches, which they judged to be excessively controversial and have often been passionately dismissed rather than theoretically discussed. Yet a number of such scholars felt compelled to at least embrace the innovative and rich terminology displayed in those audacious studies, or else realised that, notwithstanding their hypercritical results, some of the new methodologies displayed in them could be profitable in some measure and contribute to renewing the field of early Islamic studies. Moreover, this twofold attitude has made possible the appearance of the still conservative but somewhat more cautious view currently shared, though differently approached and developed, by a growing number of early Islamic scholars, who generally claim that even though the early written sources of Islam may very well date to a later period, they are reliable enough and offer us a fair picture of the events they comment upon or describe, and that the contradictions inherent in them do not preclude the veracity of the master narrative displayed by their authors, which therefore should remain unchallenged. The aforementioned works by Motzki and Donner adequately illustrate this appeasing approach, which Angelika Neuwirth, Michael Marx, and Nicolai Sinai have recently endorsed in their quranic studies as well. But judging from their supporters' overall conventional theoretical approach, it is difficult to tell whether this moderate and at times apparently sophisticated view truly offers a fresh look into the origins of Islam or merely serves to disguise the same old ideas advocated by earlier, more conservative scholars. Still, it is the view that has gained widest acceptance in the field in the past decade.

More or less sensitive to the paradigm shift encouraged by Schacht's, Lüling's, Wansbrough's, and Bashear's studies, *inter alios* – i.e., oscillating between its partial acceptance and its refusal – among the major works published in the last fifteen years, one should mention McAullife's encyclopaedia of the Qur'ān (2001–6); Cook's introduction (2001) and McAuliffe and Rippin's companions to the quranic corpus (2006); Isa Boullata's and Daniel Madigan's volumes on the religious language of the Qur'ān and the quranic self-image (2000 and 2001, respectively); Déroche's study on its written transmission and earliest manuscripts (2009, 2014); Neuwirth's several volumes on the Qur'ān as a late-antique text and the so-called Meccan suras (2007, 2010, 2011, 2015); Neuwirth, Marx, and Sinai's volume on the quranic milieu (2011); Rippin's new explorations of, and Sinai's essay on, quranic interpretation (1999, 2001, and 2009, respectively); Tottoli's study on the Bible and the Qur'ān (1999) and Reeves' volume on quranic and biblical intertextuality (2003); Amir-Moezzi's dictionary of the Qur'ān (2007); Emran El-Badawi's study on the Qur'ān and the Aramaic Gospel traditions (2014); Norman Calder, Jawid Mojaddedi, and Rippin's sourcebook of early Muslim literature (2002); Jonathan Brockopp's companion to Muḥammad (2010); Irving Zeitlin's study on the historical Muḥammad (2007); Motzki's (2000) and Andreas Goerke and Georg Schoeler's (2008) volumes on the biography of Muḥammad; Donner's and Aziz al-Azmeh's monographs on the origins of Islam (2010 and 2014, respectively); Crone's essay on the establishment of the Islamic empire (2010); Cook's (2004b) and Hawting's (2004) studies on the origins of Muslim culture and tradition and the development of Islamic ritual; Chase Robinson's essays on Islamic historiography (2003), the Muslim conquests (2004), and the formation of the Islamic state (2005); Andrew Marsham's on the early Islamic monarchy (2009); Maria Dakake's, William Tucker's, and Najam Haider's essays on early Shiite identity (2007, 2008, and 2011, respectively); Milka Levy-Rubin's study on non-Muslims in early Islam (2011); Michael Bonner's research on early Arab-Byzantine relations (2004); David Thomas's and Michael Philip Penn's volumes on the relations between Syriac Christianity and early Islam (2001 and 2015, respectively); Barbara Roggema's study on Syriac apocalyptic responses to the rise of Islam (2009); Emmanouela Grypeou, Mark Swanson, and Thomas's volumes on the encounter of eastern Christianity with early Islam (2006, 2013); Sidney Griffith's study on the cultural and intellectual life of the Christians living under early Islamic rule (2012); Fowden's recent essay (2014) on the relationship between

Graeco-Roman, Syrian Christian, Jewish, Arab, Iranian, and early Islamic cultures in late antiquity; Eger's likewise recent volume on the early Islamic-Byzantine frontier (2014); George Tamer's study on the implicit references to, and the discussion of, the Hellenistic worldview and its notion of time in pre-Islamic Arabian poetry and the Qur'ān (2008); and Jonathan Berkey's comprehensive handbook of Islamic history (2003).

At the same time, and considering that the entire narrative of Islamic origins is worth being retold, several scholars have fully assumed the need to look at things from a new perspective, and their insights have contributed to further developing various revisionist views by exploring afresh – albeit not with equally convincing results, but this is normal in any academic discipline – issues such as the relationship between method and theory in the study of Islamic origins (Berg 2003), the sectarian and cultural milieu out of which Islam emerged (Gallez 2005; Segovia and Lourié 2012; González Ferrín 2013, Zellentin 2013), and its beginnings (Nevo and Koren 2000; de Prémare 2002; Ohlig and Puin 2010; Micheau 2012); the authenticity of the Qur'ān (Sfar 2000) and its possible Syro-Aramaic subtexts (Luxenberg 2000); the origins and function of the quranic collection and the results of its contemporary study with the tools of biblical criticism (de Prémare 2004; Kropp 2007; Pohlmann 2013); the Qur'ān's historical context and its biblical subtexts (Reynolds 2008, 2010, 2011b), its complex textuality and rhetoric (Cuypers and Gobillot 2007; Azaiez 2015), its canonisation and sacred character (De Smet, Callatay, and van Reeth 2004; De Smet and Amir-Moezzi 2014); Muḥammad's biography (Powers 2011, 2014; Shoemaker 2012); the making of the early Islamic tradition (Berg 2000; Bashear 2004; Shoshan 2004; Reynolds 2011b); the reworking of biblical figures in early Islam (Dye and Nobilio 2012); and early Islamic apocalypticism (Cook 2002).

However, challenging the ordinary picture of Islam's origins is perhaps only the showiest purpose of some of these studies – the essential one being the in-depth re-examination of the complex processes that led to Islam's formation. In order to fulfil this task, however, it seems necessary to assume once and for all the methodological theses so perspicaciously formulated by Aaron Hughes (2012: 128–31):

> [1] We must cease treating Islam . . . and Islamic data as if they were somehow special or privileged objects of study. . . . [2] It is time to identify all those approaches that masquerade as critical scholarship for what they are. . . . [3] Islamic studies must appeal to the theoretical framework of other disciplines. . . . [4] Finally, Islamic studies must integrate itself with those critical discourses within the academic study of religion that are non-phenomenological.

It should also be mentioned, in conclusion, that the field of early Islamic studies is now benefiting from the progress underway in the neighbouring fields of late-antique Near-Eastern studies (Shahid 1984a, 1984b, 1989, 1995; Hoyland 2001, 2015; Jan Retsö 2003; Iwona Gajda 2009; Joëlle Beaucamp, Françoise Briquel-Chatonnet, and Christian Robin 2010; Averil Cameron and Hoyland 2011; Greg Fisher 2011; Glen Bowersock 2012, 2013; Griffith 2013; Jetse Dijkstra and Fisher 2014; and Ward 2014) as well as late-antique and early-Islamic archaeology and epigraphy (Magness 2003; Avni 2014; Talgam 2014).

My belief is that studying the quranic Noah narratives – like any other quranic narratives for that matter – may in its own right contribute to the renewed study of Islam's origins, as they provide a fascinating albeit heretofore unexplored window into Jewish-Christian polemics and their formative influence upon Islam, the textual sources of the Qur'ān, the life of the quranic prophet as mirrored/shaped in the quranic text, and the subsequent making of the Islamic prophet in the Muhammadan *evangelium* (i.e., Muḥammad's *Sīra* or "biography"). In addition, they offer a likewise overlooked but extremely suggestive glimpse into what may be described as the earliest stage of the messianic controversy out of which Islam emerged as a new religion and the subsequent development of the early Islamic community. The present study examines the form, content, implicit purpose, and sources of these narratives, which so far have never been carefully scrutinised. It also explores, again for the first time, the use that the authors of the Muhammadan *evangelium* made of the quranic Noah and the implications of this for the critical study of Islam's beginnings.

As I have indicated above, this is a field nowadays undergoing a slow but decisive transformation. Until recently, late-antique religious identities, and Islam in particular, were normally taken to be already existent from the very beginning, i.e., regardless of the intricate, dynamic, and often ambiguous processes that resulted in their formation. Against this naive view, however, it now seems clear to an increasing number of scholars that religious identity-making usually undergoes a complex threefold process before becoming something definite and compelling: (1) unclear dissemination of more or less vague identity markers against a brewing background of common ideas and practices, (2) re-dissemination of such markers along new ad hoc but still fuzzy lines or axes of crystallisation, and (3) the final promotion and consolidation of these. In short, what usually begins as a juxtaposed set of indeterminate flows gradually transforms into an agglomeration of interdependent clusters before narrowing into a few well-defined realms, be they ideas, communities, texts, or practices. And if this notion rightly applies to the formation of Jewish, Christian, and Muslim identities, it may also be used to depict the progressive shaping of their core beliefs and authoritative texts – a context in which intertextuality often plays a remarkable part.

Abraham Geiger (1833) was the first scholar to emphasise the Qur'ān's connection to biblical and parabiblical literature, thus "extend[ing] the text's frame of reference beyond the narrow confines of [the] exclusively pagan 'age of ignorance'" (Neuwirth and Sinai 2011: 4) against whose background the traditional narrative of Islam's origins willingly sets the "revelation" of the Qur'ān. Studies as different from one another as those published over the past nine decades by Josef Horowitz (1926), Heinrich Speyer (1931), John Wansbrough (1977), Roberto Tottoli (1999), John Reeves (2003), and, more recently, Gabriel Reynolds (2010) and Emran El-Badawi (2014) variously draw on Geiger's pioneer approach. Reynolds, in particular, highlights the fact that "[t]he student of the Qur'ān should be always alert to the conversation that the Qur'ān conducts with earlier texts, and in particular to its intimate conversation with Biblical literature" (2010: 36), an expression by which he implicitly means – as can be safely deduced from his treatment of many pseudepigraphic and apocryphal writings – the parabiblical literary tradition as well. Moreover, he coins the term "subtext" as a synonym for the biblical and parabiblical literary tradition either explicitly or tacitly present in the Qur'ān (2010: 23). El-Badawi, in turn, speaks of an "intertextual dialogue" (2014: 7) whose many facets should be studied in order to gain a better understanding of the quranic corpus – a view shared by Tottoli and Reeves and also, although in a more complex form, by Wansbrough, who rightly notes that doctrinal stereotypes "have discouraged examination of the document as representative of a traditional literary type" (2004: xxi). Thus the renewed attention to quranic intertextualty, to which, *inter alia*, Tottoli, Reeves, Reynold and El-Badawi witness, seems to prove how very wrong Stefan Wild was in the mid-1990s when he stated that increasing scholarly interest in the Qur'ān as a textual corpus had displaced, if not eradicated, any virtual interest in its intertextual dimension (1996: vii-ix).

On the other hand, Angelika Neuwirth and Nicolai Sinai's fear that intertextual explorations of the Qur'ān might at times be "suspected of serving an underlying political agenda, ... namely, of aiming to demonstrate that the Qur'ān is nothing but a rehash of earlier traditions in order to discredit the Islamic faith and assert Western superiority" (2011: 4), seems absurd to me. For genuine scholarship serves no other purpose than that of academic research regardless of how its results may be reused, and eventually subverted, by pseudo- or non-scholars. To put it briefly, scholarship should never subordinate itself to other concerns, whether apologetic or destructive, pious or Islamophobic: just as Islamophobic prejudices should be denounced as such, Muslim convictions, however respectful one should be of them, cannot be placed beyond rational questioning, nor can critical thinking be identified with a "colonialist" tool, as the late Edward Said (1978) and many others after him seemingly pretend.

Instead of such cautious fear, one would rather expect a work devoted to scrutinising the quranic milieu to pay at least some attention to the latter's intertextual climate (and thereby to address the topic of its *Sitz im Literatur* in addition to analysing its alleged *Sitz im Leben*); just as one would naturally expect a six-volume encyclopaedia of the Qur'ān to include an entry on quranic intertextuality (whereas McAuliffe's *Encyclopedia* simply does not provide one!).

However, the unexamined notion that most scholars and laypeople have of what the *textus receptus* of the Qur'ān actually is may be the biggest handicap anyone working on quranic (inter-)textuality must confront from the very beginning.. For what we take to be the Qur'ān is but a variant reading among others that became authoritative around the 10th century; or, to put it in even more forceful terms, a variant reading of one of the different and differing codices/recensions of an earlier document which we simply lack – supposing there was one single document right from the start, which is doubtful at best (on which see Cook 2004a). Furthermore, it is not possible to document that particular codex, in spite of all the efforts made to date it back to the mid-7th century, before the 690s, or the early 8th century, as there is no earlier manuscript that matches it in its integrity (Déroche 2014). In fact, prior to that date we only have fragments whose nature seems anything but clear. Nor is it reasonable to pretend we can easily ascertain the type of document(s?) that those earlier preserved fragments belonged to. Yet one thing is sure: projecting onto them the notion of a pre-existing "Uthmanic codex" (i.e., the concept of a pre-Marwanid canonical Qur'ān) proves an unwarranted assumption, and thus makes little sense (see further de Prémare [2002: 296–7; 2010], who basically relies on Ibn Sa'd and persuasively points to 'Abd al-Malik b. Marwān as the true compiler of the Qur'ān; cf. Robinson [2005: 100–4], who independently reaches a similar conclusion; and both Neuwirth [2007: 18–22] and Hamdan [2011], who, while retaining the notion that there actually was an "Uthmanic codex" in 'Uṯmān's times, do admit the possible undertaking of a "second *maṣāḥif* project," in Hamdan's own words, under 'Abd al-Malik's rule).[1] Yet it is upon both that highly debatable retro-projection and the idea that the so-called "Uthmanic codex" contains only Muḥammad's *ipssima verba* that the Muslim exegetical tradition overtly builds its discourse.

Against this overly inoffensive view, however, an increasing number of quranic scholars are nowadays willing to admit that we simply do not yet have a clear picture of the prehistory of the Qur'ān and its collection. There is no denying, however, that just as new religions usually take shape only after some kind of dialectal variation is explicitly or tacitly allowed within a given religious milieu (for these are always complex and dynamic in their very nature), new normative texts usually spread out of a common multidimensional stock of previous writings inside a multifaceted, and again dynamic, scribal milieu. A close examination of quranic intertextuality should thus help to re-locate the quranic corpus in its late-antique near-eastern scribal setting, whereas avoiding this necessary move would just contribute to reinforcing the notion that, in contrast to any other late-antique writing, the Qur'ān stands, and must ultimately remain, as an isolated document.

To claim as Aziz al-Azmeh does, therefore, that "prioritising intertextuality analytically and interpretatively de-contextualises Qur'anic emergence and extrudes history from the picture, . . . [thus] lend[ing] credence to the situation wonderfully described by Paul Valéry as he spoke of 'an Orient of the mind': 'a state between waking and dreaming where there is no logic nor chronology to keep the elements of our memory from attracting each other in their natural combination'" (2013: 2), obliterates the fact that the only apparent "history" that we are still repeatedly asked to rely on is the literary story so carefully elaborated by the Muslim tradition. In contrast, prioritising intertextuality on the basis, say, of the explicit or implicit quranic reuse of earlier Jewish, Christian, and Manichaean texts would just help to welcome history into the picture for once, instead of clinging to a state closer to dreaming than waking, where both logic and chronology are sacrificed on the altar of a fabricated memory and hence re-shaped in an unnatural combination. For the traditional account of the collection of the Qur'ān provided in the early Islamic sources should be regarded not so much as an embellished report but as a powerful discursive strategy, which is worth being studied with the tools of critical discourse analysis.

Additionally, it should be clear that intertextual studies need not primarily aim at unraveling a series of literary influences between two or more texts. As David Clippinger argues,

> Intertextuality is a method of reading one text against another that illuminates shared textual and ideological resonances; the assertion that all texts and ideas exist within a fabric of relations. The term "intertextuality" refers to both a method of reading that juxtaposes texts in order to discover points of similarity and differences as well as the belief that all texts are part and parcel of a fabric of historical, social, ideological, and textual relations. As a whole, intertextuality suggests an important break with prior conceptions of the text as an autonomous entity separate from ideology and history. An intertextual reading, therefore, crosses disciplinary boundaries and challenges the perceived sanctity of genre by demonstrating that all texts and ideas draw upon similar ideological sources (2001: 190).

This is not the same as to say that some texts may have influenced the composition of other texts. Rather, it means that different texts can be studied together as being different, though interconnected, strata of an ongoing intellectual tradition, or regions of a single, though complex, ideological milieu. Boundaries may not always be easy to draw between such regions, nor do we always know what exactly belongs to each and what does not. The study of Islamic origins is particularly challenging in this regard, but it must doubtless move along intertextual lines in order to move forward beyond the grand narratives to which it has usually been subjected.

Actually, the quranic text itself hints in this direction when it complicates any plain equation between "revelation" (*tanzīl*), the "writing" (*kitāb*) said to contain it, the "signs" (*āyāt*) of such "writing," and its Arabic "recitation" (*qur'ān*). In Q 10.37 the "writing" and its "recitation" are clearly to be distinguished. So too in 41:3, where the latter is said to contain and to make clear the "signs" of the former (which might – only might – be taken to be equated in 41:2–3 with the "revelation" itself). Yet 43:3–4 equates the "recitation" neither with the "writing" nor with its "signs," but with the "matrix" or the "mother of the writing" (*umm al-kitāb*), where the "recitation" itself is said to be contained – but which is equated with the "writing" in 56:78 (cf. also 85:22)! While in 3:7, after explicitly equating the "writing" with the "revelation" itself, we read that only some parts of the "writing" (namely, its purely unambiguous verses) are identical to its "matrix"! What can we make of this? That is, how are we to understand these slippery categories? Is the "recitation" an outcome of the "writing," or must we place it above the writing, together with its "matrix"? Additionally, is the recitation equal to such a "matrix," or is it different from it insofar as it is merely said to be contained in it? Furthermore, how can the "recitation" be said to be contained in it while being, at the same time, a mere outcome of the "book" (literally, an exposition of its "signs")? And what about the "writing" itself? How can it be that only some parts of it are identical to the "matrix of the book," whereas its "recitation" is said to be fully contained in such a "matrix"? Where do the discarded parts of the "book" belong? And how then can the "writing" itself be equated with its "matrix"? To put it in more forceful terms: Why is it that we get the impression – as suggested by Michel Foucault in a different context – that when we try to organise such notions, say, by their shape (i.e., by their very own definition), the very function and the logical extension of each one varies, and that we face a similar problem when we try to organise them otherwise?[2] Certainly, one could also question the exact meaning and the rich connotations of the verbs *ṣaddaqa* (to confirm) and *faṣala* (to separate?) in 10:37, as well as those of the verbs *ǧamaʿa* (to collect) and *qara'a* (to recite) in 75:17–18. We could thereby ask what relationship there is to be found between them. Likewise, one can – and perhaps should – inquire into the exact meaning of the allusions to previous revelations, warnings, and legends (maybe also writings?) contained in 10:37; 25:4–6; 53:56. In short, we may very well demand whether the Qur'ān – or at least its *Grundschriften* – originally functioned as a sort of "palimpsest," as I have elsewhere suggested (Segovia 2012: 235), and whether the concepts of "liminality" and "intertextuality" may thus be apt to define its pre-canonical – both redactional and editorial – status.

None of this amounts to dismissing its originality, however. Neuwirth and Sinai are right to say that "if a historical contextualisation of the Qur'ān is to be pursued with any methodological and intellectual credibility today, it must make a determined effort to detect and describe the ways in which the Qur'ān's theology and literary format could be deemed by the community of its adherents to outcast and outbid previous competitors on the scene of religious scriptures in such a decisive way that it became the foundational text of a new monotheistic religion, Islam" (2011: 14). Still, the process through which the Qur'ān became that foundational text was neither linear nor uniform, and it is legitimate to question whether the process itself was fully accomplished by the mid-7th century. Unless one accepts the traditional narrative of the Qur'ān's origins, it is hard to assume that there ever existed a unified document behind the so-called "Uthmanic codex." All we have are late reports about how the latter was composed after Zayd b. Ṯābit's collection of Muḥammad's revelations, either directly or indirectly, i.e., through the mediation of several transmitters. But such late reports visibly fall under the category of scriptural myth-making; to put it differently, they aim at enforcing the view that there was a single focal point at the origin of the textual process that culminated in the production of the Qur'ān and that such a process was ultimately stable. Scholars in the field of early Jewish and Christian studies would automatically reject such a view as either naive or fabricated *ad hoc* to exclude any eventual irregularity in the process of canon formation; a possible analogy to that view would be to explain the emergence of earliest Christianity and/or rabbinic Judaism as a linear process with a single, clear-cut starting point. Conversely, most scholars of early Islam believe such a straightforward description to be accurate concerning the collection of the Qur'ān and would instead label any alternative view as dangerously revisionist (see e.g. Sinai 2014; cf. Dye 2015).

The sharp implications of this "normative" view for the study of quranic intertextuality should not be overlooked. For if the Qur'ān simply goes back to Muḥammad in its totality, and from Muḥammad to Uṯmān in such an undemanding manner, then there naturally is little room to undertake any intertextual exploration of the quranic corpus that proves capable of moving beyond the plain acknowledgement that Muḥammad himself was, in his own right, either due to his contacts with the Jewish and the Christian communities of Arabia or through the heavenly inspirations that he received, well acquainted with the themes and writings of the biblical tradition. In other words, such a view tends to equate the study of quranic intertextuality with that of Muḥammad's hypothetical sources, and thereby with the study of the pre-history of the Qur'ān (see once more Wild 1996: vii-ix). But then, how is it that certain quranic narratives that seem to be dependant on a non-quranic subtext (e.g., the Alexander legend in Q 18:83–102, as van Bladel 2008 perspicaciously shows) can only be dated after the 630s? Or that others (e.g., the story about Mary's pregnancy and Jesus' birth in Q 19, as Dye 2012 convincingly suggests) need to be linked to the Christian liturgical and scriptural traditions peculiar to the Kathisma church in Palestine? Moreover, would not Syria-Palestine, on the one hand, and Iraq-Iran, on the other hand, be a more reasonable scenario than the pre-Islamic Arabian peninsula for the encouragement of scribal, i.e., intertextual exchanges between Muslims, Christians, Jews, Manichaeans, and Zoroastrians? And would not be the time elapsing between the beginnings of Muḥammad's career in the Ḥiǧāz and the 690s or the 710s, when the new Arab state was fully formed and Islam promoted as a new religion by the Marwanids, represent a more natural timeframe than Muḥammad's own lifetime alone for the implementation of such exchanges?

My purpose in the present book, however, is not to explore these fascinating issues but to examine a number of heretofore unnoticed intertextual connections between the Qur'ān and several Jewish and Christian writings as regards one particular literary character that is repeatedly employed in the quranic corpus as a model for the quranic prophet, in order to stress the latter's eschatological credentials in a way that his prophetic profile could easily match that of the distinctive prophets and/or charismatic figures in the late-antique sectarian milieu out of which Islam gradually emerged. This was a model that was also later used in the *Sīra* literature and elsewhere to strengthen Muḥammad's eschatological, even messianic, credentials. Thus both my approach and my method in this book are different from what I have published so far in matters of quranic intertextuality and Muslim identity formation, as can be easily inferred from the following remarks.

I have earlier dealt with the study of some crucial issues concerning the complex processes of religious identity formation in late antiquity and a number of overlapping intertextual trajectories therein, and also with the study of the Qur'ān within that specific setting. I have tried to prove, for instance, that the quranic portrayal of Jesus' birth in Q 3:46 and 19:29–30 echoes the Arabic Gospel of the Infancy 1:2, which must in turn be read as an adaptation of a previous Noahic motif that goes back to the Second Temple Period and was later applied to Jesus in both the New Testament and the New Testament apocrypha (Segovia 2011; see also chapter two below). Originally set out in the Enochic corpus and other related writings as a kind of messianic symbol, this motif made its way well into late antique times and was reused in different contexts to describe Melchizedek, Jesus, and Moses alongside other related motifs that were likewise used to describe these and other figures. In short, the quranic portrayal of Jesus' birth in Q 3:46 and 19:29–30 must be placed in an ongoing tradition of variant textual reinterpretations of a single motif whose ideological background is, however, much more complex. In a second chapter included in a volume that I edited with Basil Lourié in memory of John Wansbrough (Segovia and Lourié 2012), I explored the parabolic use of natural order as opposed to human disobedience in the prologue to the Book of the Watchers and its fragmentary quranic parallels, more specifically the quranic reuse of 1Enoch 1–5 for paraenetic purposes in Q 7:36; 10:6; 16:81; and 24:41,44,46 (Segovia 2012). My aim, therefore, was to place these seemingly unrelated quranic passages within a well-known and continuing intellectual tradition that goes back, once more, to the Second Temple Period, and of which one may find numerous textual examples in the prophetic, apocalyptic, and wisdom literature of that period; yet this required outlining the more probable source of its quranic instantiation, which in my view should be searched for in 1Enoch 1–5 (especially 2:1–5:4). Finally, I have recently devoted a third and somewhat more complex article to the symptomatic rereading of Q 56:1–56 in light of Apocalypse of Abraham 21–2 (Segovia 2015b). My purpose here was not merely to show that Q 56:1–56 draws almost verbatim on ApAb 21–2 (especially 21:7; 22:1,3–5), but also that Paul's Abrahamic argument as reinterpreted in an overtly supersessionist fashion by the Church is subliminally reused against the Jews in the quranic passage in order to lay the foundations of a new founding (and again supersessionist) myth – a new myth that is fully indebted, however, to the post-Pauline Jewish discussion of Paul's Abrahamic argument in the Apocalypse of Abraham (on which see also Segovia 2014).

Again, my aim here is to (re)place the Qur'ān at the crossroads of the conversations and controversies of old to which its texts witness, but now also to symptomatically (re)read it in light of some of the events that it mirrors and/or to which it provides a literary and conceptual framework, be they episodes in the life of an anonymous prophet, portions on the shaping of a new charismatic figure, or phases in the development of a new religious community. A word about the method I follow in my research seems necessary, therefore, at this juncture.

My point of departure is a *symptomatic reading* of Q 11:35 and 49, where Noah and the quranic prophet unexpectedly exchange their roles and identities. To be sure, the quranic Noah narratives provide a type for the end of time as preached by the quranic prophet (on which see Shoemaker 2012: 118–96), and thus are susceptible to a *typological reading*. Therefore, Noah himself may be said to implicitly function as a type for the quranic prophet, who is repeatedly modelled in the Qur'ān upon various biblical figures (e.g., Abraham, Joseph, and Moses; see Tottoli 1999). Yet Q 11:35 and 49 go even beyond such implicit identification in that they explicitly substitute one character for another, which represents an unparalleled move in the whole quranic corpus. This made me aware that there is seemingly more to the quranic Noah narratives than has been hitherto noticed, and therefore helped me establish the working premise of the inquiry that has ultimately led to the composition of this book. Additionally, rereading several passages of Ibn Hišām's *Sīrat Rasūl Allāh* – especially those concerning Muḥammad's birth and confrontation with the Meccans – one gets the impression that the quranic Noah was also a key figure behind Muḥammad's description. So I have decided to expand my research by exploring at some length the apparent links existing between these three literary characters.

Noah obviously fits that category quite easily – that is to say, he is no more than a literary figure who appears and reappears rather frequently in the biblical and parabiblical literature of late antiquity, usually as an apocalyptic type, as is also the case in the Qur'ān. Conversely, the quranic prophet and Muḥammad, while being literary figures as well – since they are the main characters of two independent writings: the Qur'ān and Ibn Hišām's *Sīra* – should instead be regarded as historical figures, or – as the Muslim tradition and most scholars of early Islam would have it – as a single historical figure. My point, of course, is not to deny their historicity; in this study I am chiefly interested in their literary presentations. In addition, I should not like to give the impression that, in my view, the quranic prophet and Muḥammad are to be envisaged as two distinct historical characters. Certainly, the quranic prophetical *logia* go back to a prophet, and it is very likely that such a prophet was no other than Muḥammad himself. But it is nonetheless important to acknowledge that he is only named in the Qur'ān four/five times (Q 3:144; 33:40; 47:2; 48:29; and 61:6 as Aḥmad). Now, these verses may well be later interpolations, as David Powers (2011) has recently suggested *apropos* Q 33:40; but even if they are not, they cannot be read as providing an absolute clue to the character who is anonymously addressed in the quranic corpus as (merely) "you," unless one assumes that the Qur'ān is a uniform text containing only Muḥammad's *ipssima verba* – a view which I have already discussed in the preceding pages (see also Berg 2006). To put it differently, from a purely literary standpoint – and again, it is such a point of view that interests me here – the Qur'ān mostly remains (like "John's" gospel, for that matter) an anonymous document. Moreover, how can we be sure that there is only one prophet behind the prophetical *logia* contained in the quranic corpus? The fact is that we cannot, even if we pretend otherwise; for again, such a reduction would imply reading the Qur'ān in light of the Muslim tradition, which may prove for the historian of late-antique religion as problematic as reading the texts gathered in the New Testament in light of the Christian theological tradition. And yet there are hints in the quranic corpus itself that point in this direction, as I will later argue. So I am not claiming here that there actually are several quranic prophets instead of just one. However, for coherence's sake, I think it is necessary to bear all these notions in mind, and therefore to distinguish between the quranic prophet and Muḥammad as two literary figures and to understand that the prophetical *logia* of the Qur'ān are a puzzle that we still need to work out in some very crucial aspects. This is why I have decided to denominate the prophet repeatedly alluded to in the Qur'ān as "the quranic prophet," without further qualification, and Hišām's literary hero as "Muḥammad."

Once the connections between both of these figures and Noah become apparent, the next step is to survey the Noahic narratives in the Qur'ān and to carefully select the passages worthy of consideration in order to explore the Noahic shaping of the quranic prophet therein. Undoubtedly, a preliminary distinction needs to be made between those quranic passages that simply mention Noah and those that build upon the Noah story at some length, retell it in different ways, and provide new insights on it. Likewise, distinguishing between core themes and motifs and secondary features seems essential to me. So the first task I undertake in the present book is to work out and classify all such conceptual elements and literary units. Next, it seems to me necessary to analyse their possible interrelations, both formal and thematic. I offer the results of this *methodical cross-examination* in chapter three.

Setting apart the quranic Noah narratives from those passages that simply mention Noah also entails examining the literary frame and rhetorical conventions of each one, as well as unraveling formulaic repetitions and eventual variations in tone and style. Simultaneously, I feel some attention ought to be paid to the particular distribution of themes and motifs in each narrative and to the way in which each one seems to reflect a common purpose. The conclusions reached through this *selective literary analysis* are given in chapter four.

Little by little, however, one notices that behind such an overall purpose each narrative apparently serves a specific intent, and that to decipher this one needs to discover its thematic emphasis, which is in turn singled out by the rhetorical dynamism peculiar to each narrative. Examining this issue implies undertaking a *second symptomatic reading*, now of the quranic Noah narratives themselves, individually considered. Additionally, I try to apply that dynamic and symptomatic lens to the full set of the quranic Noah narratives to check whether they can somehow be said to interact reciprocally and put forward different parts of a single progressive story. I then attempt to examine whether such a symptomatic development could contribute to clarifying the typological presentation of the quranic prophet in the Qur'ān and a few relevant episodes of his biography. The results of this textual exploration are offered in chapter five.

It seems clear from the start, however, that the quranic Noah has features that resemble other Noah stories found in the pseudepigraphic, apocryphal, and patristic literature of late antiquity. Quite naturally, the next move is to test those parallels. Yet two criteria must be met. One consists in determining which specific texts ought to be examined. My view is that, just as new religions usually take shape only after some kind of dialectal variation is explicitly or tacitly allowed within a given religious milieu (for these are always complex and dynamic in their very nature), new normative texts usually spread out of a common stock of writings circulating inside a composite, and hence multifaceted, scribal setting. Sectarian divisions may influence certain choices, but normally the selection of useful subtexts and intertexts operates on a broader basis. Hence I take into consideration all meaningful texts regardless of their confessional circumscription, which entails surveying a considerable number of Jewish, Christian, Gnostic, and Manichaean writings. The other methodological criterion is to distinguish between textual precedents and plausible textual sources of the quranic Noah. Proximity in time and space seem at first a reliable premise on which to build that comprehensive survey. Yet the study of Islam's beginnings has undergone so many changes in recent years that it is hard to establish with accuracy which documents actually belonged to the scribal milieu out of which Islam emerged. Nevertheless, some provisional conclusions are provided in chapter six.

Lastly, I undertake the study of Ibn Hišām's *Sīra* in light of the results achieved throughout my research on the quranic Noah narratives so as to determine to what extent he, or Ibn Isḥāq before him, used these narratives as a subtext on which to build their picture of Muḥammad's life. This means applying an intertextual and symptomatic lens as well. While pondering this, however, it is hard to avoid the impression that Muḥammad's representation in Ibn Hišām's *Sīra* also draws, albeit obliquely, on the non-quranic Noah literature, and moreover, that Muḥammad is implicitly depicted therein as a Noahic "messiah." This finding and its fascinating implications are presented in both chapter seven and the afterword to the present book, where I additionally canvass a series of medieval Muslim writings to reinforce the view that, at least in certain Muslim circles, Muḥammad was either actually seen as a new Messiah or as having been given messianic traits – a provocative view that hitherto has not received due attention.

If I am right in this concluding assumption, it would then be possible to see either Ibn Isḥāq's original work or Ibn Hišām's recension as representing a transitory albeit decisive step in the development of the Islamic community: a step that would mark, or rather validate, the transition from an originally Christian milieu to a new religious setting. Transition from the quranic prophet as the herald of the eschaton to Muḥammad as the founder of a new messianic community – I suggest – should probably be read as its once tentative, though later abandoned, corollary; for that early messianic community finally transformed into a more or less standardised religious community, whose social and political concerns became prevalent over its former eschatological beliefs. Be that as it may, intertextuality and religious identity formation – which is also at stake, nonetheless, in the Noahic shaping of the quranic prophet – interplay at this particular point in a very remarkable manner, and my major goal in the present study is to explore some of their interconnections within, and implications for, the making of the Islamic religion.

Accordingly, the line of the argument in the book divides into seven parts. Chapter two explores the apocalyptic image of Noah in the literature of pre-Islamic Judaism and Christianity by way of introduction to the argument put forward in chapter seven and in the afterword regarding Muḥammad's messiahship. In turn, chapter three provides the reader with an overview of all the quranic passages that mention Noah; it also unfolds the basic structure of the quranic Noah narratives and examines Noah's distinctive traits in the Qur'ān in contrast to his biblical counterpart. In chapter four I undertake a multifaceted analysis of the quranic Noah narratives based upon their adaptation of classical prophetic and apocalyptic literary forms and themes, contextual placement within each *sūra* (where applicable), and primary meaning. Chapter five explores the intertwining between the quranic Noah and the quranic prophet, i.e., the way in which the latter is symptomatically modelled after the former; a few additional remarks on the plausible *Urtext* of the two major quranic Noah narratives (Q 11:25–49; 71) and on the apparent scribal background of the Qur'ān are given in that chapter as well. Chapter six, for its part, aims at exploring the precedents and sources of the quranic Noah narratives; as noted above, the distinction between mere precedents and hypothetical textual sources, on the one hand, and – I shall now add – differentiation between parallel themes, motifs, and literary *topoi*, on the other hand, is essential to the argument put forward in this chapter. Conversely, in chapter seven I investigate the use that the authors of the earliest "biography" of Muḥammad (i.e., Ibn Isḥāq and his editor Ibn Hišām) made of the quranic Noah narratives, and I contend that the quranic Noah helped them not only to enhance Muhammad's eschatological credentials, but also to subliminally represent him as a new Messiah..

Hence the present study formulates a threefold hypothesis that may be summarised as follows: (1) the Noah narratives are used in the Qur'ān to depict the life and preachings of the quranic prophet and to stress his eschatological credentials; (2) similarly, they were later re-used by the authors of Muḥammad's "biography" to inscribe their own view of Muḥammad's life and preaching and to likewise stress his eschatological credentials; additionally, exploring the intertwining of the quranic Noah narratives and the Muhammadan *evangelium* further suggests that (3) either the quranic prophet, or Muḥammad himself, was not initially conceived of as just a prophet: quite probably he was also, if tentatively, regarded as new Messiah by some of his followers.

To be sure, endorsing the view that Muḥammad might have been thought of as a new Messiah by a number of his adherents adds a new, challenging aspect to the scholarly conversation on the many mysteries surrounding Islam's origins.

# Chapter 2 / Tracing the Apocalyptic Noah in Pre-Islamic Jewish and Christian Literature

The apocalyptic literature of early Judaism has deeply influenced both Christianity and Islam. One of its most salient features is the profusion of eschatological mediators – be they angels or humans – who are variously commissioned to either instruct a human figure, imprison the rebellious angels and destroy their progeny, or renovate the earth (so Sariel, Raphael, Michael, and Gabriel in 1Enoch 10, respectively). They may be alternatively depicted, however, as those who communicate the events of the eschaton to the righteous (so Enoch in most parts of 1Enoch and Abraham in the Apocalypse that bears his name). Furthermore, a single eschatological mediator may be introduced as he who shall gloriously arise at the end of time, vindicate the righteous, sit upon God's throne to preside over the divine judgment, and disclose all the secrets of wisdom (so the Chosen One, who, as is widely known, receives other various names and attributes, in 1En 46; 48–51; 61–2); or – to mention another outstanding illustration, and as we shall see below – as he who will cleanse the earth of evil and whose seed shall endure beyond destruction. Obviously, this enumeration makes no claim to exhaustivity; yet it points to the complex framework of apocalyptic imagery (on which see Collins 1998).

Occasionally these figures appear to be closely interrelated. A given figure may be simply modelled upon another one whose specific characters it re-adapts, whereas other figures develop some features not included in any previous model (cf. Charles 1902: 35; Peters 2008: 9). A twofold hybrid procedure can be documented as well: adoption (reinterpretation) and innovation (which can sometimes depend on a former reinterpretation) may well converge at times. Be that as it may, one must quite often deal with either explicit or implicit "transpositions" – a term which I propose here to understand in light of its musical meaning: the same motif can be transposed to a different key and thus produce a virtual analogon.

Upon these considerations, the present chapter aims at tracing the picture of the apocalyptic Noah in the literature of pre-Islamic Judaism and Christianity by way of introducing the argument put forward in chapter seven and the afterword to this book – namely, that Muḥammad himself was tentatively thought of as a new Messiah by a number of his followers, and that this was partly due to his tacit identification with an apocalyptic Noah figure that differs from the mainstream biblical Noah considerably. In my view, the interpretative key to such an identification ultimately lies in the messianic symbol applied to Noah in 1En 106–7 and other parallel texts, a symbol that we find again in the Qur'ān and the Muhammadan *evangelium* as a means to depict Jesus and Muḥammad, respectively. Hence, if one blends together these three separate instantiations, one can easily discern the tacit proposal audaciously made by Muḥammad's "biographers." But prior to that, it is essential to recover in their own right the textual traces of the apocalyptic Noah. Therefore, those Jewish and Christian writings which merely follow or comment on the biblical narrative of the flood will not be mentioned in what follows.The Noah story in 1Enoch, the Genesis Apocryphon (1QapGen), 4Q534–6, and 1Q19–19bis should thus be mentioned in the first instance.

*The Birth of Noah (1 Enoch 106–7).* 1Enoch 106–7 recounts (a) the miraculous birth of Noah (106:1–3); (b) Lamech's surprise and *méfiance* towards him (106:4a); (c) the latter's appeal to Methuselah, begging him to ask Enoch about the newborn child (106:4b-7); (d) Methuselah's speech to Enoch (106:8–12); and both (e) Enoch's answer to Methuselah – through which we learn that Noah will be righteous and blameless, that he will temporarily withdraw all iniquity from the earth and be Lamech's remnant, and that accordingly he and his sons will be saved from the flood (106:13–107:2) – and (f) Methuselah's consequent answer to Lamech (107:3c); to which (g) a brief explanation of Noah's name is appended (107:3d). Noah's astonishing qualities (106:2–3) are most remarkable:[1] "(106:2b) His body was whiter than snow and redder than a rose, (106:2c) his hair was all white and like white wool and curly. (106:2d) Glorious <was his face>. (106.2e) When he opened his eyes, the house shone like the sun. (106:3a) And he stood up from the hands of the midwife, (106:3b) and he opened his mouth and praised the Lord <of eternity>" (cf. 106:10c-11). We shall again find some of these prominent traits – by means of which Noah is outlined as an eschatological mediator[2] – ascribed to other figures. The idea that the end of time will somehow resemble the flood – which is described as the "first end" in 93:4c (cf. Luke 17:26) – has encouraged certain transpositions of the Noah story, from which the Enochic tradition possibly developed itself as such (see below the comments on 1QapGen, 4Q534–6, and 1Q19–19bis), and of which 1 Enoch still offers other various accounts.

*The Book of the Watchers (1Enoch 10:1–3).* The first of these is found in the Book of the Watchers. In 1Enoch 10:1–3 Sariel reveals to Noah that the earth is about to perish so that he may preserve himself alive and escape from the deluge. We then read that "from him a plant will be planted, and [that] his seed will endure for all the generations of eternity" (10:3), which closely parallels Abraham's description in 93:5b-c.

*The Similitudes of Enoch (1 Enoch 60:1–10,23–5; 65:1–69:1).* In 1Enoch 65:9,6–8,10–12 it is Enoch who instructs Noah after being petitioned by the latter (65:2,4–5,3) prior to the imminent destruction of the earth (65:1). Noah is introduced in 65:11c as pure and blameless and his name is included among the holy ones (65:2a). We are also told that he will be preserved among those who dwell on the earth (65:12b), and that a fountain of the righteous and the holy will flow from his progeny (65:12d-e). Vv. 1–3 of chap. 67 offer a shorter and slightly different version of Noah's blessing in the form of a divine oracle. Noah's vision of the flood follows in 67:4–69:1; cf. Enoch's vision of the flood and the final judgment in 60:23,1–10,24–5.

*The Book of Dreams (1Enoch 83–4; 89:1–8).* In the first dream vision, Enoch narrates to Methuselah his dialogue with his grandfather, Mahalalel, and his vision of the flood (83), which leads him to pray to God (84). The Animal Apocalypse also draws on the Noah story (89:1–8); Noah is now said to be born a bull (i.e., a man) who later became a man (a heavenly being?; see Porter 1983: 53; Tiller 1993: 259, 295–6; Nickelsburg 2001: 375) by means of an angelic instruction (89:1a-b; cf. 70:1–2; 71:14; 2Enoch 21:2–22:10).

*The Epistle of Enoch (1Enoch 93:4–5,8).* As noted above 1En 93.4 refers to the flood as a "first end" (93:4c); cf. additionally 93:4d and 93:8d. The plant symbol formerly applied to Noah is transposed in 93.5b to Abraham.

*The Genesis Apocryphon and other Dead Sea Scrolls presumably related to the Apocalypse of Noah (1QapGen, 4Q534–6, and 1Q19–19bis).* 1QapGen 1–5:25 parallels 1Enoch 106–7. A reference to "the Book of the Words of Noah" (5:29) is then made to introduce the second major part of the scroll (up to cols. 17/18), in which Noah summarises his life and relates a series of visions concerning the fault of the rebellious angels and his mission before dividing the earth among his sons; the symbolism of the righteous plant is used in the extant fragments of cols. 13–15. The claim that 1QapGen cols. 1–5 or 5–17/18 and 1 En 106–7 could draw on a previous Book – or, as labelled by Robert Henry Charles (1893: 14, 19, 25, 33, 61, 71, 86, 106, 146.), Apocalypse – of Noah, which Florentino García Martínez (1981: 195–232; 1992: 1–44; 1999: 94–5) has repeatedly identified with 4Q534, and which has frequently been posited since August Dillmann (1853) as the point of departure of some of the earliest Enochic writings (namely 1 En 6–11, on which see e.g. Milik 1976: 55; Sacchi 1990: 101, 103, 108, 110, 156–7, 210, 242, 266, 273) is disputed – as is the relationship between 4Q534–6 and 1Q19–19bis (Baxter 2006: 179–94). If such dependence were confirmed, however, one would be somewhat compelled to consider the Noah story as the eldest explicit apocalyptic-like motif in Second Temple literature.

It goes without saying that this motif underwent different adaptations in Jewish and Christian literature of late antiquity, from the 1st century CE onwards. What follows is an attempt to survey them concisely.[3]

*2Enoch 71–2.* The story of Melchizedek in 2Enoch 71–2 is, as I have suggested, modelled upon the Noah story in 1 En 106–7. A fundamental difference is to be observed, however, in the account of Melchizedek's virginal birth – as well as in his and Nir's priestly condition. It should also be noted that 2En 71:18 reproduces more or less verbatim 1 En 106.3b: "he [= the new born child] spoke . . . and blessed the Lord." Additionally, the analogy between the flood and the eschaton – which is already present, e.g. in 1En 93:4–5 and 8–10 – is amplified in 2En 72:6 through the reference there contained to "another Melchizedek" who will be born at the end of time.

*Apocalypse of Abraham 11:2, Joseph and Aseneth 22:7, and Revelation 1:14.* YHWH's angel and Abraham's guide to the heavenly realm is described in Apocalypse of Abraham 11:2 as having "the hair of his head [white] as snow." This description is dependent upon Noah's portrayal in 1Enoch 106:2a – rather than upon Dan 7:9 – insofar as the figure thus depicted is not YHWH himself but an angel. The very same motif occurs again in Joseph and Aseneth 22:7, where it is used to describe Jacob, i.e. Joseph's father. We read that "his [= Jacob's] head was snow-white, and the hairs of his head . . . extremely thick," a possible allusion to their "woolen" nature (cf. 1En 106:2a). Likewise, Revelation 1:14 portrays Christ in the following terms: "His hair was as white as snow-white wool, and his eyes flamed like fire" (REB). The parallelism with 1En 106:2 (not only 106:2a, but also 106:2b) is even closer in this case.

*Matthew 1:18–19.* Joseph's cautiousness towards Mary's mysterious pregnancy in Matthew 1:18–19 runs parallel to – in spite of not being identical with – Lamech's suspicion of his wife in 1QapGen 2 (cf. 1En 106:4a).

*Matthew 1:20, Luke 1–2, and Protoevangelium of James 19:2.* Jesus's miraculous and supernatural conception – which contrasts with its denial in the case of Noah in 1Enoch 106:18b; 107:2 – is also reminiscent of the Noah story.

In addition, it is possible to find some echoes of the newborn Noah's ability to speak in two writings where this ability is transferred to the newborn Jesus.

*Arabic Gospel of the Infancy 1:2, and Qur'ān 3:46; 19:29–30.* We read in the former that "Jesus spoke when he was lying in the cradle and said to his mother: 'Verily I am Jesus, the Son of God, the Word [of God], whom thou hast brought forth as Gabriel the angel announced to thee. My father has sent me for the salvation of the world.'" The affinities between the opening sentence and the Noah story in 1En 106:3 are evident in spite of their differences: Noah stood up (or, according to the Ethiopic version, was taken) from the hands of the midwife and then praised the Lord (or else spoke to/with the Lord of righteousness); Jesus, in turn, spoke to his mother while lying in his cradle. An echo of this very same motif is also found twice in the Qur'ān: cf. Q 3:46: "He [= Jesus] will speak to people in the cradle and in his adulthood, and he shall be among the righteous;" and 19:29–30: "She [= Mary] pointed at him [= the newborn Jesus]; but they said: 'How can we speak to one who is in the cradle, [and hence to] a little child?' He [= Jesus] said: 'I am God's servant; He has given me the Scripture and made me a prophet.'" The concluding statement in Q 3:46 is especially noteworthy, for its allusion to the righteous (pl.): ومن الصلحين *wa min al-ṣāliḥīn*, "And he will be counted amidst the righteous," implicitly evokes the Ethiopic text of 1 En 106:3b, where "righteousness" (ጽድቅ: *ṣədq*) is attributed to God (see n. 1 above).

Yet there is no reasonable way to demonstrate the influence of the Ethiopic text of 1 Enoch 106:3 upon Qur'ān 3:46; the difference between the two verbal roots from which the Ethiopic noun ጽድቅ *ṣədq* and the Arabic active participle صلحون derive could easily be an objection. Still, it is possible to see in Q. 3:46; 19:29–30 an indirect, fragmentary, yet fascinating echo of the apocalyptic Noah story; indirect because it concerns Jesus rather than Noah, and fragmentary because there is something missing in the Qur'ān: namely, the light motif, which nonetheless made its way, as we shall see, into the very core of the Muhammadan *evangelium*.

There are other additional, in fact remarkable connections between Noah, the quranic prophet, and Muḥammad; so much so that one wonders whether the quranic prophet and Muḥammad are, so to speak, just two among a number of late-antique Noahic *reflections*; that is, whether they were almost entirely modelled after Noah – since he had often been envisaged as the herald of the past and future eschaton – to enhance their own eschatological credentials. I shall now turn to such additional connections, and more broadly to the quranic view of Noah, and analyse the way in which Noah, the quranic prophet, and Muḥammad seem to overlap, like the various faces of a single character, before I revisit the instantiation of Noah's messianic symbol in the Muhammadan *evangelium*.

## Excursus. A Lost Apocalypse of Noah?

As Darrell Hannah (2007: 472–3) writes regarding 1Enoch 37–71, "[s]cholars who accept that portions of a 'Book of Noah' have been either interpolated into the text of the Parables or have served as source material for the original composition of the Parables include both earlier commentators such as August Dillmann, Heinrich Ewald, Robert Henry Charles, and François Martin, and more recent scholars as Albert-Marie Denis, George Nickelsburg, Ephraim Isaac, Siegbert Uhlig, Matthew Black, Florentino García Martínez, and John Collins. Thus," he adds, "the existence of material from a Noah apocryphon within the text of the Parables continues to be widely recognized today, and probably represents the majority view."

This statement can be also applied to other sections of the Enochic corpus, 1Enoch 106–7 among them. Yet the idea that 1 Enoch could draw upon a previous Book or Apocalypse of Noah has not been undisputed in recent scholarship (see Dimant 2006). I shall now attempt to briefly re-examine this subject in light of some of the methodological and conceptual distinctions made by Dorothy Peters in a recent and useful book (2008: 29–61). However,I will not assume her conclusion concerning the hypothetical existence of a Book of Noah, a possibility that she seems to deny (following Devorah Dimant), whereas I, on the contrary, regard its existence as quite plausible.

While addressing the problem of the "Noahic" characterisation of Enoch in 1Enoch, Peters proposes to distinguish between (*a*) the oral and literary Noah traditions that may have influenced the composition of certain parts of 1Enoch, (*b*) the role played by Noah in those oral/literary traditions and in the Enochic corpus, and (*c*) the hypothetical existence of a Book of Noah that could draw upon those very same oral/literary traditions and moreover be considered as the source of a number of Noahic narratives and motifs present in 1 Enoch.

Her conclusions regarding this complex question are as follows: (1) When the Noah narratives present in the earliest strata of 1Enoch (e.g., in chaps. 6–11) were re-contextualised into the final form of the Enochic corpus, some Noahic traits were transferred to Enoch, insofar as in the previous oral/literary Noah traditions from which such traits were originally taken by the authors of 1Enoch, Noah himself was implicitly – and hence somewhat problematically – depicted as a giant. (2) The late Noahic narratives in 1Enoch (e.g., those found in chaps. 106–7) were in turn patterned after the Enoch narratives already developed in earlier parts of the corpus, and Enoch's traits were thus transferred back to Noah. Peters supports her first conclusion, which seems to me very likely, by noting the omission of Noah's transformation into a heavenly being in 4Q206 and also with her own reading of the original Noah traditions – provided they once existed –

against the background of the giant flood narratives found in 6Q8 and other related documents, such as the Midrash of Shemhazai and 'Aza'el studied by Loren Stuckenbruck (1997; 2004) and John Reeves (1993: 110–15), whose interpretations she basically follows. Regarding the existence of a Book or Apocalypse of Noah, however, she sides with Dimant, according to whom such a hypothetical book, if it ever existed, would have been written – judging from its alleged quotations in 1En 6–11 – in "third person style and not, as one would expect of a *Book of Noah* or an *Apocalypse of Noah*, in an autobiographic style" (2006: 234). Thus Peters considers it unlikely that 1En 106–7 could draw on a previous Noah apocryphon, inasmuch as the latter must be considered, in all probability, a fictitious book; from this she draws her second conclusion.

However, this negative argument regarding the Apocalypse of Noah, and thereby Peters's second conclusion, are far from being convincing. The style of the Noahic fragments in 1Enoch 6–11 need not be the style of their textual source. In other words, the incorporation of certain materials taken from one text into another may be done quite freely. The third person style narrative characteristic of 1En 6–11 tells us nothing about the style of the Book of Noah; it only tells us something – which is altogether different – about the style of 1En 6–11.

As Michael Stone reminds us, "the burden of the proof falls [indeed] on those scholars who would deny the authenticity of the Book of Noah titles and sections *a priori* and not on those who would assert it" (2006: 17). It seems well within the scope of the evidence to conclude, therefore, that an Apocalypse of Noah could have existed after all, regardless of the distinctions that ought be made between such a hypothetical book, the Noah traditions included in it and in other various texts such as 1Enoch 106–7, and the role played by Noah in each of them.

Additionally, it should be also noted that if an Apocalypse of Noah – or at least certain parts of it – is either preserved or implicitly referred to in 1Q19–19bis and 4Q534–6, as García Martínez has persuasively argued, this would not only force us to see in 1En 10:1–3; 60:1–10,23–5; 65:1–69:1; 83–4; 89:1–8; 93:4–5,8; 106–7, on the one hand, and in 1QapGen 1–17/18, on the other hand, more or less clear reminiscences of and/or direct borrowings from that book; it would also contribute to place it – given the references to the "Chosen One of God," who is also said to be the "Light to the nations," and his opponents contained in 4Q534 1:9–10 – within the broader history of reciprocal relations existing between Jewish apocalyptic literature and the Isaianic corpus (on which see Charles 1893: 26; Hanson 1979; Blenkinsopp 2006; and the cross-references to the Isaianic corpus in Nickelsburg 2001: 582). Judging from this and from what will be said in the next section, the importance of the Noah apocalyptic tradition can hardly be dismissed, in spite of its unclear origins, nuanced transmission, and fragmentary witnesses.

# Chapter 3 / Noah in the Qur'ān: An Overview

Noah is repeatedly mentioned in the Qur'ān.[1] In addition to some brief, discrete but significant allusions to: (*i*) his own time and the events that followed;[2] (*ii*) his divine election,[3] inspiration,[4] and guidance;[5] (*iii*) his role as a prophet,[6] messenger,[7] and/or servant[8] of God; (*iv*) the words by which he admonished his contemporaries;[9] (*v*) their rejection of his mission;[10] and (*vi*) his qualities as a model/ *exemplum* for the quranic prophet[11] – all of which are disseminated through thirty-two verses belonging to twenty-one apparently unrelated suras (Arab. *suwar*, chapters)[12] – he is the subject of seven major quranic narratives (hereinafter quranic Noah narratives I–VII),[13] including a whole quranic *sūra* of twenty-eight verses.[14]

Very likely such major narrative units, as also the brief allusions to Noah outside these, should be taken – like most of the materials in the Qur'ān, for that matter – as "distinct pericopes of essentially homiletic purpose . . . [that were] incorporated more or less intact into the canonical compilation . . . [and] unified by means of a limited number of rhetorical conventions" (Wansbrough 2004: 20–1, 47). The fact that they ought to be envisaged as independent pericopes does not necessarily mean they were originally unconnected, however.

It is indeed difficult to know what precisely the Qur'ān is and when it acquired its present form. Testimonies about its different versions/recensions are well documented in the Islamic sources themselves; so too are reports about its textual additions and suppressions and the date of its alleged "Uthmanic" collection (de Prémare 2004, 2010; Gilliot 2006). Likewise, its origins are far from clear. Recent scholarship on the Qur'ān shows that its alleged unity, background, and chronology posit many problems if approached from a historio-critical perspective, thus highlighting questions long overlooked in the interpretation of the Muslim scripture, such as: "What layers does it contain and how should they be studied?" "Which was their original character and function?" "What complex redactional process did they undergo?" "Which specific historical/cultural settings must one have in mind when addressing these issues?" (see Wansbrough 2004; Kropp 2007; Reynolds 2008, 2011b; de Prémare 2010; Pohlmann 2013). Hence it is also difficult to know how the different quranic texts that mention Noah, and more particularly the aforementioned quranic Noah narratives, came to be gathered in the quranic corpus, and what their original nature and intent was; the same holds true regarding the larger pericopes within which they are often included. Yet this does not preclude them from being studied.

It is worth mentioning, to begin with, that the quranic Noah narratives present several peculiar traits, which are unparalleled in the biblical Noah narrative (Gen 6:8–9:28):

(1) not all of them are written in third person; six out of seven contain either short or relatively long monologues (by Noah) and dialogues (between Noah and his opponents or else between Noah and God);
(2) they all basically follow a regular, stereotypical prophetic pattern, which is lacking in the biblical narrative: ($\alpha$) commission, ($\beta$) admonition, ($\gamma$) prediction of disaster, ($\delta$) contestation, and ($\varepsilon$) justification (both often duplicated and once reported in indirect speech),[15] followed by ($\zeta$) a monologue/dialogue and ($\eta$) a twofold – and not less typical – apocalyptic theme: punishment of the wicked and salvation of the righteous, to which ($\theta$) an eschatological coda is frequently appended (see Table 1 below);
(3) except in quranic Noah narratives nos. III–IV and VI, the story of the flood generally plays a secondary role in comparison to the one apparently assigned to Noah's confrontation with his opponents in nos. I–II, V, and especially VII (where the flood story goes unmentioned);
(4) as I will suggest in the next chapter, a strong eschatological atmosphere pervades almost all quranic Noah narratives;
(5) finally, their main character, i.e. Noah, differs from his biblical counterpart in that:

a. he is commissioned by God as his apostle (nos. I, IV–V, VII);
b. he warns his contemporaries so as to make them repent and turn to God (nos. I–V, VII);
c. he is mocked and/or rejected by them (in all quranic Noah narratives);
d. he implores God's help and mercy (nos. III–VII) and is comforted by him (no. III);
e. he asks God to punish the wicked (no. VII).

Elements a, b, c, and d (and/or other similar ones) are inherent in the quranic portrayal of Noah outside the quranic Noah narratives as well (see Table 2 below), whereas element e is exclusive to them. It must also be noted that elsewhere in the Qur'ān, Noah is mentioned as the first in a list of prophets that includes *inter alios* Abraham, Moses, and Jesus – a list which is traditionally understood to end with Muḥammad. Moreover, he is also singled out in the Qur'ān as a model/*exemplum* for the quranic prophet himself (Q 4:163; 6:90; 22:42; 25:41; 33:7; 42:13). While this can also be found in quranic Noah narratives nos. II and III (cf. Q 10:72; 11:49), the latter goes even further by symptomatically erasing the boundaries between the two prophets (11:35). Hence Noah is additionally, if tentatively, presented in the quranic Noah narratives:

f. as the quranic prophet himself (no. III).

I shall come back to this crucial issue in chapters five and seven.

Table 1 below provides the rhetorical scheme followed in the quranic Noah narratives, whereas Table 2 summarises Noah's distinctive traits in the Qur'ān, both in and outside these narratives.

**Table 1:** *The rhetorical scheme in the quranic Noah narratives*

| | Q 7:59–64 (QNN I) | Q 10:71–4 (QNN II) | Q 11:25–49 (QNN III) | Q 23:23–30 (QNN IV) | Q 26:105–22 (QNN V) | Q 54:9–17 (QNN VI) | Q 71:1–28 (QNN VII) |
|---|---|---|---|---|---|---|---|
| *α* | 7:59 | – | 11:25 | 23:23 | – | – | 71:1 |
| *β* | 7:59 | 10:71–2 | 11:25–6 | 23:23 | 26:106–10 | – | 71:2–4 (+10–20) |
| *γ* | 7:59 | 10:72 | 11:26 | – | – | – | 71:4 |
| *δ* | (1) 7:60<br>(2) 7:64 | 10:73 | (1) 11:27<br>(2) 11:32<br>(3) 11:43 | 23:24 | (1) 26:111<br>(2) 26:116 | 54:9 | (71:7,21–3) |
| *ε* | (1) 7:61–3<br>(2) – | – | (1) 11:28–31<br>(2) 11:33–4 | – | (1) 26:112<br>(2) – | – | – |
| *ζ* | – | – | 11:45–7 | 23:26 | 26:117–18 | 54:10 | 71:5–28 |
| *η* | 7:64 | 10:73 | 11:36–48 | 23:27–9 | 26:119–20 | 54:11–14 | (71:25) |
| *θ* | – | 10:73–4 | 11:49 | 23:30 | 26:121–2 | 54:15–17 | – |

Key to Table 1:
*α* = prophetic commission
*β* = admonition by the prophet
*γ* = warning and/or prediction of disaster, made by the prophet
*δ* = contestation/rejection of his warning by his opponents (*or* by one of his sons)
*ε* = justification of his own mission by the prophet
*ζ* = prophetic monologue addressed to God, or else dialogue between the prophet and God
*η* = salvation of the righteous and divine punishment of the wicked
*θ* = eschatological coda

**Table 2:** *Noah's distinctive traits in the Qur'ān* (references to the quranic Noah narratives in bold type)

| A | B | C | D | E | F | G | H | I | J | K | L | M | N | O | P |
|---|---|---|---|---|---|---|---|---|---|---|---|---|---|---|---|
| 3:33 | | | | | | | | | | | | | | | |
| | 4:163 | | 4:163 | 4:163 | | | | 4:163 | | | | | | | |
| | | | | | 4:164 | | | | | | | | | | |
| | | 6:84 | | | | | | | | | | | | | |
| 6:87 | | | | | | 6:88 | | | | | | | | | |
| | | | 6:90 | | | | | 6:90 | | | | | | | |
| | | | | | 7:59 | | | | | **7:59** | | | | | |
| | | | | | | | | | | **7:60** | **7:60** | | | | |
| | | | | | **7:61** | | | | | **7:61** | | | | | |
| | | | | | | | | | | **7:62** | | | | | |
| | | | | | | | | | | **7:63** | | | | | |
| | | | | | | | | | | | **7:64** | | | | |
| | | | | | 9:70 | | | | | | | | | | |
| | | | | | | | | | | **10:71** | | | | | |
| | | | | | | | **10:72** | | | **10:72** | | | | | |
| | | | | | | | | | | | **10:73** | | | | |
| | | | | | | | | | | **11:25** | | | | | |
| | | | | | | | | | | **11:26** | | | | | |
| | | | | | | | | | | **11:27** | **11:27** | | | | |
| | | | | | | | | | | **11:28** | | | | | |
| | | | | | | | | | | **11:29** | | | | | |
| | | | | | | | | | | **11:30** | | | | | |
| | | | | | | | | | | **11:31** | | | | | |
| | | | | | | | | | | **11:32** | **11:32** | | | | |
| | | | | | | | | | | **11:33** | | | | | |
| | | | | | | | | | | **11:34** | | | | | |
| | | | | | | | | | **11:35** | | | | | | |
| | | | | | | | | | | | | | | **11:36** | |
| | | | | | | | | | | ***11:42*** | | | | | |
| | | | | | | | | | | ***11:43*** | ***11:43*** | | | | |
| | | | | | | | | | | | | | | | **11:45** |
| | | | | | | | | | | | | | | | **11:47** |
| | | | | | | | | **11.49** | | | | | | | |
| | | | | | 14:9 | | | | | 14:9 | 14:9 | | | | |
| | | | | | | | | | | 14:10 | | | | | |
| | | | | | | | | | | 14:11 | | | | | |
| | | | | | | | | | | 14:12 | | | | | |
| | | | | | | | | | | 14:13 | | | | | |
| | | | | | | | | | | | | 14:15 | | | |
| | | | | | | 17:3 | | | | | | | | | |

**Table 2** (continuation)

| A | B | C | D | E | F | G | H | I | J | K | L | M | N | O | P |
|---|---|---|---|---|---|---|---|---|---|---|---|---|---|---|---|
| 19:58 | | 19:58 | 19:58 | | | | | | | | | | | | |
| | | | | | | | | | | | | | | | 21:76 |
| | | | | | | | | 22:42 | | | 22:42 | | | | |
| | | | | | 23:23 | | | | | **23:23** | | | | | |
| | | | | | | | | | | **23:24** | **23:24** | | | | |
| | | | | | | | | | | **23:25** | **23:25** | | | | |
| | | | | | | | | | | | | **23:26** | | | |
| | | | | | 25:37 | | | | | | 25:37 | | | | |
| | | | | | | | | 25:41 | | | | | | | |
| | | | | | 26:105 | | | | | | **26:105** | | | | |
| | | | | | | | | | | **26:106** | | | | | |
| | | | | | 26:107 | | | | | **26:107** | | | | | |
| | | | | | | | | | | **26:108** | | | | | |
| | | | | | | | | | | **26:109** | | | | | |
| | | | | | | | | | | **26:110** | | | | | |
| | | | | | | | | | | **26:111** | **26:111** | | | | |
| | | | | | | | | | | **26:112** | | | | | |
| | | | | | | | | | | **26:113** | | | | | |
| | | | | | | | | | | **26:114** | | | | | |
| | | | | | | | | | | **26:115** | | | | | |
| | | | | | | | | | | **26:116** | **26:116** | | | | |
| | | | | | | | | | | | | **26:117** | | | **26:117** |
| | | | | | | | | | | | | **26:118** | | | **26:118** |
| | | | | | 29:14 | | | | | | | | | | |
| | | | | | 29:15 | | | | | | | | | | |
| | | | 33:7 | 33:7 | | | | 33:7 | | | | | | | |
| | | | | | | | | | | | | | | | 37:75 |
| | | | | | | 37:81 | | | | | | | | | |
| | | | | | | | | | | | 38:11 | | | | |
| | | | | | 40:5 | | | | | | 40:5 | | | | |
| 42:13 | | | | | | | | 42:13 | | | | | | | |
| | | | | | | | | | | | 50:12 | | | | |

**Table 2** (continuation)

| A | B | C | D | E | F | G | H | I | J | K | L | M | N | O | P |
|---|---|---|---|---|---|---|---|---|---|---|---|---|---|---|---|
| | | | | | | | | | | | **54:9** | | | | |
| | | | 57:26 | 57:26 | 57:26 | | | | | | | | | | |
| | | | | 57:27 | | | | | | | | | | | |
| | | | | | | 66:10 | | | | | | | | | |
| | | | | | **71:1** | | | | | | | | | | |
| | | | | | | | | | | **71:2** | | | | | |
| | | | | | | | | | | **71:3** | | | | | |
| | | | | | | | | | | **71:4** | | | | | |
| | | | | | | | | | | **71:5** | | **71:5** | | | |
| | | | | | | | | | | **71:6** | | **71:6** | | | |
| | | | | | | | | | | **71:7** | **71:7** | **71:7** | | | |
| | | | | | | | | | | **71:8** | | **71:8** | | | |
| | | | | | | | | | | **71:9** | | **71:9** | | | |
| | | | | | | | | | | **71:10** | | **71:10** | | | |
| | | | | | | | | | | **71:11** | | **71:11** | | | |
| | | | | | | | | | | **71:12** | | **71:12** | | | |
| | | | | | | | | | | **71:13** | | **71:13** | | | |
| | | | | | | | | | | **71:14** | | **71:14** | | | |
| | | | | | | | | | | **71:15** | | **71:15** | | | |
| | | | | | | | | | | **71:16** | | **71:16** | | | |
| | | | | | | | | | | **71:17** | | **71:17** | | | |
| | | | | | | | | | | **71:18** | | **71:18** | | | |
| | | | | | | | | | | **71:19** | | **71:19** | | | |
| | | | | | | | | | | **71:20** | | **71:20** | | | |
| | | | | | | | | | | | **7:21** | **71:21** | | | |
| | | | | | | | | | | | **7:22** | **71:22** | | | |
| | | | | | | | | | | | **7:23** | **71:23** | | | |
| | | | | | | | | | | | | **71:24** | **71:24** | | |
| | | | | | | | | | | | | **71:25** | | | |
| | | | | | | | | | | | | **71:26** | **71:26** | | |
| | | | | | | | | | | | | **71:27** | **71:27** | | |
| | | | | | | | | | | | | | **71:28** | | **71:28** |

Key to Table 2:

A = Noah is elected by God
B = Noah is divinely inspired
C = Noah is divinely guided
D = Noah is commissioned by God as a prophet

E = Noah is the first on a prophetic list that includes *inter alios* Abraham, Moses, and Jesus
F = Noah is commissioned by God as his apostle/messenger
G = Noah is depicted as God's servant
H = Noah is depicted as a Muslim
I = Noah is depicted as a model/*exemplum* for the quranic prophet
J = Noah is tentatively identified with the quranic prophet
K = Noah argues with the people (*or* with one of his sons)
L = Noah's warning is rejected by them (*or* by his rebellious son)
M = Noah implores God's help against the idolaters
N = Noah asks God to punish them
O = God comforts Noah
P = Noah implores God's mercy on him and his family

Hence we have in the Qur'ān (1) an *amplified* account – or rather a *series* of seven independent but interrelated expanded accounts (together with their parallels and *marginalia*) – plus (2) a *typological* and *eschatological* reading of the Noah story. Obviously the rich if heretofore almost overlooked implications of the latter for the shaping of the Muhammadan *evangelium* and what would thereby become a new "salvation history" (on which see Wansborugh 2006) are more than remarkable. But before examining these a more detailed analysis of the form, content, context, purpose, sources and textual precedents of the quranic Noah narratives – to which unfortunately very little attention has so far been paid in spite of their relevance – might prove helpful. Accordingly in chapters 4–6 I will attempt at exploring afresh such matters.

# *Excursus A*. Full text and translation of the quranic Noah narratives

The following table reproduces side by side the full text of the quranic Noah narratives, followed by their translation.

**Table 3:** *The quranic Noah narratives*

| Q 7:59–64 (QNN I) | Q 10:71–4 (QNN II) | Q 11:25–49 (QNN III) | Q 23:23–30 (QNN IV) | Q 26:105–22 (QNN V) | Q 54:9–17 (QNN VI) | Q 71:1–28 (QNN VII) |
|---|---|---|---|---|---|---|
| Q 7:59:<br>لَقَدْ أَرْسَلْنَا نُوحًا<br>إِلَىٰ قَوْمِهِ فَقَالَ يَا<br>قَوْمِ اعْبُدُوا اللَّهَ<br>مَا لَكُمْ مِنْ إِلَٰهٍ<br>غَيْرُهُ إِنِّي أَخَافُ<br>عَلَيْكُمْ عَذَابَ<br>يَوْمٍ عَظِيمٍ | Q 10:71:<br>وَاتْلُ عَلَيْهِمْ نَبَأَ<br>نُوحٍ إِذْ قَالَ لِقَوْمِهِ<br>يَا قَوْمِ إِنْ كَانَ<br>كَبُرَ عَلَيْكُمْ مَقَامِي<br>وَتَذْكِيرِي بِآيَاتِ<br>اللَّهِ فَعَلَى اللَّهِ<br>تَوَكَّلْتُ فَأَجْمِعُوا<br>أَمْرَكُمْ وَشُرَكَاءَكُمْ<br>ثُمَّ لَا يَكُنْ أَمْرُكُمْ<br>عَلَيْكُمْ غُمَّةً ثُمَّ<br>اقْضُوا إِلَيَّ وَلَا<br>تُنْظِرُونِ | Q 11:25:<br>وَلَقَدْ أَرْسَلْنَا نُوحًا إِلَىٰ<br>قَوْمِهِ إِنِّي لَكُمْ نَذِيرٌ<br>مُبِينٌ | Q 23:23:<br>وَلَقَدْ أَرْسَلْنَا نُوحًا<br>إِلَىٰ قَوْمِهِ فَقَالَ<br>يَا قَوْمِ اعْبُدُوا<br>اللَّهَ مَا لَكُمْ مِنْ<br>إِلَٰهٍ غَيْرُهُ ۖ أَفَلَا<br>تَتَّقُونَ | Q 26:105:<br>كَذَّبَتْ قَوْمُ نُوحٍ<br>الْمُرْسَلِينَ | Q 54:9:<br>كَذَّبَتْ قَبْلَهُمْ<br>قَوْمُ نُوحٍ فَكَذَّبُوا<br>عَبْدَنَا وَقَالُوا<br>مَجْنُونٌ وَازْدُجِرَ | Q 71:1:<br>إِنَّا أَرْسَلْنَا نُوحًا<br>إِلَىٰ قَوْمِهِ أَنْ أَنْذِرْ<br>قَوْمَكَ مِنْ قَبْلِ أَنْ<br>يَأْتِيَهُمْ عَذَابٌ أَلِيمٌ |
| Q 7:60:<br>قَالَ الْمَلَأُ مِنْ<br>قَوْمِهِ إِنَّا لَنَرَاكَ<br>فِي ضَلَالٍ مُبِينٍ | Q 10:72:<br>فَإِنْ تَوَلَّيْتُمْ فَمَا<br>سَأَلْتُكُمْ مِنْ أَجْرٍ ۖ<br>إِنْ أَجْرِيَ إِلَّا عَلَى<br>اللَّهِ ۖ وَأُمِرْتُ أَنْ<br>أَكُونَ مِنَ الْمُسْلِمِينَ | Q 11:26:<br>أَنْ لَا تَعْبُدُوا إِلَّا اللَّهَ<br>ۖ إِنِّي أَخَافُ عَلَيْكُمْ<br>عَذَابَ يَوْمٍ أَلِيمٍ | Q 23:24:<br>فَقَالَ الْمَلَأُ الَّذِينَ<br>كَفَرُوا مِنْ قَوْمِهِ<br>مَا هَٰذَا إِلَّا بَشَرٌ<br>مِثْلُكُمْ يُرِيدُ أَنْ<br>يَتَفَضَّلَ عَلَيْكُمْ<br>وَلَوْ شَاءَ اللَّهُ<br>لَأَنْزَلَ مَلَائِكَةً مَا<br>سَمِعْنَا بِهَٰذَا فِي<br>آبَائِنَا الْأَوَّلِينَ | Q 26:106:<br>إِذْ قَالَ لَهُمْ أَخُوهُمْ<br>نُوحٌ أَلَا تَتَّقُونَ | Q 54:10:<br>فَدَعَا رَبَّهُ أَنِّي<br>مَغْلُوبٌ فَانْتَصِرْ | Q 71:2:<br>قَالَ يَا قَوْمِ إِنِّي لَكُمْ<br>نَذِيرٌ مُبِينٌ |
| Q 7:61:<br>قَالَ يَا قَوْمِ لَيْسَ<br>بِي ضَلَالَةٌ<br>وَلَٰكِنِّي رَسُولٌ<br>مِنْ رَبِّ<br>الْعَالَمِينَ | Q 10:73:<br>فَكَذَّبُوهُ فَنَجَّيْنَاهُ<br>وَمَنْ مَعَهُ فِي<br>الْفُلْكِ وَجَعَلْنَاهُمْ<br>خَلَائِفَ وَأَغْرَقْنَا<br>الَّذِينَ كَذَّبُوا بِآيَاتِنَا<br>ۖ فَانْظُرْ كَيْفَ كَانَ<br>عَاقِبَةُ الْمُنْذَرِينَ | Q 11:27:<br>فَقَالَ الْمَلَأُ الَّذِينَ<br>كَفَرُوا مِنْ قَوْمِهِ مَا<br>نَرَاكَ إِلَّا بَشَرًا مِثْلَنَا<br>وَمَا نَرَاكَ اتَّبَعَكَ إِلَّا<br>الَّذِينَ هُمْ أَرَاذِلُنَا بَادِيَ<br>الرَّأْيِ وَمَا نَرَىٰ لَكُمْ<br>عَلَيْنَا مِنْ فَضْلٍ بَلْ<br>نَظُنُّكُمْ كَاذِبِينَ | Q 23:25:<br>إِنْ هُوَ إِلَّا رَجُلٌ<br>بِهِ جِنَّةٌ فَتَرَبَّصُوا<br>بِهِ حَتَّىٰ حِينٍ | Q 26:107:<br>إِنِّي لَكُمْ رَسُولٌ<br>أَمِينٌ | Q 54:11:<br>فَفَتَحْنَا أَبْوَابَ<br>السَّمَاءِ بِمَاءٍ<br>مُنْهَمِرٍ | Q 71:3:<br>أَنِ اعْبُدُوا اللَّهَ<br>وَاتَّقُوهُ وَأَطِيعُونِ |

**Table 3** (continuation)

| Q 7:59–64 (QNN I) | Q 10:71–4 (QNN II) | Q 11:25–49 (QNN III) | Q 23:23–30 (QNN IV) | Q 26:105–22 (QNN V) | Q 54:9–17 (QNN VI) | Q 71:1–28 (QNN VII) |
|---|---|---|---|---|---|---|
| Q 7:62: أُبَلِّغُكُمْ رِسَالَاتِ رَبِّي وَأَنْصَحُ لَكُمْ وَأَعْلَمُ مِنَ اللَّهِ مَا لَا تَعْلَمُونَ | Q 10:74: ثُمَّ بَعَثْنَا مِنْ بَعْدِهِ رُسُلًا إِلَىٰ قَوْمِهِمْ فَجَاءُوهُمْ بِالْبَيِّنَاتِ فَمَا كَانُوا لِيُؤْمِنُوا بِمَا كَذَّبُوا بِهِ مِنْ قَبْلُ ۚ كَذَٰلِكَ نَطْبَعُ عَلَىٰ قُلُوبِ الْمُعْتَدِينَ | Q 11:28: قَالَ يَا قَوْمِ أَرَأَيْتُمْ إِنْ كُنْتُ عَلَىٰ بَيِّنَةٍ مِنْ رَبِّي وَآتَانِي رَحْمَةً مِنْ عِنْدِهِ فَعُمِّيَتْ عَلَيْكُمْ أَنُلْزِمُكُمُوهَا وَأَنْتُمْ لَهَا كَارِهُونَ | Q 23:26: قَالَ رَبِّ انْصُرْنِي بِمَا كَذَّبُونِ | Q 26:108: فَاتَّقُوا اللَّهَ وَأَطِيعُونِ | Q 54:12: وَفَجَّرْنَا الْأَرْضَ عُيُونًا فَالْتَقَى الْمَاءُ عَلَىٰ أَمْرٍ قَدْ قُدِرَ | Q 71:4: يَغْفِرْ لَكُمْ مِنْ ذُنُوبِكُمْ وَيُؤَخِّرْكُمْ إِلَىٰ أَجَلٍ مُسَمًّى ۚ إِنَّ أَجَلَ اللَّهِ إِذَا جَاءَ لَا يُؤَخَّرُ ۖ لَوْ كُنْتُمْ تَعْلَمُونَ |
| Q 7:63: أَوَعَجِبْتُمْ أَنْ جَاءَكُمْ ذِكْرٌ مِنْ رَبِّكُمْ عَلَىٰ رَجُلٍ مِنْكُمْ لِيُنْذِرَكُمْ وَلِتَتَّقُوا وَلَعَلَّكُمْ تُرْحَمُونَ | | Q 11:29: وَيَا قَوْمِ لَا أَسْأَلُكُمْ عَلَيْهِ مَالًا ۖ إِنْ أَجْرِيَ إِلَّا عَلَى اللَّهِ ۚ وَمَا أَنَا بِطَارِدِ الَّذِينَ آمَنُوا ۚ إِنَّهُمْ مُلَاقُو رَبِّهِمْ وَلَٰكِنِّي أَرَاكُمْ قَوْمًا تَجْهَلُونَ | Q 23:27: فَأَوْحَيْنَا إِلَيْهِ أَنِ اصْنَعِ الْفُلْكَ بِأَعْيُنِنَا وَوَحْيِنَا فَإِذَا جَاءَ أَمْرُنَا وَفَارَ التَّنُّورُ ۙ فَاسْلُكْ فِيهَا مِنْ كُلٍّ زَوْجَيْنِ اثْنَيْنِ وَأَهْلَكَ إِلَّا مَنْ سَبَقَ عَلَيْهِ الْقَوْلُ مِنْهُمْ ۖ وَلَا تُخَاطِبْنِي فِي الَّذِينَ ظَلَمُوا ۖ إِنَّهُمْ مُغْرَقُونَ | Q 26:109: وَمَا أَسْأَلُكُمْ عَلَيْهِ مِنْ أَجْرٍ ۖ إِنْ أَجْرِيَ إِلَّا عَلَىٰ رَبِّ الْعَالَمِينَ | Q 54:13: وَحَمَلْنَاهُ عَلَىٰ ذَاتِ أَلْوَاحٍ وَدُسُرٍ | Q 71:5: قَالَ رَبِّ إِنِّي دَعَوْتُ قَوْمِي لَيْلًا وَنَهَارًا |
| Q 7:64: فَكَذَّبُوهُ فَأَنْجَيْنَاهُ وَالَّذِينَ مَعَهُ فِي الْفُلْكِ وَأَغْرَقْنَا الَّذِينَ كَذَّبُوا بِآيَاتِنَا ۚ إِنَّهُمْ كَانُوا قَوْمًا عَمِينَ | | Q 11:30: وَيَا قَوْمِ مَنْ يَنْصُرُنِي مِنَ اللَّهِ إِنْ طَرَدْتُهُمْ ۚ أَفَلَا تَذَكَّرُونَ | Q 23:28: فَإِذَا اسْتَوَيْتَ أَنْتَ وَمَنْ مَعَكَ عَلَى الْفُلْكِ فَقُلِ الْحَمْدُ لِلَّهِ الَّذِي نَجَّانَا مِنَ الْقَوْمِ الظَّالِمِينَ | Q 26:110: فَاتَّقُوا اللَّهَ وَأَطِيعُونِ | Q 54:14: تَجْرِي بِأَعْيُنِنَا جَزَاءً لِمَنْ كَانَ كُفِرَ | Q 71:6: فَلَمْ يَزِدْهُمْ دُعَائِي إِلَّا فِرَارًا |
| | | Q 11:31: وَلَا أَقُولُ لَكُمْ عِنْدِي خَزَائِنُ اللَّهِ وَلَا أَعْلَمُ الْغَيْبَ وَلَا أَقُولُ إِنِّي مَلَكٌ وَلَا أَقُولُ لِلَّذِينَ تَزْدَرِي أَعْيُنُكُمْ لَنْ يُؤْتِيَهُمُ اللَّهُ خَيْرًا ۖ اللَّهُ أَعْلَمُ بِمَا فِي أَنْفُسِهِمْ ۖ إِنِّي إِذًا لَمِنَ الظَّالِمِينَ | Q 23:29: وَقُلْ رَبِّ أَنْزِلْنِي مُنْزَلًا مُبَارَكًا وَأَنْتَ خَيْرُ الْمُنْزِلِينَ | Q 26:111: قَالُوا أَنُؤْمِنُ لَكَ وَاتَّبَعَكَ الْأَرْذَلُونَ | Q 54:15: وَلَقَدْ تَرَكْنَاهَا آيَةً فَهَلْ مِنْ مُدَّكِرٍ | Q 71:7: وَإِنِّي كُلَّمَا دَعَوْتُهُمْ لِتَغْفِرَ لَهُمْ جَعَلُوا أَصَابِعَهُمْ فِي آذَانِهِمْ وَاسْتَغْشَوْا ثِيَابَهُمْ وَأَصَرُّوا وَاسْتَكْبَرُوا اسْتِكْبَارًا |

**Table 3** (continuation)

| Q 7:59–64 (QNN I) | Q 10:71–4 (QNN II) | Q 11:25–49 (QNN III) | Q 23:23–30 (QNN IV) | Q 26:105–22 (QNN V) | Q 54:9–17 (QNN VI) | Q 71:1–28 (QNN VII) |
|---|---|---|---|---|---|---|
| | | Q 11:32:<br>قَالُوا يَا نُوحُ قَدْ جَادَلْتَنَا<br>فَأَكْثَرْتَ جِدَالَنَا فَأْتِنَا<br>بِمَا تَعِدُنَا إِنْ كُنْتَ مِنَ<br>الصَّادِقِينَ | Q 23:30:<br>إِنَّ فِي ذَٰلِكَ<br>لَآيَاتٍ وَإِنْ كُنَّا<br>لَمُبْتَلِينَ | Q 26:112:<br>قَالَ وَمَا عِلْمِي<br>بِمَا كَانُوا يَعْمَلُونَ | Q 54:16:<br>فَكَيْفَ كَانَ<br>عَذَابِي وَنُذُرِ | Q 71:8:<br>ثُمَّ إِنِّي دَعَوْتُهُمْ<br>جِهَارًا |
| | | Q 11:33:<br>قَالَ إِنَّمَا يَأْتِيكُمْ بِهِ<br>اللَّهُ إِنْ شَاءَ وَمَا أَنْتُمْ<br>بِمُعْجِزِينَ | | Q 26:113:<br>إِنْ حِسَابُهُمْ إِلَّا<br>عَلَىٰ رَبِّي ۖ لَوْ<br>تَشْعُرُونَ | Q 54:17:<br>وَلَقَدْ يَسَّرْنَا<br>الْقُرْآنَ لِلذِّكْرِ<br>فَهَلْ مِنْ مُدَّكِرٍ | Q 71:9:<br>ثُمَّ إِنِّي أَعْلَنْتُ لَهُمْ<br>وَأَسْرَرْتُ لَهُمْ<br>إِسْرَارًا |
| | | Q 11:34:<br>وَلَا يَنْفَعُكُمْ نُصْحِي<br>إِنْ أَرَدْتُ أَنْ أَنْصَحَ<br>لَكُمْ إِنْ كَانَ اللَّهُ يُرِيدُ<br>أَنْ يُغْوِيَكُمْ ۚ هُوَ رَبُّكُمْ<br>وَإِلَيْهِ تُرْجَعُونَ | | Q 26:114:<br>وَمَا أَنَا بِطَارِدِ<br>الْمُؤْمِنِينَ | | Q 71:10:<br>فَقُلْتُ اسْتَغْفِرُوا<br>رَبَّكُمْ إِنَّهُ كَانَ<br>غَفَّارًا |
| | | Q 11:35:<br>أَمْ يَقُولُونَ افْتَرَاهُ ۖ<br>قُلْ إِنِ افْتَرَيْتُهُ فَعَلَيَّ<br>إِجْرَامِي وَأَنَا بَرِيءٌ<br>مِمَّا تُجْرِمُونَ | | Q 26:115:<br>إِنْ أَنَا إِلَّا نَذِيرٌ<br>مُبِينٌ | | Q 71:11:<br>يُرْسِلِ السَّمَاءَ<br>عَلَيْكُمْ مِدْرَارًا |
| | | Q 11:36:<br>وَأُوحِيَ إِلَىٰ نُوحٍ أَنَّهُ<br>لَنْ يُؤْمِنَ مِنْ قَوْمِكَ إِلَّا<br>مَنْ قَدْ آمَنَ فَلَا تَبْتَئِسْ<br>بِمَا كَانُوا يَفْعَلُونَ | | Q 26:116:<br>قَالُوا لَئِنْ لَمْ تَنْتَهِ<br>يَا نُوحُ لَتَكُونَنَّ<br>مِنَ الْمَرْجُومِينَ | | Q 71:12:<br>وَيُمْدِدْكُمْ بِأَمْوَالٍ<br>وَبَنِينَ وَيَجْعَلْ لَكُمْ<br>جَنَّاتٍ وَيَجْعَلْ لَكُمْ<br>أَنْهَارًا |
| | | Q 11:37:<br>وَاصْنَعِ الْفُلْكَ بِأَعْيُنِنَا<br>وَوَحْيِنَا وَلَا تُخَاطِبْنِي<br>فِي الَّذِينَ ظَلَمُوا ۚ إِنَّهُمْ<br>مُغْرَقُونَ | | Q 26:117:<br>قَالَ رَبِّ إِنَّ<br>قَوْمِي كَذَّبُونِ | | Q 71:13:<br>مَا لَكُمْ لَا تَرْجُونَ<br>لِلَّهِ وَقَارًا |
| | | Q 11:38:<br>وَيَصْنَعُ الْفُلْكَ وَكُلَّمَا<br>مَرَّ عَلَيْهِ مَلَأٌ مِنْ قَوْمِهِ<br>سَخِرُوا مِنْهُ ۚ قَالَ إِنْ<br>تَسْخَرُوا مِنَّا فَإِنَّا نَسْخَرُ<br>مِنْكُمْ كَمَا تَسْخَرُونَ | | Q 26:118:<br>فَافْتَحْ بَيْنِي<br>وَبَيْنَهُمْ فَتْحًا<br>وَنَجِّنِي وَمَنْ<br>مَعِيَ مِنَ<br>الْمُؤْمِنِينَ | | Q 71:14:<br>وَقَدْ خَلَقَكُمْ أَطْوَارًا |
| | | Q 11:39:<br>فَسَوْفَ تَعْلَمُونَ مَنْ<br>يَأْتِيهِ عَذَابٌ يُخْزِيهِ<br>وَيَحِلُّ عَلَيْهِ عَذَابٌ<br>مُقِيمٌ | | Q 26:119:<br>فَأَنْجَيْنَاهُ وَمَنْ<br>مَعَهُ فِي الْفُلْكِ<br>الْمَشْحُونِ | | Q 71:15:<br>أَلَمْ تَرَوْا كَيْفَ<br>خَلَقَ اللَّهُ سَبْعَ<br>سَمَاوَاتٍ طِبَاقًا |

**Table 3** (continuation)

| Q 7:59–64 (QNN I) | Q 10:71–4 (QNN II) | Q 11:25–49 (QNN III) | Q 23:23–30 (QNN IV) | Q 26:105–22 (QNN V) | Q 54:9–17 (QNN VI) | Q 71:1–28 (QNN VII) |
|---|---|---|---|---|---|---|
| | | Q 11:40:<br>حَتَّىٰ إِذَا جَاءَ أَمْرُنَا<br>وَفَارَ التَّنُّورُ قُلْنَا احْمِلْ<br>فِيهَا مِنْ كُلٍّ زَوْجَيْنِ<br>اثْنَيْنِ وَأَهْلَكَ إِلَّا مَنْ<br>سَبَقَ عَلَيْهِ الْقَوْلُ وَمَنْ<br>آمَنَ ۚ وَمَا آمَنَ مَعَهُ<br>إِلَّا قَلِيلٌ | | Q 26:120:<br>ثُمَّ أَغْرَقْنَا بَعْدُ<br>الْبَاقِينَ | | Q 71:16:<br>وَجَعَلَ الْقَمَرَ<br>فِيهِنَّ نُورًا وَجَعَلَ<br>الشَّمْسَ سِرَاجًا |
| | | Q 11:41:<br>وَقَالَ ارْكَبُوا فِيهَا بِسْمِ<br>اللَّهِ مَجْرَاهَا وَمُرْسَاهَا ۚ<br>إِنَّ رَبِّي لَغَفُورٌ رَحِيمٌ | | Q 26:121:<br>إِنَّ فِي ذَٰلِكَ لَآيَةً ۖ<br>وَمَا كَانَ أَكْثَرُهُمْ<br>مُؤْمِنِينَ | | Q 71:17:<br>وَاللَّهُ أَنْبَتَكُمْ مِنَ<br>الْأَرْضِ نَبَاتًا |
| | | Q 11:42:<br>وَهِيَ تَجْرِي بِهِمْ فِي<br>مَوْجٍ كَالْجِبَالِ وَنَادَىٰ<br>نُوحٌ ابْنَهُ وَكَانَ فِي<br>مَعْزِلٍ يَا بُنَيَّ ارْكَبْ<br>مَعَنَا وَلَا تَكُنْ مَعَ<br>الْكَافِرِينَ | | Q 26:122:<br>وَإِنَّ رَبَّكَ لَهُوَ<br>الْعَزِيزُ الرَّحِيمُ | | Q 71:18:<br>ثُمَّ يُعِيدُكُمْ فِيهَا<br>وَيُخْرِجُكُمْ إِخْرَاجًا |
| | | Q 11:43:<br>قَالَ سَآوِي إِلَىٰ جَبَلٍ<br>يَعْصِمُنِي مِنَ الْمَاءِ ۚ<br>قَالَ لَا عَاصِمَ الْيَوْمَ<br>مِنْ أَمْرِ اللَّهِ إِلَّا مَنْ<br>رَحِمَ ۚ وَحَالَ بَيْنَهُمَا<br>الْمَوْجُ فَكَانَ مِنَ<br>الْمُغْرَقِينَ | | | | Q 71:19:<br>وَاللَّهُ جَعَلَ لَكُمُ<br>الْأَرْضَ بِسَاطًا |
| | | Q 11:44:<br>وَقِيلَ يَا أَرْضُ ابْلَعِي<br>مَاءَكِ وَيَا سَمَاءُ أَقْلِعِي<br>وَغِيضَ الْمَاءُ وَقُضِيَ<br>الْأَمْرُ وَاسْتَوَتْ عَلَى<br>الْجُودِيِّ ۖ وَقِيلَ بُعْدًا<br>لِلْقَوْمِ الظَّالِمِينَ | | | | Q 71:20:<br>لِتَسْلُكُوا مِنْهَا سُبُلًا<br>فِجَاجًا |
| | | Q 11:45:<br>وَنَادَىٰ نُوحٌ رَبَّهُ فَقَالَ<br>رَبِّ إِنَّ ابْنِي مِنْ أَهْلِي<br>وَإِنَّ وَعْدَكَ الْحَقُّ<br>وَأَنْتَ أَحْكَمُ الْحَاكِمِينَ | | | | Q 71:21:<br>قَالَ نُوحٌ رَبِّ إِنَّهُمْ<br>عَصَوْنِي وَاتَّبَعُوا<br>مَنْ لَمْ يَزِدْهُ مَالُهُ<br>وَوَلَدُهُ إِلَّا خَسَارًا |

**Table 3** (continuation)

| Q 7:59–64 (QNN I) | Q 10:71–4 (QNN II) | Q 11:25–49 (QNN III) | Q 23:23–30 (QNN IV) | Q 26:105–22 (QNN V) | Q 54:9–17 (QNN VI) | Q 71:1–28 (QNN VII) |
|---|---|---|---|---|---|---|
| | | Q 11:46:<br>قَالَ يَا نُوحُ إِنَّهُ لَيْسَ<br>مِنْ أَهْلِكَ ۖ إِنَّهُ عَمَلٌ<br>غَيْرُ صَالِحٍ ۖ فَلَا تَسْأَلْنِ<br>مَا لَيْسَ لَكَ بِهِ عِلْمٌ ۖ<br>إِنِّي أَعِظُكَ أَنْ تَكُونَ<br>مِنَ الْجَاهِلِينَ | | | | Q 71:22:<br>وَمَكَرُوا مَكْرًا<br>كُبَّارًا |
| | | Q 11:47:<br>قَالَ رَبِّ إِنِّي أَعُوذُ<br>بِكَ أَنْ أَسْأَلَكَ مَا لَيْسَ<br>لِي بِهِ عِلْمٌ ۖ وَإِلَّا تَغْفِرْ<br>لِي وَتَرْحَمْنِي أَكُنْ مِنَ<br>الْخَاسِرِينَ | | | | Q 71:23:<br>وَقَالُوا لَا تَذَرُنَّ<br>آلِهَتَكُمْ وَلَا تَذَرُنَّ<br>وَدًّا وَلَا سُوَاعًا<br>وَلَا يَغُوثَ وَيَعُوقَ<br>وَنَسْرًا |
| | | Q 11:48:<br>قِيلَ يَا نُوحُ اهْبِطْ<br>بِسَلَامٍ مِنَّا وَبَرَكَاتٍ<br>عَلَيْكَ وَعَلَىٰ أُمَمٍ مِمَّنْ<br>مَعَكَ ۚ وَأُمَمٌ سَنُمَتِّعُهُمْ<br>ثُمَّ يَمَسُّهُمْ مِنَّا عَذَابٌ<br>أَلِيمٌ | | | | Q 71:24:<br>وَقَدْ أَضَلُّوا كَثِيرًا ۖ<br>وَلَا تَزِدِ الظَّالِمِينَ<br>إِلَّا ضَلَالًا |
| | | Q 11:49:<br>تِلْكَ مِنْ أَنْبَاءِ الْغَيْبِ<br>نُوحِيهَا إِلَيْكَ ۖ مَا كُنْتَ<br>تَعْلَمُهَا أَنْتَ وَلَا قَوْمُكَ<br>مِنْ قَبْلِ هَٰذَا ۖ فَاصْبِرْ ۖ<br>إِنَّ الْعَاقِبَةَ لِلْمُتَّقِينَ | | | | Q 71:25:<br>مِمَّا خَطِيئَاتِهِمْ<br>أُغْرِقُوا فَأُدْخِلُوا<br>نَارًا فَلَمْ يَجِدُوا<br>لَهُمْ مِنْ دُونِ اللَّهِ<br>أَنْصَارًا |
| | | | | | | Q 71:26:<br>وَقَالَ نُوحٌ رَبِّ لَا<br>تَذَرْ عَلَى الْأَرْضِ<br>مِنَ الْكَافِرِينَ دَيَّارًا |
| | | | | | | Q 71:27:<br>إِنَّكَ إِنْ تَذَرْهُمْ<br>يُضِلُّوا عِبَادَكَ وَلَا<br>يَلِدُوا إِلَّا فَاجِرًا<br>كَفَّارًا |
| | | | | | | Q 71:28:<br>رَبِّ اغْفِرْ لِي<br>وَلِوَالِدَيَّ وَلِمَنْ<br>دَخَلَ بَيْتِيَ مُؤْمِنًا<br>وَلِلْمُؤْمِنِينَ<br>وَالْمُؤْمِنَاتِ وَلَا تَزِدِ<br>الظَّالِمِينَ إِلَّا تَبَارًا |

**Table 3** (continuation)

| **Q 7:59–64 (QNN I)** | **Q 10:71–4 (QNN II)** | **Q 11:25–49 (QNN III)** | **Q 23:23–30 (QNN IV)** | **Q 26:105–22 (QNN V)** | **Q 54:9–17 (QNN VI)** | **Q 71:1–28 (QNN VII)** |
|---|---|---|---|---|---|---|
| Q 7:59: *We sent Nūḥ* (= Noah) *to his people, and he said: "My people, serve God, for you have no god other than him! I fear for you the punishment of a dreadful day."* | Q 10:71: *Tell them the story of Nūḥ when he said to his people: "My people, if my stay and my reminding you of the signs of God has become too burdensome upon you, then I put my trust in God: Do resolve upon your plan and* [call upon] *your associates, and let not your plan be a worry to you; make your decision on me and respite me not!* | Q 11:25: *We sent Nūḥ to his people* [and he said to them]*: "I am to you a warner* [and I tell you]: | Q 23:23: *We sent Nūḥ to his people and he said* [to them]: *"My people, worship God, for he is your only god – will you not fear him?"* | Q 26:105: *The people of Nūḥ, too, denied the messengers.* | Q 54:9: *The people of Nūḥ denied* [the truth] *before them; they rejected our servant saying: "He is possessed!" – and he was rebuked.* | Q 71:1: *We sent Nūḥ to his people*[, saying]: *"Warn your people before a painful punishment comes to them!"* |
| Q 7:60: *But the leaders of his people said: "Clearly you are in error – so we believe."* | Q 10:72: *But if you turn away* [from my advice] – *well, I have asked no reward from you: my reward falls upon God alone and I have been commanded to be of those who surrender to him."* | Q 11:26: *Worship no one but God – for* [otherwise] *I fear for you the punishment of a painful day!"* | Q 23:24: *But the leading disbelievers among his people said: "He is just a man like yourselves trying to take precedence over you. If God willed* [to send a messenger] *he would have sent down angels instead. Besides, we never heard of anything like this from our forefathers.* | Q 26:106: *Their brother Nūḥ said to them: "Will you not fear God?* | Q 54:10: *So he called out to his Lord and said: "I am vanquished, so help me!"* | Q 71:2: *And so he said: "My people, I am to you a clear warner.* |

**Table 3** (continuation)

| **Q 7:59–64 (QNN I)** | **Q 10:71–4 (QNN II)** | **Q 11:25–49 (QNN III)** | **Q 23:23–30 (QNN IV)** | **Q 26:105–22 (QNN V)** | **Q 54:9–17 (QNN VI)** | **Q 71:1–28 (QNN VII)** |
|---|---|---|---|---|---|---|
| Q 7:61: *He said: "My people, there is no error in me – I am rather a messenger from the Lord of the Worlds!* | Q 10:73: *But they rejected him, so we saved him and those who were with him in the ark and let them survive, and we drowned those who denied our signs. Now, behold how was the end of those who were thus forewarned!* | Q 11:27: *But the leading disbelievers among his people said: "We do not see you but as a man like ourselves, and it is patent that only the vilest of us follow you; we do not see that you are any better than we are – in fact we think you are liars* [sic]*."* | Q 23:25: *He is just a demon-possessed man, so let's wait and see what happens to him."* | Q 26:107: *I am to you a trustworthy messenger,* | Q 54:11: *We opened the gates of heaven with rain pouring down* | Q 71:3: *Worship God, fear him and obey me!* |
| Q 7:62: *I am delivering to you the messages of my Lord and giving you sincere advise, for I know from God what you ignore.* | Q 10:74: *Then, after him, we sent forth messengers to their peoples and they brought them clear signs; but they would not believe that which they had formerly denied. So we seal the hearts of the transgressors!* | Q 11:28: *He said: "My people, think: suppose I do have with me a clear sign from my Lord, and that he has bestowed his mercy upon me, but that this has been obscured for you – could we force you to accept it against your will?* | Q 23:26: [Nūḥ] *said: "My Lord, support me, for they deny me!"* | Q 26:108: *so fear God and obey me!* | Q 54:12: *and made the earth to burst with springs. And the waters met for a matter already decreed.* | Q 71:4: *He will forgive you your sins and spare you until the time he has appointed; then, when it arrives, it will not be delayed – if only you understood!"* |

**Table 3** (continuation)

| Q 7:59–64 (QNN I) | Q 10:71–4 (QNN II) | Q 11:25–49 (QNN III) | Q 23:23–30 (QNN IV) | Q 26:105–22 (QNN V) | Q 54:9–17 (QNN VI) | Q 71:1–28 (QNN VII) |
|---|---|---|---|---|---|---|
| Q 7:63: *Do you wonder that a message from your Lord should come to you through a man from among you so that he may warn you and you may fear God and thus be given mercy?"* | | Q 11:29: *My people, I ask no reward from you for this – my reward falls upon God alone. I will not drive away the faithful – surely they shall meet their Lord; but I see you are an ignorant people.* | Q 23:27: *And so we inspired him: "Build the ark under our eyes and inspiration. When our command comes and the oven boils, load upon the ark two of every kind together with your family – save those against whom the verdict has already been rendered – and do not plead with me concerning those who have wronged, for they shall be drowned!* | Q 26:109: *I ask no reward from you, for my reward falls upon the Lord of the Worlds;* | Q 54:13: *We carried him upon [a vessel] of planks and nails* | Q 71:5: *He said: "My Lord, I have called my people night and day;* |
| Q 7:64: *But they called him a liar, so we saved him and those who were with him in the ark; and we drowned those who denied our signs – assuredly they were a blind people!* | | Q 11:30: *My people, who would help me against God if I were to drive them away? Will you not take heed?* | Q 23:28: *And when you and your companions are settled on the ark, say: 'Praise to God who has saved us from the wrongdoers!';* | Q 26:110: *so fear God and obey me!"* | Q 54:14: *running before our eyes – a reward for he who had been denied.* | Q 71:6: *yet my calling has only increased them in flight:* |

**Table 3** (continuation)

| **Q 7:59–64 (QNN I)** | **Q 10:71–4 (QNN II)** | **Q 11:25–49 (QNN III)** | **Q 23:23–30 (QNN IV)** | **Q 26:105–22 (QNN V)** | **Q 54:9–17 (QNN VI)** | **Q 71:1–28 (QNN VII)** |
|---|---|---|---|---|---|---|
| | | Q 11:31:<br>*I am not telling you that I hold God's treasures, or that I know what is hidden, or that I am an angel; nor do I say that God will grant no good to those who are despised in your eyes: God knows best what is in their souls! – Otherwise I would be among the wrongdoers."* | Q 23:29:<br>*and also: 'My Lord, let me land in a blessed harbour, for you are the best of all protectors.'"* | Q 26:111:<br>*They replied: "Why should we believe you when only the vilest follow you?"* | Q 54:15:<br>*We left this as a sign – will anyone remember?* | Q 71:7:<br>*every time I called them, so that you may forgive them, they put their fingers in their ears and covered themselves with their garments; they persisted* [in their rebellion] *and proved arrogant and defiant.* |
| | | Q 11:32:<br>*They said: "Nūḥ, you have long argued with us. Bring down on us the punishment you have threaten us with if you are speaking the truth!"* | Q 23:30:<br>*Surely there are signs in this, for we always put* [people] *to the test.* | Q 26:112:<br>*He said: "And what is my knowledge of what they have done?* | Q 54:16:<br>*How* [terrible] *my punishment was – and* [the fulfilment of] *my warning!* | Q 71:8:<br>*I have called them openly;* |
| | | Q 11:33:<br>*He said: "It is God who will bring it down if he wishes, and you will not be able to cause him to fail.* | | Q 26:113:<br>*Their account falls upon my Lord alone – if only you could see!* | Q 54:17:<br>*We have made the Qur'ān easy to remember – will anyone take heed?* | Q 71:9:<br>*I have preached to them in public and talked to them in private.* |
| | | Q 11:34:<br>*Although I do want to advise you, my advice will be of no use to you if he is willing to leave you in your delusions. He is your Lord and to him you shall be returned!"* | | Q 26:114:<br>*I will not drive away the faithful.* | | Q 71:10:<br>*I told them: 'Ask forgiveness of your Lord, for he is all-forgiving!* |

**Table 3** (continuation)

| Q 7:59–64 (QNN I) | Q 10:71–4 (QNN II) | Q 11:25–49 (QNN III) | Q 23:23–30 (QNN IV) | Q 26:105–22 | Q 54:9–17 (QNN VI) | Q 71:1–28 (QNN VII) |
|---|---|---|---|---|---|---|
| | | Q 11:35:<br>*If they say: "He has forged it," say: "If I have forged it, then my sin falls upon me, but I am innocent of what you do."* | | Q 26:115:<br>*I am but a plain warner."* | | Q 71:11:<br>*He will send down from above abundant* [rain] *for you,* |
| | | Q 11:36:<br>*And it was revealed to Nūḥ: "None of your people will believe, except those who have already done so; hence do not be distressed by what they may do.* | | Q 26:116:<br>*They answered: "Nūḥ, if you do not desist, then for sure you will be stoned."* | | Q 71:12:<br>*and give you wealth and sons, and provide you with gardens and rivers!* |
| | | Q 11:37:<br>*Build the ark under our eyes and inspiration and do not plead with me concerning those who have wronged – for they shall be drowned!"* | | Q 26:117:<br>*He said: "My Lord, my people have but rejected me;* | | Q 71:13:<br>*What is the matter with you? Why do you not accept God's greatness,* |
| | | Q 11:38:<br>*So he built the ark, and whenever the leaders of his people passed by they mocked him. He said: "You may deride us now, but we will come to deride you in the same manner,* | | Q 26:118:<br>*so judge between me and them and save me and the believers who are with me!"* | | Q 71:14:<br>*when it is stage by stage that he has created you?* |
| | | Q 11:39:<br>*and then you will find out who will get a humiliating punish-ment and upon whom a lasting suffering will alight."* | | Q 26:119:<br>*We saved him and his followers in the laden ark,* | | Q 71:15:<br>*Have you never wondered how God created seven heavens one upon another,* |

**Table 3** (continuation)

| Q 7:59–64 (QNN I) | Q 10:71–4 (QNN II) | Q 11:25–49 (QNN III) | Q 23:23–30 (QNN IV) | Q 26:105–22 (QNN V) | Q 54:9–17 (QNN VI) | Q 71:1–28 (QNN VII) |
|---|---|---|---|---|---|---|
| | | Q 11:40: *When our command came and the oven boiled, we said: "Load upon the ark two of every kind together with your own family – save those against whom the verdict has already been rendered – and those who have believed." But only a few had believed with him.* | | Q 26:120: *and drowned the others.* | | Q 71:16: *and placed the moon as a light and the sun as a lamp therein?* |
| | | Q 11:41: *He said: "Embark therein! In the name of God it shall sail and anchor – for surely my Lord is all-forgiving and merciful."* | | Q 26:121: *Surely there is a sign in this – yet most of them do not believe.* | | Q 71:17: *Or how he has made you grow out of the earth* |
| | | Q 11:42: *It sailed with them amidst waves like mountains; and Nūḥ called to his son who stood apart* [from them]*: "My son, get on board with us and do not stay with the disbelievers!"* | | Q 26:122: *Indeed your God alone is the Almighty, the Merciful!* | | Q 71:18: *and how he will return you into it and then bring you out again?* |

**Table 3** (continuation)

| Q 7:59–64 (QNN I) | Q 10:71–4 (QNN II) | Q 11:25–49 (QNN III) | Q 23:23–30 (QNN IV) | Q 26:105–22 (QNN V) | Q 54:9–17 (QNN VI) | Q 71:1–28 (QNN VII) |
|---|---|---|---|---|---|---|
| | | Q 11:43: *But he replied: "I will take refuge on a mountain to save me from the water!'"* [Nūḥ] *said: "There is no refuge today from God's command but for those on whom he has mercy!" The waves came between them and he was among the drowned.* | | | | Q 71:19: *Or how he has laid the earth for you* |
| | | Q 11:44: *Then it was said: "Earth, swallow your water!; and heaven, withhold* [your rain]*!" The waters subsided and the matter was accomplished. The ark settled on* [Mount] *al-Ǧūdiyy and it was said: "Gone are the wrongdoers!"* | | | | Q 71:20: *so that you can walk along it?'"* |
| | | Q 11:45: *Nūḥ called out to his Lord and said: "My Lord, my son is from my family. So if your promise is true and you are indeed the justest of all judges –"* | | | | Q 71:21: *Then Nūḥ said: "My Lord, they have disobeyed me and followed those whose riches and children will increase but their ruin,* |

**Table 3** (continuation)

| Q 7:59–64 (QNN I) | Q 10:71–4 (QNN II) | Q 11:25–49 (QNN III) | Q 23:23–30 (QNN IV) | Q 26:105–22 (QNN V) | Q 54:9–17 (QNN VI) | Q 71:1–28 (QNN VII) |
|---|---|---|---|---|---|---|
| | | Q 11:46: *He said: "Nūḥ, he is not of your family; what he did was not right. But do not ask me things you know nothing about. I advise you, lest you be counted among the ignorant."* | | | | Q 71:22: *who have laid a plot* [against me] |
| | | Q 11:47: *He said: "My Lord, I take refuge with you from asking that about which I have no knowledge! And unless you forgive me and have mercy on me I shall be among the losers!"* | | | | Q 71:23: *saying: 'Do not leave your gods! Do not leave Wadd, Suwā', Yagūṯ, Ya'ūq or Nasr!'* |
| | | Q 11:48: *It was said: "Nūḥ, disembark in peace from us with blessings upon you and upon the nations that shall spring from those who are with you. To other nations we will grant enjoyment for a time; then a painful punishment from us will touch them."* | | | | Q 71:24: *They have already misled many.* [Therefore, my Lord,] *I ask you not to increase the wrongdoers save in error!"* |
| | | Q 11:49: *That is from the news of the unseen which we reveal to you; neither you nor your people knew it before this; so be patient, for the* [best] *outcome belongs to the god-fearers.* | | | | Q 71:25: *Because of their sins they were drowned and thrown into the Fire, and they found no one to help them against God.* |

**Table 3** (continuation)

| Q 7:59–64 (QNN I) | Q 10:71–4 (QNN II) | Q 11:25–49 (QNN III) | Q 23:23–30 (QNN IV) | Q 26:105–22 (QNN V) | Q 54:9–17 (QNN VI) | Q 71:1–28 (QNN VII) |
|---|---|---|---|---|---|---|
| | | | | | | Q 71:26: *Nūḥ said: "My Lord, do not leave upon the earth even one of the disbelievers,* Q 71:27: *for otherwise they will mislead your servants and beget only sinners and disbelievers.* Q 71:28: *My Lord, forgive me, my parents and whoever enters my house as a believer, and all the believers, men and women alike; and do not increase the wrongdoers save in destruction."* |

# *Excursus B*. Quranic allusions to Noah outside the quranic Noah narratives

As shown above (see chapter one and Table 2) allusions to Noah in the Qur'ān are not limited to the seven quranic Noah narratives examined in this book. Outside these, one finds Noah mentioned in the following thirty-two quranic verses, of which only the excerpts specifically referring to him are translated below:

Q 3:33:

إِنَّ اللَّهَ اصْطَفَىٰ آدَمَ وَنُوحًا وَآلَ إِبْرَاهِيمَ وَآلَ عِمْرَانَ عَلَى الْعَالَمِينَ

*God chose Ādam* (= Adam), *Nūḥ* (= Noah), *Ibrāhīm's* (= Abraham's) *family and Imrān's* (= Amram's/Joachim's) *family over all other men.*

Q 4:163:

إِنَّا أَوْحَيْنَا إِلَيْكَ كَمَا أَوْحَيْنَا إِلَىٰ نُوحٍ وَالنَّبِيِّينَ مِنْ بَعْدِهِ ۚ وَأَوْحَيْنَا إِلَىٰ إِبْرَاهِيمَ وَإِسْمَاعِيلَ وَإِسْحَاقَ وَيَعْقُوبَ وَالْأَسْبَاطِ وَعِيسَىٰ وَأَيُّوبَ
وَيُونُسَ وَهَارُونَ وَسُلَيْمَانَ ۚ وَآتَيْنَا دَاوُودَ زَبُورًا

*Indeed, we have revealed to you as earlier to Nūḥ and the prophets after him . . .*

Q 6:84:

وَوَهَبْنَا لَهُ إِسْحَاقَ وَيَعْقُوبَ ۚ كُلًّا هَدَيْنَا ۚ وَنُوحًا هَدَيْنَا مِنْ قَبْلُ ۖ وَمِنْ ذُرِّيَّتِهِ دَاوُودَ وَسُلَيْمَانَ وَأَيُّوبَ وَيُوسُفَ وَمُوسَىٰ وَهَارُونَ ۚ
وَكَذَٰلِكَ نَجْزِي الْمُحْسِنِينَ

*We gave to him* [i.e. Ibrāhīm] *Isḥāq* (= Isaac) *and Ya'qūb* (= Jacob), *each of whom we guided as we had earlier guided Nūḥ . . .*

Q 9:70:

أَلَمْ يَأْتِهِمْ نَبَأُ الَّذِينَ مِنْ قَبْلِهِمْ قَوْمِ نُوحٍ وَعَادٍ وَثَمُودَ وَقَوْمِ إِبْرَاهِيمَ وَأَصْحَابِ مَدْيَنَ وَالْمُؤْتَفِكَاتِ ۚ أَتَتْهُمْ رُسُلُهُمْ بِالْبَيِّنَاتِ ۖ فَمَا كَانَ اللَّهُ
لِيَظْلِمَهُمْ وَلَٰكِنْ كَانُوا أَنْفُسَهُمْ يَظْلِمُونَ

*Have they never heard the stories of their predecessors – the peoples of Nūḥ, 'Ād, Ṯamūd, Ibrāhīm, and Madyan* (= Midian) *– and the ruined cities? Their messengers came to them with clear proof that God would never wrong them, but they wronged themselves!*[16]

Q 14:9:

أَلَمْ يَأْتِكُمْ نَبَأُ الَّذِينَ مِنْ قَبْلِكُمْ قَوْمِ نُوحٍ وَعَادٍ وَثَمُودَ ۛ وَالَّذِينَ مِنْ بَعْدِهِمْ ۛ لَا يَعْلَمُهُمْ إِلَّا اللَّهُ ۚ جَاءَتْهُمْ رُسُلُهُمْ بِالْبَيِّنَاتِ فَرَدُّوا أَيْدِيَهُمْ فِي
أَفْوَاهِهِمْ وَقَالُوا إِنَّا كَفَرْنَا بِمَا أُرْسِلْتُمْ بِهِ وَإِنَّا لَفِي شَكٍّ مِمَّا تَدْعُونَنَا إِلَيْهِ مُرِيبٍ

*Have you not heard the stories of those who were before you – the peoples of Nūḥ, 'Ād, Ṯamūd and those who came after them? . . .*

Q 17:3:

ذُرِّيَّةَ مَنْ حَمَلْنَا مَعَ نُوحٍ ۚ إِنَّهُ كَانَ عَبْدًا شَكُورًا

*Oh you* [Children of Israel], *descendants of those we carried with Nūḥ! – He surely was a grateful servant.*

Q 17:17:

وَكَمْ أَهْلَكْنَا مِنَ الْقُرُونِ مِنْ بَعْدِ نُوحٍ ۗ وَكَفَىٰ بِرَبِّكَ بِذُنُوبِ عِبَادِهِ خَبِيرًا بَصِيرًا

*How many generations have we destroyed since Nūḥ! . . .*

Q 19:58:

أُولَٰئِكَ الَّذِينَ أَنْعَمَ اللَّهُ عَلَيْهِمْ مِنَ النَّبِيِّينَ مِنْ ذُرِّيَّةِ آدَمَ وَمِمَّنْ حَمَلْنَا مَعَ نُوحٍ وَمِنْ ذُرِّيَّةِ إِبْرَاهِيمَ وَإِسْرَائِيلَ وَمِمَّنْ هَدَيْنَا وَاجْتَبَيْنَا ۚ إِذَا تُتْلَىٰ عَلَيْهِمْ آيَاتُ الرَّحْمَٰنِ خَرُّوا سُجَّدًا وَبُكِيًّا

*Those were the prophets upon whom God bestowed his blessing from among Ādam's descendants, those we carried with Nūḥ, the seed of Ibrāhīm and Isrā'īl* (= Israel) *and those we guided and chose . . .*

Q 21:76:

وَنُوحًا إِذْ نَادَىٰ مِنْ قَبْلُ فَاسْتَجَبْنَا لَهُ فَنَجَّيْنَاهُ وَأَهْلَهُ مِنَ الْكَرْبِ الْعَظِيمِ

*Earlier we answered Nūḥ when he cried out to us: we saved him and his family from the flood*

Q 21:77:

وَنَصَرْنَاهُ مِنَ الْقَوْمِ الَّذِينَ كَذَّبُوا بِآيَاتِنَا ۚ إِنَّهُمْ كَانُوا قَوْمَ سَوْءٍ فَأَغْرَقْنَاهُمْ أَجْمَعِينَ

*and we helped him against the people who had denied our signs – they were wicked people, so we drowned them all together!*

Q 22:42:

وَإِنْ يُكَذِّبُوكَ فَقَدْ كَذَّبَتْ قَبْلَهُمْ قَوْمُ نُوحٍ وَعَادٌ وَثَمُودُ

*And if they deny you, so too . . . did the people of Nūḥ, and those of ʿĀd and Ṯamūd.*

Q 25:37:

وَقَوْمَ نُوحٍ لَمَّا كَذَّبُوا الرُّسُلَ أَغْرَقْنَاهُمْ وَجَعَلْنَاهُمْ لِلنَّاسِ آيَةً ۖ وَأَعْتَدْنَا لِلظَّالِمِينَ عَذَابًا أَلِيمًا

*And the people of Nūḥ: when they denied the messengers* [sic] *we drowned them and made them a sign to all people – since we have prepared a painful torment for the wicked!*

Q 29:14:

وَلَقَدْ أَرْسَلْنَا نُوحًا إِلَىٰ قَوْمِهِ فَلَبِثَ فِيهِمْ أَلْفَ سَنَةٍ إِلَّا خَمْسِينَ عَامًا فَأَخَذَهُمُ الطُّوفَانُ وَهُمْ ظَالِمُونَ

*We sent Nūḥ to his people: he lived among them a thousand years minus fifty years; but when the flood seized them they were still wrongdoers.*

Q 29:15:

فَأَنْجَيْنَاهُ وَأَصْحَابَ السَّفِينَةِ وَجَعَلْنَاهَا آيَةً لِلْعَالَمِينَ

*We saved him and those with him in the ark, and made this a sign to all people!*

Q 33:7:

وَإِذْ أَخَذْنَا مِنَ النَّبِيِّينَ مِيثَاقَهُمْ وَمِنكَ وَمِن نُّوحٍ وَإِبْرَاهِيمَ وَمُوسَىٰ وَعِيسَى ابْنِ مَرْيَمَ ۖ وَأَخَذْنَا مِنْهُم مِّيثَاقًا غَلِيظًا

*We have taken a pledge from the prophets: from you, Nūḥ, Ibrāhīm, Mūsà* (= Moses) *and ʻĪsà* (= Jesus) *the son of Maryam* (= Mary) – *from all of you!*

Q 37:75:

وَلَقَدْ نَادَانَا نُوحٌ فَلَنِعْمَ الْمُجِيبُونَ

*Nūḥ called to us – and how excellent our response was!*

Q 37:76:

وَنَجَّيْنَاهُ وَأَهْلَهُ مِنَ الْكَرْبِ الْعَظِيمِ

*We saved him and his family from great distress*

Q 37:77:

وَجَعَلْنَا ذُرِّيَّتَهُ هُمُ الْبَاقِينَ

*and let his offspring last* [for many ages].

Q 37:78:

[17]و بركنا عليه فى الأخرين

*We have bestowed our blessing upon him in the last days.*[18]

Q 37:79:

سَلَامٌ عَلَىٰ نُوحٍ فِي الْعَالَمِينَ

*Peace upon Nūḥ among all men!*[19]

Q 37:80:

إِنَّا كَذَٰلِكَ نَجْزِي الْمُحْسِنِينَ

*Thus do we reward the righteous,*

Q 37:81:

إِنَّهُ مِنْ عِبَادِنَا الْمُؤْمِنِينَ

*for he is to be counted among our faithful servants.*

Q 37:82:

ثُمَّ أَغْرَقْنَا الْآخَرِينَ

*Whereas we drowned all others.*

Q 40:5:

كَذَّبَتْ قَبْلَهُمْ قَوْمُ نُوحٍ وَالْأَحْزَابُ مِنْ بَعْدِهِمْ ۖ وَهَمَّتْ كُلُّ أُمَّةٍ بِرَسُولِهِمْ لِيَأْخُذُوهُ ۖ وَجَادَلُوا بِالْبَاطِلِ لِيُدْحِضُوا بِهِ الْحَقَّ فَأَخَذْتُهُمْ ۖ فَكَيْفَ كَانَ عِقَابِ

. . . [T]*he people of Nūḥ denied* [the truth] *and so did the* [disbelieving] *parties after them. Every community has conspired to seize its own messenger and striven to deny the truth with falsehood. But I destroyed them – and how* [terrible] *my punishment was!*

Q 40:30:

وَقَالَ الَّذِي آمَنَ يَا قَوْمِ إِنِّي أَخَافُ عَلَيْكُمْ مِثْلَ يَوْمِ الْأَحْزَابِ

*Then the believer said: 'My people, I fear for you* [a fate] *akin to the fate of those who opposed* [the prophets]*:*

Q 40:31:

مِثْلَ دَأْبِ قَوْمِ نُوحٍ وَعَادٍ وَثَمُودَ وَالَّذِينَ مِنْ بَعْدِهِمْ ۚ وَمَا اللَّهُ يُرِيدُ ظُلْمًا لِلْعِبَادِ

*hence similar to the fate of the people of Nūḥ, 'Ād, Ṯamūd and those who came after them . . .' . . .*

Q 42:13:

شَرَعَ لَكُمْ مِنَ الدِّينِ مَا وَصَّىٰ بِهِ نُوحًا وَالَّذِي أَوْحَيْنَا إِلَيْكَ وَمَا وَصَّيْنَا بِهِ إِبْرَاهِيمَ وَمُوسَىٰ وَعِيسَىٰ ۖ أَنْ أَقِيمُوا الدِّينَ وَلَا تَتَفَرَّقُوا فِيهِ ۚ كَبُرَ عَلَى الْمُشْرِكِينَ مَا تَدْعُوهُمْ إِلَيْهِ ۚ اللَّهُ يَجْتَبِي إِلَيْهِ مَنْ يَشَاءُ وَيَهْدِي إِلَيْهِ مَنْ يُنِيبُ

*He has laid down for you in matters of faith what he already charged Nūḥ with, what we have revealed to you and he previously charged Ibrāhīm, Mūsà and 'Īsà with . . .*

Q 50:12:

كَذَّبَتْ قَبْلَهُمْ قَوْمُ نُوحٍ وَأَصْحَابُ الرَّسِّ وَثَمُودُ

*The people of Nūḥ disbelieved long before them . . .*

Q 51:46:

وَقَوْمَ نُوحٍ مِنْ قَبْلُ ۖ إِنَّهُمْ كَانُوا قَوْمًا فَاسِقِينَ

*Before that* [we destroyed] *the people of Nūḥ – they were a truly rebellious people!*

Q 53:52:

وَقَوْمَ نُوحٍ مِنْ قَبْلُ ۖ إِنَّهُمْ كَانُوا هُمْ أَظْلَمَ وَأَطْغَىٰ

*And before that the people of Nūḥ – they were exceedingly unjust and insolent!*

Q 57:26:

وَلَقَدْ أَرْسَلْنَا نُوحًا وَإِبْرَاهِيمَ وَجَعَلْنَا فِي ذُرِّيَّتِهِمَا النُّبُوَّةَ وَالْكِتَابَ ۖ فَمِنْهُمْ مُهْتَدٍ ۖ وَكَثِيرٌ مِنْهُمْ فَاسِقُونَ

*We sent Nūḥ and Ibrāhīm and gave prophethood and the Book to their offspring . . .*

Q 66:10:

ضَرَبَ اللَّهُ مَثَلًا لِلَّذِينَ كَفَرُوا امْرَأَتَ نُوحٍ وَامْرَأَتَ لُوطٍ ۖ كَانَتَا تَحْتَ عَبْدَيْنِ مِنْ عِبَادِنَا صَالِحَيْنِ فَخَانَتَاهُمَا فَلَمْ يُغْنِيَا عَنْهُمَا مِنَ اللَّهِ
شَيْئًا وَقِيلَ ادْخُلَا النَّارَ مَعَ الدَّاخِلِينَ

*God has given a similitude for the unbelievers: the wives of Nūḥ and Lūṭ* (= Lot), *who married two of our righteous servants but then betrayed them; yet their husbands were unable to help them against God! . . .*

# Chapter 4 / The Quranic Noah Narratives: Form, Content, Context, and Primary Meaning

The quranic Noah narratives have been studied at some length by Erica Martin (2010), who focuses her analysis on some of their micro-components or "story elements," examines their development within each particular narrative and the major sections in these, investigates their relationship to the *Straflegenden* or "punishment stories" within which they are placed, and gives some hints as to their more immediate intent, close interdependence, rhetorical qualities, and explicit meaning, but does not fully inquire into their literary form, dynamic structure, and overall implicit purpose. Nor does she systematically explore the parallels of such elements elsewhere in the Qur'ān, their hypothetical sources and precedents outside the quranic corpus, and their implications for the Muhammadan *evangelium*.

On the other hand, while Martin must certainly be credited with having gone beyond all previous studies on the subject (Welch 2000; Tottoli 2002; Wheeler 2002, 2006; Brinner 2003; Addas 2007b; Brown 2007; Chabbi 2008), some of her own premises and conclusions seem to me highly doubtful. Thus according to her, "the most ubiquitous element, appearing in six of the seven sūras [namely quranic Noah narratives nos. I–VI], is 'Noah argues with the people.'" In fact, this element is lacking in quranic Noah narrative no. VI (where only Noah's rejection by his opponents is mentioned in v. 9), not in VII (where it is extensively reported by Noah himself in vv. 2–22). Moreover, Martin fails to notice so decisive an element as Noah's rejection by his opponents, which indeed is the only element fully contained in all narratives – and an essential motif in the shaping of the Muhammadan *evangelium* after the quranic Noah narratives, as we shall see. In short, there is still much more to be argued about the quranic Noah narratives, their constitutive elements and motifs, and the way in which these are displayed, as also about the ideological background and tacit purpose of the different narratives that they inform, which Martin roughly limits to the more shallow and explicit purpose of prophetic monotheistic preaching.

Hence in this chapter I will undertake a multifaceted analysis of the quranic Noah narratives based upon their adaptation of classical prophetic and apocalyptic literary forms and themes, contextual placement within each *sūra* (where applicable), and primary meaning.

According to the number of verses in each narrative, quranic Noah narrative no. VII is the longest, followed by nos. III, V, VI, IV, I, and II, whereas in terms of the number of words, no. III is the longest, followed by nos. VII, IV, V, II, I, and VI (see Table 4, columns A and B, below).[1] An additional division can also be made as to the number of formal segments (on which see Table 1 above) into which each narrative divides: conforming to this principle, no. III is also the longest one, followed by nos. I, II, IV, V, and both VI and VII (see Table 4, column C, below).

**Table 4:** *Comparative length of the quranic Noah narratives*

| | (A) length by number of verses | (B) absolute length | (C) length by number of formal segments |
|---|---|---|---|
| + | QNN VII (28) | QNN III | QNN III (8) |
| | QNN III (25) | QNN VII | Quranic Noah narratives I, II, IV, V (6) |
| | QNN V (18) | QNN IV | Quranic Noah narratives VI, VII (4) |
| | QNN VI (9) | QNN V | |
| | QNN IV (8) | QNN II | |
| | QNN I (6) | QNN I | |
| – | QNN II (4) | QNN VI | |

Furthermore, and as suggested above, all quranic Noah narratives follow a similar though flexible formal pattern, which I shall now try to set out.

## *Quranic Noah narrative no. I* (Q 7:59–64 / *Sūrat al-Aʿrāf*):

This narrative comprises Noah's commission (v. 59a); his admonition to his people, whom he encourages to turn to God (v. 59b); Noah's warning: if they do not turn to God, they will suffer punishment at the day of judgment (v. 59c); the people's rejection of Noah, whom they accuse of talking nonsense (v. 60); Noah's reply: far from talking nonsense, he claims, he has been commissioned by God to instruct them (vv. 61–3); and a brief final account in which we are told that he was once more rejected, that God saved him together with those who did believe him, and that God drowned all of the others, for they were but a blind people unable to understand his signs (v. 64). Its literary form, therefore, is that of a six-part *Straf-legend* that includes the following formal segments: ($\alpha$) a prophetic commission (v. 59); ($\beta$) the prophet's admonition (v. 59); ($\gamma$) his warning and prediction of disaster (v. 59); ($\delta$) the rejection of his mission (v. 60, but which is alluded to again in v. 64); ($\varepsilon$) the prophet's own justification (vv. 61–3); and ($\eta$) a short narrative about the salvation of the righteous and the divine punishment of the wicked (v. 64).

Vv. 59a and 64 (i.e., the introduction and the conclusion to the story) are of a narrative nature, whereas vv. 59b-63 reproduce (by narrating it, cf. vv. 59a, 61a) Noah's dialogue with his contemporaries, and especially Noah's own words (vv. 59b-c, 61–3). There is no monologue by Noah here, nor does he talk to God. On the other hand, the eschatological coda found in almost all other quranic Noah narratives is also lacking in quranic Noah narrative no. I: the episode merely informs us of what happened to Noah and his people. Nevertheless, the story is preceded by a more general warning (7:26–58), and other legends similar to that of Noah are told immediately afterwards (7:65–93) as a sign of the fate that awaits the unbelievers (7:94–102). Thus an eschatological mood is easily discernible. Finally, the obvious connection between 7:59–64 and 182–8, and within it the striking parallel between 7.60 (where Noah is accused of talking nonsense) and 184 (where the quranic prophet is likewise accused of being possessed, cf. 23:25; 54:9), add to this and prove that the Noah story is here more than just a legend (cf. also 10:94–109; 11:12–24,35,38,49).

## *Quranic Noah narrative no. II* (Q 10:71–4 / *Sūrat Yūnus*):

This narrative basically divides into the same formal segments characteristic of the first one, save the prophet's commission, which is substituted by an express command given to the quranic prophet ("Tell them [lit. recite/relate to them] the story of Noah! . . ." [v. 71a]) and his own justification. Thus it comprises the prologue/*incipit*; ($\beta$) the prophet's admonition (vv. 71b-e + 2b-d), in the midst of which ($\gamma$) his warning is abruptly inserted (v. 72a) with an implicit prediction of disaster ("If you turn away! –" ); and ($\delta$, $\eta$) a short narrative about the rejection of his mission, the salvation of the righteous, and the divine punishment of the wicked (v. 73a-b), to which ($\theta$) an eschatological coda is appended (vv. 73c-74). So this time we have a six-part *Straflegend*. Again there is no monologue by Noah, nor does he talk to God. Overall the formal structure is very similar, therefore, to that of quranic Noah narrative no. I: between the introduction and the conclusion to the story we find Noah's words, though this time the words of his opponents go unmentioned. It must also be stressed that, in contrast to no. I, no. II not only informs us of what happened to Noah and his people, but a coda in which the reader is reminded of the fate of those who are reluctant to accept the words of God's messengers and warned of the fact that he has sealed the hearts of the transgressors bestows an incisive eschatological tone to the story. In turn, vv. 10:94–109 shed light upon the use that the quranic prophet was expected to make of the Noah story, and hence upon what I have earlier called the prologue/*incipit* to no. II (cf. 7:182–8; 11:12–24,35,38,49).

## *Quranic Noah narrative no. III* (Q 11:25–49 / *Sūrat Hūd*):

This narrative is, by far, the longest and most complete, and also, together with no. VII, the most complex of all of the quranic Noah narratives. Save a prologue/*incipit* similar to that of quranic Noah narrative no. II, it has all the segments found in the preceding accounts, including those missing in quranic Noah narrative no. II: ($\alpha$) a prophetic commission (v. 25a); ($\beta$) the prophet's admonition (vv. 25b-26a); ($\gamma$) his warning and prediction of disaster (v. 26b); ($\delta$) this time a threefold rejection of his warning, twice by its addressees (vv. 27, 32) who even mock him (v. 38), and then later by one of his sons (v. 43); ($\varepsilon$) a twofold justification of his mission by the prophet himself (vv. 28–31, 33–4); ($\eta$) an expanded narrative about the salvation of the righteous and the divine punishment of the wicked (vv. 36–48) that includes God's instructions to Noah (v. 37), the story of the flood (vv. 40–8), and ($\zeta$) a short but apparently misplaced dialogue between Noah and God (for it is strangely placed after the flood!) in which the prophet asks God to have mercy on him and his family and then submits to his will (vv. 45–7); and again, ($\theta$) an eschatological coda that further strengthens the connection between Noah and the quranic prophet (v.49). Therefore quranic Noah narrative no. III should be read as an eight-part *Straflegend* in which Noah's (vv. 25–34, 38–9, 41, 42b-c, 43b, 45, 47), his opponents' (vv. 27, 32, 43a), and even God's (vv. 35–7, 40, 44, 46, 48) words are now extensively reported. It must be highlighted that v. 35, which seems to be addressed to the quranic prophet rather than Noah (cf. 11:13), breaks off the narrative and prefigures the content of v. 49, in which the former is comforted by God, who asks him to be patient and assures him that the judgment of the wicked and the salvation of the righteous will take place at the appointed time (cf. 7:182–8; 10:94–109; 11:12–24, as well as the command given to the quranic prophet in 10:71).

## *Quranic Noah narrative no. IV* (Q 23:23–30 / *Sūrat al Mu'minūn*):

This is a much simpler narrative, as it lacks altogether segments $\gamma$ and $\varepsilon$. Thus it is a six-part *Straflegend* composed of: ($\alpha$) a prophetic commission (v. 23a); ($\beta$) the prophet's admonition (v. 23b-c); ($\delta$) the rejection of his mission by the people (vv. 24–5), who once more mock him (v. 25); ($\zeta$) a short monologue by Noah, who asks God to help him (v. 26); ($\eta$) God's instructions to Noah (vv. 27–9); and ($\theta$) a short eschatological coda that reads Noah's story as a divine sign (v. 30) and hence as a divine instruction. Interestingly enough, four out of six parts of the story are entirely framed as two consecutive dialogues: one between Noah's and his opponents (vv. 23b-25), and the other one between a frustrated Noah, who implores divine assistance, and God, who instructs him (vv. 26–9). It should also be observed that Noah's opponents accuse him not just of talking nonsense (like in 7:60) but of being a "demon-possessed" man (*rağul bihi ğinna*); cf. 11:38, where he is mocked by them, and 54:9, where once more he is accused of being "possessed" (but also 7:184; 37:36; 44:14; 52:29 and 68:51, where the quranic prophet is likewise accused of being "possessed" [*mağnūn*]; 51:39, where that very same term is applied to Moses; 51:52, where it applies to all previous rejected prophets; and 6:10, where we read that these and the quranic prophet were mocked, too). Moreover, he is said to be a man just like anyone else (v. 24); cf. 11:27 (as well as the references to the quranic prophet in 3:144; 6:8–10; 7:188; 11:12; 16:103). I will come back to these accusations later on.

## *Quranic Noah narrative no. V* (Q 26:105–22 / *Sūrat aš-Šu'arā*):

This narrative lacks the prophet's commission and his warning to the people, but like no. III it presents a rather complex structure, since the rejection of the prophet's mission (though not his own justification, as one would expect) is here twofold. So in this case we have a six-part *Straflegend* formed of: ($\beta$) the prophet's admonition (vv. 106–10); ($\delta$) the twofold rejection of his mission by the people (vv. 111 and 116, respectively); ($\varepsilon$) the prophet's own justification (v. 112); ($\zeta$) a monologue by Noah, who once more asks God to help him (vv. 117–18); ($\eta$) the story about the salvation of the righteous and the condemnation of the wicked (vv. 119–20); and ($\theta$) an eschatological coda akin to, but somewhat longer than, that found in no. IV (vv. 121–2).

## *Quranic Noah narrative no. VI* (Q 54:9–17 / *Sūrat al-Qamar*):

This is the shortest of all the quranic Noah *Straflegenden* and presents a quite simple fourfold structure: ($\delta$) the rejection of the prophetic mission (v. 9); ($\zeta$) a very short monologue by Noah, who asks God to help him (v. 10); ($\eta$) a narrative about the flood and the salvation of the righteous (vv. 11–14); and ($\theta$) an eschatological coda (vv. 15–17) that echoes and expands those found in nos. IV and V. (The refrain in vv. 16–17 is reproduced almost verbatim in 54:21–2,30,32,39–40,51, where it functions as a coda to other similar stories and thereby as a foreword to the eschatological warning in vv. 43–55; notice also the reference in v. 9 to the warning contained in vv. 1–8.)

## *Quranic Noah narrative no. VII* (Q 71 / *Sūrat Nūḥ*):

This narrative is very peculiar on its own in that, in spite of some close affinities with no. IV (most of VII consists of a dialogue between Noah and the people [vv. 2–4], followed by a very long monologue by Noah [vv. 5–28] that includes an expanded account of the former [vv. 10–23]), it mainly focuses on Noah's personal frustration and thoughts; so much so that it is Noah himself who asks God to punish those reluctant to accept his warnings (vv. 26–8). Thus we have a six-part *Straflegend* formed by the following observable segments: (*α*) the prophetic commission (v. 1); (*β*) Noah's admonition (vv. 2–4a, 10–20); (*γ*) his warning (v. 4b-c); (*δ*) the rejection of his mission by his contemporaries (vv. 7, 21–3); (*ζ*) Noah's monologue (vv. 5–28); and (*η*) a seemingly misplaced and succinct reference (for Noah's monologue continues afterwards) to the punishment of the wicked (v. 25a). Such apparent misplacement echoes 11:45–7 (see above) and has been singled out as indicating a possible connection between the two narratives (Martin 2010: 256–7).

Overall, it is interesting to note that a flood narrative proper is only found in quranic Noah narratives no. III and (to a lesser extent) no. VI, whereas dialogues between Noah and his contemporaries are present in nos. I, III, IV, and V; dialogues between Noah and God in nos. III, IV, V, VI, and VII; and monologues by Noah in nos. IV, V, VI, and (especially) VII.

A word now about the context, immediate intent, and additional purpose of these overlapping narratives. The quranic Noah narratives present the story of Noah along with other early prophetic legends that aim to make several peoples acknowledge and turn to the true God, or else realise that they will be punished if they do not. Therefore they are meant (*a*) to provide typological instruction to the unbelievers and the *mu'minūn* alike (i.e., to menace the infidels and encourage the faithful with predictions about their fate [quranic Noah narratives nos. I–VI]) and (*b*) to comfort the quranic prophet (whose own frustration and thoughts might be reflected in no. VII) against his opponents (cf. no. I and 7:182–8; no. II and 10:94–109; and no. III, especially v. 49, and 11.12–24).

I will comment more on *b* in the next chapter, but I think it might be useful at this point to provide the reader with a table of the verses in which the quranic prophet is either explicitly or implicitly alluded to within the quranic Noah narratives (see Table 5 below).

**Table 5:** *Explicit (and implicit) allusions to the quranic prophet within the quranic Noah narratives*

| QNN I | QNN II | QNN III | QNN IV | QNN V | QNN VI | QNN VII |
|---|---|---|---|---|---|---|
| (7:60)<br>cf. 6:10<br>cf. 7:184<br>cf. 11:38<br>cf. 23:25<br>cf. 37:36<br>cf. 44:14<br>cf. 52:29<br>cf. 54:9<br>cf. 68:51 | 10:71 | (11:27)<br>cf. 3:144<br>cf. 7:188<br>cf. 11:12<br>cf. 16:103<br>cf. 23:24 | (23:24)<br>cf. 3:144<br>cf. 6:8<br>cf. 6:9<br>cf. 7:188<br>cf. 11:12<br>cf. 11:27<br>cf. 16:103 | – | (54:9)<br>cf. 6:10<br>cf. 7:60<br>cf. 7:184<br>cf. 11:38<br>cf. 23:25<br>cf. 37:36<br>cf. 44:14<br>cf. 52:29<br>cf. 68:51 | – |
| | | 11:35<br>cf. 11:13 | (23:25)<br>cf. 6:10<br>cf. 7:60<br>cf. 7:184<br>cf. 11:38<br>cf. 37:36<br>cf. 44:14<br>cf. 52:29<br>cf. 54:9<br>cf. 68:51 | | | |
| | | (11:38) | | | | |
| | | 11:49 | | | | |

# *Excursus*. Reworked texts in the quranic Noah narratives

Formulaic duplications (often multiple repetitions of distinctive formulae) attest to the widespread usage of rhetorical conventions in the Qur'ān and/or its *Grundschriften* – and also to the highly plausible homiletic, liturgical, and exegetical context in which they were produced and consumed. Whereas it is relatively easy to recognise some of these duplications (cf. e.g. Q 11:37,40; 23:27), others may escape the reader (cf. e.g. Q 66:10; 71:25).

Table 6 below marks in grey those verses in the quranic Noah narratives that include such formulaic repetitions, regardless of whether their mirrors are to be found inside or outside the quranic Noah narratives themselves. Interpolations are also singled out in italics.

**Table 6:** *Verses containing formulaic duplications and repetitions inside the quranic Noah narratives*

| Q 7:59–64 (QNN I) | Q 10:71–4 (QNN II) | Q 11:25–49 (QNN III) | Q 23:23–30 (QNN IV) | Q 26:105–22 (QNN V) | Q 54:9–17 (QNN VI) | Q 71:1–28 (QNN VII) |
|---|---|---|---|---|---|---|
| **7:59** | *10:71* | **11:25** | **23:23** | **26:105** | **54:9** | **71:1** |
| 7:60 | **10:72** | **11:26** | 23:24 | **26:106** | **54:10** | **71:2** |
| 7:61 | **10:73** | **11:27** | **23:25** | **26:107** | 54:11 | **71:3** |
| 7:62 | 10:74 | 11:28 | **23:26** | **26:108** | 54:12 | **71:4** |
| 7:63 | | **11:29** | **23:27** | **26:109** | 54:13 | 71:5 |
| **7:64** | | **11:30** | 23:28 | **26:110** | 54:14 | 71:6 |
| | | 11:31 | 23:29 | **26:111** | **54:15** | 71:7 |
| | | 11:32 | **23:30** | 26:112 | **54:16** | 71:8 |
| | | 11:33 | | **26:113** | **54:17** | 71:9 |
| | | 11:34 | | **26:114** | | 71:10 |
| | | *11:35* | | **26:115** | | **71:11** |
| | | 11:36 | | 26:116 | | **71:12** |
| | | **11:37** | | **26:117** | | **71:13** |
| | | 11:38 | | 26:118 | | **71:14** |
| | | 11:39 | | **26:119** | | **71:15** |
| | | **11:40** | | **26:120** | | **71:16** |
| | | 11:41 | | **26:121** | | **71:17** |
| | | 11:42 | | **26:122** | | **71:18** |
| | | 11:43 | | | | **71:19** |
| | | 11:44 | | | | **71:20** |
| | | **11:45** | | | | 71:21 |
| | | 11:46 | | | | **71:22** |
| | | 11:47 | | | | 71:23 |
| | | 11:48 | | | | **71:24** |

**Table 6** (continuation)

| Q 7:59–64 (QNN I) | Q 10:71–4 (QNN II) | Q 11:25–49 (QNN III) | Q 23:23–30 (QNN IV) | Q 26:105–22 (QNN V) | Q 54:9–17 (QNN VI) | Q 71:1–28 (QNN VII) |
|---|---|---|---|---|---|---|
| | | *11:49* | | | | **71:25** |
| | | | | | | 71:26 |
| | | | | | | 71:27 |
| | | | | | | **71:28** |

# Chapter 5 / Reading Between the Lines: The Quranic Noah Narratives as Witnesses to the Life of the Quranic Prophet?

A close analysis of the dynamic structure of each quranic Noah narrative and the tacit ideological connections between them may help to unravel their purposes, that is, the purpose particular to each narrative as well as the overall purpose; lacking any further information as to why the narratives were collected and partially unified within the quranic text, this overall purpose can nonetheless be tentatively assigned to the series they form within the latter. Unless I am very much mistaken, they are not independent stories gathered together into the quranic collection with the sole purpose of illustrating the reliability of God's promises to his prophets and their followers and/or the way in which he punishes those who mock them – which is commonly adduced as the basic purpose of these kinds of stories – but independent stories that were composed for some very concrete reason in the manner that we now have them and were later collected into the Qur'ān according to a more general plan. My thesis is that each narrative or group of narratives underpins a specific message, and that a more extensive message may be elicited if they are put together in a sequence.[1] Lest this procedure be judged too speculative, one should recall that some imagination is necessary to reconstruct the meaning of a text whose key we lack, and that drawing it from the text itself is a much more reasonable move than projecting onto it external criteria that prove to be arbitrary at the very least.

I will now try to prove that, regardless of the chronology and textual development of the quranic Noah narratives themselves, on which very little can be said with some certainty (see the comments below on quranic Noah narratives nos. III and VII), they offer a fascinating albeit heretofore unexplored window into the life of the quranic prophet as mirrored/shaped in the Qur'ān by providing something like a logical sequence for, and hence a plausible chronology of, what I would venture to typecast as its two key episodes. In other words, they may be read as witnesses to his career, exhibiting that he went through opposition first, then distress, and thereafter vindication.

But let us look at them a bit more closely with these notions in mind:

*Quranic Noah narrative no. I* (Q 7:59–64). On my reading, a careful analysis of this narrative's three-part dynamic structure discloses its implicit, underlying message. First, we have Noah's commission and warning and his rejection by the people in vv. 59–60 (*i*); then comes Noah's justification in vv. 61–3 (*ii*); and lastly the conclusion to the story in v. 64 (*iii*), at the beginning of which the rejection of Noah's mission is mentioned again (in v. 64a). This markedly symmetrical division, with Noah's justification lying at its very centre (v. 61–3), therefore surrounded by his rejection (vv. 60, 64a), the prologue (v. 59) and the epilogue (v. 64b-c), may be schematised as follows:

(Introduction) ⊣ Rejection | *Justification* | Rejection ⊢ (Conclusion)
C O N F R O N T A T I O N

(the introduction consisting of the prophet's commission and warning and the conclusion including the flood narrative). Read in this way, the prophet's CONFRONTATION, which is moreover present in all of the six verses (i.e., from v. 59b to v. 64) and further highlighted by the concatenation of first-person speeches reported in vv. 59, 60, and 61, seems to be the core of the message in this narrative.

*Quranic Noah narrative no. VI* (Q 54:9–17). While the rejection of Noah's mission is also specifically referred to in its first verse (v. 9), the implicit message in this narrative rather gravitates around Noah's COMPLAINT, which is introduced in v. 10, followed (like Noah's justification in the former narrative) by a flood narrative (this time longer, vv. 11–14) and an eschatological coda (in contrast to no. I, vv. 15–17). Noah's complaint is also the most salient feature in this particular narrative, and additionally the one that seems to motivate God's resolution (and his actions). Thus we have the following dynamic scheme:

(Introduction) ⊣ Rejection | *COMPLAINT* ⇒ Conclusion ⊢ (Coda)

(the introduction consisting of the brief reference to vv. 54:1–8 and the conclusion including, as in quranic Noah narrative no. I, the flood narrative).

A few remarks on the message thus implied in quranic Noah narratives nos. I and VI might prove useful at this juncture, i.e., before examining nos. II, III, IV, V, and VII. First, it should be noted that the confrontation between the prophet and his opponents (which is the main point in quranic Noah narrative I) and the prophet's complaint (as endorsed in quranic Noah narrative no. VI) are intrinsically dependant upon one another, as one would naturally expect the prophet's frustration to entail some kind of complaint on his part. Second, they both stand (together with Noah's commission as a prophet) as the major distinguishing themes of the quranic Noah story, to which all other themes (e.g., the rejection of Noah's mission, Noah's own words of justification, etc.) are implicitly connected. All in all it seems fair to suppose that they must constitute the earliest elements in the life of the quranic prophet, as well; and hence witness to an episode that ought to be placed at the beginning of his career and to which no. IV points, too (albeit presenting not just a more lengthy narrative but also a more complex structure than either quranic Noah narrative I or VI). Accordingly I shall label it "Episode 1" (hereinafter *E1*) and distinguish within it Noah's confrontation ($E1^a$) and his subsequent complaint ($E1^b$). In contrast, nos. II and V seem to reuse the Noah story in order to give full credit to, and thereby confirm the role of, the quranic prophet, perhaps at a time when increasing opposition against him made such overt support necessary (see the comments on both narratives below). Therefore I take this motif to represent a later episode (hereinafter "Episode 2" [*E2*]) in the career of the quranic prophet. Some further contrast, however, must be made as regards (*a*) he who grants trustworthiness to the quranic prophet, either implicitly the prophet himself ($E2_{QP}$) or explicitly God ($E2_G$), and (*b*) the means by which trustworthiness is thus granted to him, either through more or less explicit authentication ($E2_{+/-}$) or through identification of the quranic prophet with Noah ($E2_{QP=N}$). Upon closer examination, it is easy to observe that *E2* is enhanced in no. III, whereas no. VII signals once more to the prophet's complaint ($E1^b$), as brought forth in nos. IV and VI (some indications as to the hypothetical original narrative underlying nos. III and VII will be provided below). Finally, no. IV recapitulates *E1*, while at the same time pointing to *E2*.

*Quranic Noah narrative no. IV* (Q 23:23–30). The two major themes inherent in the previous narratives are picked up again in vv. 23–6. Yet unlike I and VI, in no. IV God's words are inscribed at the opening of its two main, equal-length sections, i.e,. at the very beginning of vv. 23 (ولقد أرسلنا نوحا . . . 'We sent Noah . . .') and 27 (فأوحينا إليه . . . 'We inspired him . . .'), thus resulting a dynamic sequence akin to this:

⇉ ⇉

*Divine commission* < Rejection | Complaint > *Divine assistance* ⊦ (Coda)
∵ Twofold divine sanction or APPROVAL ∴

Therefore, this time it is God's own (twofold) APPROVAL of Noah's mission that is at stake in the narrative. Accordingly, a first if tacit step towards the confirmation of the quranic prophet as Noah *redivivus* (or as a second Noah) is undertaken.[2]

*Quranic Noah narrative no. II* (Q 10:71–4). From the point of view of its rhetoric, the message in this narrative turns on the transition from its second to its third verse, which marks the passage from one portion to another of the two basic parts into which the whole narrative divides: the former (v. 71–2) recounting Noah's warning, the latter (vv. 73–4) his rejection and the events that followed (both in his own time and afterwards). I take Noah's quite emphatic and extensive WARNING in vv. 71–2 to be the thematic linchpin in the narrative. What is even more important in v. 71 (i.e., at the very opening of the narrative), is that the quranic prophet is symptomatically if indirectly appointed as the addressee of God's (or the Angel's) words (see the initial command: ... واتل عليهم 'Recite/relate to them ... !'). This very unique feature points to a concomitant yet unmistakable DIVINE AUTHENTICATION of the quranic prophet's mission that will be made blatant in quranic Noah narrative no. V (note also the unparalleled typological reference to Noah as a Muslim in the same verse). One could perhaps describe the arrangement of these notions as follows:

⇒*Unmatched incipit* = *DIVINE AUTHENTICATION OF THE Q.P.* ⊣ WARNING | (Rejection +) Conclusion ⊦ (Addendum)

(the conclusion consisting of the flood story and the addendum including other later and similar events).

*Quranic Noah narrative no. V* (Q 26:105–22). This narrative addresses all themes mentioned so far, i.e., Noah's warning (vv. 106–10, 112–15), the rejection of his mission (vv. 105, 111, 116), the prophet's frustrated complaint (vv. 117–18), the happy end to the whole story – i.e., God's saving of Noah and his associates – (vv. 119–20), and the already familiar coda (vv. 121–2). However, it is interesting to observe Noah's insistence on introducing himself not just as God's messenger but as someone who is to be obeyed on God's behalf (vv. 108, 110), an issue unparalleled in all previous quranic Noah narratives (cf. 7:61–2) and only found again in 26:125–6,131,143–4,150,162–3,178–9 and partly quranic Noah narrative VII (cf. 71:3). On my reading this equally rare feature, which is doubtless very significant, points in turn (cf. the comments made above apropos no. II) to the SELF-AUTHENTICATION of the quranic prophet, very likely provided here (and elsewhere within *Sūrat al-Šuʿarā*) as a supplement to his divine approval. To illustrate this, I would suggest the following diagram:

All other themes ⇐ *SELF-AUTHENTICATION OF THE Q.P.* ⇒ All other themes ⊦ (Coda)

Hence in quranic Noah narratives nos. II and V, the Noah story is seemingly used – as I have already hinted– in order to give full credit to the quranic prophet at a time when increasing opposition against him might have urged such straightforward, conspicuous support. This is quite evident in quranic Noah narrative no. II, whose first verse betrays unspecified but increasing tension between the quranic prophet and his audience (وَاتْلُ عَلَيْهِمْ نَبَأَ نُوحٍ إِذْ قَالَ لِقَوْمِهِ يَا قَوْمِ إِنْ كَانَ كَبُرَ عَلَيْكُمْ مَقَامِي وَتَذْكِيرِي بِآيَاتِ اللَّهِ فَعَلَى اللَّهِ تَوَكَّلْتُ فَأَجْمِعُوا أَمْرَكُمْ وَشُرَكَاءَكُمْ ثُمَّ لَا يَكُنْ أَمْرُكُمْ عَلَيْكُمْ غُمَّةً ثُمَّ اقْضُوا إِلَيَّ وَلَا تُنْظِرُونِ 'My people, if my stay and my reminding you of the signs of God has become too burdensome upon you, then I put my trust in God: Do resolve upon your plan and [call upon] your associates, and let not your plan be a worry to you; make your decision on me and give me no respite!'). According to the Islamic tradition, opposition to Muḥammad in Mecca became quite strong after 615. It could be, then, that quranic Noah narratives nos. II and V allude to that period.[3] Yet the traditional depiction of Muḥammad's career in Mecca is too late and probably too biased to be taken at face value as a genuine historical record, and therefore cannot be said to provide a reliable referent that would help one fathom with some accuracy the early preaching of the quranic prophet.[4] Be that as it may, on my reading nos. II and V introduce us to a second focal episode in his life, which is undertaken again in no. III.

*Quranic Noah narrative no. III* (Q 11:25–49). There is almost nothing new in this narrative, in which Noah's commission, warning, and rejection are extensively reported in vv. 25–34, followed by God's words of comfort and instruction (vv. 36–7) and the expanded flood narrative that comprises vv. 38–48 – save that in vv. 35 and 49 the quranic prophet is (after the model provided in no. II?) expressly addressed and comforted. Now this occurs in such a telling and forthright manner (see the comments on no. III in chapter four above) that it is even hard to properly distinguish between both figures! In other words, the point is not that the quranic prophet is once more in sight here (as he indeed is in no. II), or implicitly identified with Noah (as in no. V, on my reading); the point now is that the two personalities are strangely confused, as though they were interchangeable (a point already observed by aṭ-Ṭabarī in his *Ǧāmiʿ al-Bayān fī Tafsīr al-Qur'ān*; cf. Martin 2010: 259, 271). Therefore it is the disruption of the narrative rather than its development after a given keynote (as in nos. I, II, IV and VI) or keynotes (as in no. V) that provides inner tension and implicit meaning to the story in no. III, whose dynamic focus thus unexpectedly shifts from an already well-known tale to the IDENTIFICATION of the quranic prophet with his hero (Noah). This fascinating fact, together with the seemingly embellished qualities of this narrative (note for instance God's repeated initiative to commission Noah [v. 25], comfort him [v. 36], instruct him [v. 37, 40], and even correct him when he tries in vain to have his rebellious son pardoned and saved [v. 46]), could suggest that this narrative postdates nos. II and V, but here as elsewhere there is no reason to suppose that the shorter a narrative, the older it must be as well.[5] Traces of elaborate composition, however, are detectable in the multi-layered nature of the flood narrative in vv. 36–48. Possibly this narrative originally consisted of vv. 25–34 + Noah's complaint, now found in 71:5–28 + vv. 36–41 + v. 48. Once Noah's (main) complaint was removed from that hypothetical original narrative (hereinafter quranic Noah narrative IIIa+VIIa), vv. 42–7 were probably appended to it as a kind of excursus to replace Noah's missing complaint with a dialogue between Noah and God instead of a monologue by the prophet, while vv. 35 and 49 were likely added to that reworked narrative at a later stage.

*Quranic Noah narrative no. VII* (Q 71). As in no. VI, Noah's COMPLAINT is also the chief thematic element in this particular narrative. On the other hand, as I have just suggested – and as was argued by Martin in 2010 – this narrative, or at least vv. 5–28, could very well have once been joined to an earlier version of quranic Noah narrative no. III (see the comments above on quranic Noah narrative IIIa+VIIa). If so, it was later detached from it, quite probably before the addition of vv. 35, 42–7, and 49 to the modified rendition of no. III. Notice that vv. 5–28 in no. VII may easily be inserted right after v. 34 and before v. 36 in no. III, i.e., instead of v. 35. Therefore it might be that quranic Noah narrative IIIa+VIIa did not originally include the identification of the quranic prophet with Noah, as introduced in v. 35 of no. III; likewise, the quranic prophet is neither mentioned nor implicitly alluded to in no. VII. Lacking such explicit identification between the two figures, quranic Noah narrative IIIa+VIIa – if it ever existed, that is – might have also predated nos. II and V, in which case it could be more or less contemporary with nos. I, IV, and VI. Yet the chronology susceptible to being assigned to the episodes in the life of the quranic prophet as reflected in the quranic Noah narratives, on the one hand, and the eventual chronology of the quranic Noah narratives themselves, on the other, should not be confused; for it is one thing to suppose that the quranic prophet went through opposition first, then distress and vindication, and another thing to suppose that the chronology of the quranic Noah narratives should follow that sequence. Speculation about the textual development of the quranic Noah narratives ought therefore to be limited, in my view, to the way in which quranic Noah narratives nos. III and VII may be hypothetically linked – and to their possible layers.

Accordingly a kind of (anonymous) "prophetic saga" is set out in the quranic Noah narratives. Still, such a reconstruction must remain tentative, as it depends upon the premise that there is a *single* quranic prophet behind all of the quranic Noah narratives – which need not be so (see chapter seven below).

Table 7 below shows the intertwining between Noah and the quranic prophet in the quranic Noah narratives, the major themes that are to be recognised in these, and the two episodes in the life of the quranic prophet which they implicitly allude to.

**Table 7:** *Intertwining between Noah and the quranic prophet in the quranic Noah narratives, major themes in these and episodes in the life of the quranic prophet thus hinted at*

| | | | | | | | |
|---|---|---|---|---|---|---|---|
| Noah | Confrontation between Noah and his opponents | Complaint made by Noah (plus the previous theme) | Divine corroboration of Noah's mission (plus the two previous themes) | Noah's warning to the people | All previous themes | | Complaint made by Noah |
| The quranic prophet | | | | Indirect authentication of the quranic prophet (as "you") | Direct authentication of the quranic prophet (as "I") | Explicit exchange between Noah and the quranic prophet | |
| Quranic Noah narratives | QNN I | QNN VI | QNN IV | QNN II | QNN V | QNN III | QNN VII |
| Episodes in the life of the quranic prophet & | *E1*[a] | *E1*[b] | *E1+E2* | *E2* | *E2* | $E2_{QP=N}$ | *E1*[b] |

Thus implicit correlation between Noah and the quranic prophet is discernible in the quranic Noah narratives.[6] He suffers opposition (maybe even persecution), he is mocked by his opponents, but in the end he is authenticated and moreover vindicated by God. Whether this is what the quranic prophet experienced himself or what the Qur'ān intends its readers to believe he experienced (in the manner of a biblical prophet, as Wansbrough thought) cannot be firmly established. What we do know, however, is that the quranic prophet seems to be authenticated in the quranic Noah narratives and that his Noahic portrayal, as set out in these, was later used by the authors of the *Sīra* literature to produce the Muhammadan *evangelium*, i.e., the so-called "biography" of Muḥammad – just as Jesus' "biography" in the canonical and apocryphal Gospels (as also, albeit indirectly, in the Qur'ān!) was partially modelled after Noah's portrayal in several para-biblical and pseudepigraphic writings.[7] I will comment further on these rewriting techniques in chapter seven, as some additional remarks on the sources and precedents of the quranic Noah are due now.

# *Excursus A*. The original story behind the Noah narratives in Q 11 and 71

As I argued above, I take it that the *Urtext* of quranic Noah narratives nos. III and VII (= quranic Noah narrative IIIa+VIIa) consisted of Noah's commission, warning, and rejection, as found in Q 11:25–34, + Noah's complaint, as now found in Q 71:5–28, + God's words of comfort and instruction to Noah, currently displayed in Q 11:36–7, + the flood narrative presently contained in Q 11:38–41 and 48. In my view, Noah's complaint was later replaced by the dialogue between Noah and God now found in Q 11:42–7, while vv. 35 and 49 in Q 11 were likely added at a later stage. In other words, I consider it very likely that the *text receptus* of quranic Noah narratives nos. III and VII underwent a three-stage redactional process that may be described as follows:

• Stage I (the original quranic Noah narrative IIIa+VIIa = Q 11:25–34 + 71:5–28 + 11:36–41):
→ ($A_1$) Q 11:25–34

[Q 11:25]

وَلَقَدْ أَرْسَلْنَا نُوحًا إِلَىٰ قَوْمِهِ إِنِّي لَكُمْ نَذِيرٌ مُّبِينٌ

*We sent Nūḥ* (= Noah) *to his people* [and he said to them]*: "I am to you a warner* [and I tell you]*:*

[Q 11:26]

أَن لَّا تَعْبُدُوا إِلَّا اللَّهَ ۖ إِنِّي أَخَافُ عَلَيْكُمْ عَذَابَ يَوْمٍ أَلِيمٍ

*Worship no one but God – for* [otherwise] *I fear for you the punishment of a painful day!"*

[Q 11:27]

فَقَالَ الْمَلَأُ الَّذِينَ كَفَرُوا مِن قَوْمِهِ مَا نَرَاكَ إِلَّا بَشَرًا مِّثْلَنَا وَمَا نَرَاكَ اتَّبَعَكَ إِلَّا الَّذِينَ هُمْ أَرَاذِلُنَا بَادِيَ الرَّأْيِ وَمَا نَرَىٰ لَكُمْ عَلَيْنَا مِن
فَضْلٍ بَلْ نَظُنُّكُمْ كَاذِبِينَ

*But the leading disbelievers among his people said: "We do not see you but as a man like ourselves, and it is patent that only the vilest of us follow you; we do not see that you are any better than we are – in fact we think you are liars* [sic]*."*

[Q 11:28]

قَالَ يَا قَوْمِ أَرَأَيْتُمْ إِن كُنتُ عَلَىٰ بَيِّنَةٍ مِّن رَّبِّي وَآتَانِي رَحْمَةً مِّنْ عِندِهِ فَعُمِّيَتْ عَلَيْكُمْ أَنُلْزِمُكُمُوهَا وَأَنتُمْ لَهَا كَارِهُونَ

*He said: "My people, think: suppose I do have with me a clear sign from my Lord, and that he has bestowed his mercy upon me, but that this has been obscured for you – could we force you to accept it against your will?*

[Q 11:29]
وَيَا قَوْمِ لَا أَسْأَلُكُمْ عَلَيْهِ مَالًا ۖ إِنْ أَجْرِيَ إِلَّا عَلَى اللَّهِ ۚ وَمَا أَنَا بِطَارِدِ الَّذِينَ آمَنُوا ۚ إِنَّهُمْ مُلَاقُو رَبِّهِمْ وَلَٰكِنِّي أَرَاكُمْ قَوْمًا تَجْهَلُونَ
*My people, I ask no reward from you for this – my reward falls upon God alone. I will not drive away the faithful – surely they shall meet their Lord; but I see you are an ignorant people.*

[Q 11:30]
وَيَا قَوْمِ مَنْ يَنْصُرُنِي مِنَ اللَّهِ إِنْ طَرَدْتُهُمْ ۚ أَفَلَا تَذَكَّرُونَ
*My people, who would help me against God if I were to drive them away? Will you not take heed?*

[Q 11:31]
وَلَا أَقُولُ لَكُمْ عِنْدِي خَزَائِنُ اللَّهِ وَلَا أَعْلَمُ الْغَيْبَ وَلَا أَقُولُ إِنِّي مَلَكٌ وَلَا أَقُولُ لِلَّذِينَ تَزْدَرِي أَعْيُنُكُمْ لَنْ يُؤْتِيَهُمُ اللَّهُ خَيْرًا ۖ اللَّهُ أَعْلَمُ
بِمَا فِي أَنْفُسِهِمْ ۖ إِنِّي إِذًا لَمِنَ الظَّالِمِينَ
*I am not telling you that I hold God's treasures, or that I know what is hidden, or that I am an angel; nor do I say that God will grant no good to those who are despised in your eyes: God knows best what is in their souls! – Otherwise I would be among the wrongdoers."*

[Q 11:32]
قَالُوا يَا نُوحُ قَدْ جَادَلْتَنَا فَأَكْثَرْتَ جِدَالَنَا فَأْتِنَا بِمَا تَعِدُنَا إِنْ كُنْتَ مِنَ الصَّادِقِينَ
*They said: "Nūḥ, you have long argued with us. Bring down on us the punishment you have threatened us with if you are speaking the truth!"*

[Q 11:33]
قَالَ إِنَّمَا يَأْتِيكُمْ بِهِ اللَّهُ إِنْ شَاءَ وَمَا أَنْتُمْ بِمُعْجِزِينَ
*He said: "It is God who will bring it down if he wishes, and you will not be able to cause him to fail.*

[Q 11:34]
وَلَا يَنْفَعُكُمْ نُصْحِي إِنْ أَرَدْتُ أَنْ أَنْصَحَ لَكُمْ إِنْ كَانَ اللَّهُ يُرِيدُ أَنْ يُغْوِيَكُمْ ۚ هُوَ رَبُّكُمْ وَإِلَيْهِ تُرْجَعُونَ
*Although I do want to advise you, my advice will be of no use to you if he is willing to leave you in your delusions. He is your Lord and to him you shall be returned!"*

→ ($B_1$) Q 75:5–28 (instead of the verses now found in Q 11:35–9):

[Q 71:5]
قَالَ رَبِّ إِنِّي دَعَوْتُ قَوْمِي لَيْلًا وَنَهَارًا
*He said: "My Lord, I have called my people night and day;*

[Q 71:6]
فَلَمْ يَزِدْهُمْ دُعَائِي إِلَّا فِرَارًا
*yet my calling has only increased them in flight:*

[Q 71:7]

وَإِنِّي كُلَّمَا دَعَوْتُهُمْ لِتَغْفِرَ لَهُمْ جَعَلُوا أَصَابِعَهُمْ فِي آذَانِهِمْ وَاسْتَغْشَوْا ثِيَابَهُمْ وَأَصَرُّوا وَاسْتَكْبَرُوا اسْتِكْبَارًا

*every time I called them, so that you may forgive them, they put their fingers in their ears and covered themselves with their garments; they persisted* [in their rebellion] *and proved arrogant and defiant.*

[Q 71:8]

ثُمَّ إِنِّي دَعَوْتُهُمْ جِهَارًا

*I have called them openly;*

[Q 71:9]

ثُمَّ إِنِّي أَعْلَنْتُ لَهُمْ وَأَسْرَرْتُ لَهُمْ إِسْرَارًا

*I have preached to them in public and talked to them in private.*

[Q 71:10]

فَقُلْتُ اسْتَغْفِرُوا رَبَّكُمْ إِنَّهُ كَانَ غَفَّارًا

*I told them: 'Ask forgiveness of your Lord, for he is all-forgiving!*

[Q 71:11]

يُرْسِلِ السَّمَاءَ عَلَيْكُمْ مِدْرَارًا

*He will send down from above abundant* [rain] *for you,*

[Q 71:12]

وَيُمْدِدْكُمْ بِأَمْوَالٍ وَبَنِينَ وَيَجْعَلْ لَكُمْ جَنَّاتٍ وَيَجْعَلْ لَكُمْ أَنْهَارًا

*and give you wealth and sons, and provide you with gardens and rivers!*

[Q 71:13]

مَا لَكُمْ لَا تَرْجُونَ لِلَّهِ وَقَارًا

*What is the matter with you? Why do you not accept God's greatness,*

[Q 71:14]

وَقَدْ خَلَقَكُمْ أَطْوَارًا

*when it is stage by stage that he has created you?*

[Q 71:15]

أَلَمْ تَرَوْا كَيْفَ خَلَقَ اللَّهُ سَبْعَ سَمَاوَاتٍ طِبَاقًا

*Have you never wondered how God created seven heavens one upon another,*

[Q 71:16]

وَجَعَلَ الْقَمَرَ فِيهِنَّ نُورًا وَجَعَلَ الشَّمْسَ سِرَاجًا

*and placed the moon as a light and the sun as a lamp therein?*

[Q 71:17]

وَاللَّهُ أَنْبَتَكُمْ مِنَ الْأَرْضِ نَبَاتًا

*Or how he has made you grow out of the earth*

[Q 71:18]

ثُمَّ يُعِيدُكُمْ فِيهَا وَيُخْرِجُكُمْ إِخْرَاجًا

*and how he will return you into it and then bring you out again?*

[Q 71:19]

وَاللَّهُ جَعَلَ لَكُمُ الْأَرْضَ بِسَاطًا

*Or how he has laid the earth for you*

[Q 71:20]

لِتَسْلُكُوا مِنْهَا سُبُلًا فِجَاجًا

*so that you can walk along it?'"*

[Q 71:21]

قَالَ نُوحٌ رَبِّ إِنَّهُمْ عَصَوْنِي وَاتَّبَعُوا مَنْ لَمْ يَزِدْهُ مَالُهُ وَوَلَدُهُ إِلَّا خَسَارًا

*Then Nūḥ said: "My Lord, they have disobeyed me and followed those whose riches and children will increase but their ruin,*

[Q 71:22]

وَمَكَرُوا مَكْرًا كُبَّارًا

*who have laid a plot* [against me]

[Q 71:23]

وَقَالُوا لَا تَذَرُنَّ آلِهَتَكُمْ وَلَا تَذَرُنَّ وَدًّا وَلَا سُوَاعًا وَلَا يَغُوثَ وَيَعُوقَ وَنَسْرًا

*saying: 'Do not leave your gods! Do not leave Wadd, Suwāʿ, Yaġūṯ, Yaʿūq or Nasr!'*

[Q 71:24]

وَقَدْ أَضَلُّوا كَثِيرًا ۖ وَلَا تَزِدِ الظَّالِمِينَ إِلَّا ضَلَالًا

*They have already misled many.* [Therefore, my Lord,] *I ask you not to increase the wrongdoers save in error!"*

[Q 71:25]

مِمَّا خَطِيئَاتِهِمْ أُغْرِقُوا فَأُدْخِلُوا نَارًا فَلَمْ يَجِدُوا لَهُمْ مِنْ دُونِ اللَّهِ أَنْصَارًا

*Because of their sins they were drowned and thrown into the Fire, and they found no one to help them against God.*

[Q 71:26]

وَقَالَ نُوحٌ رَبِّ لَا تَذَرْ عَلَى الْأَرْضِ مِنَ الْكَافِرِينَ دَيَّارًا

*Nūḥ said: "My Lord, do not leave upon the earth even one of the disbelievers,*

[Q 71:27]

إِنَّكَ إِنْ تَذَرْهُمْ يُضِلُّوا عِبَادَكَ وَلَا يَلِدُوا إِلَّا فَاجِرًا كَفَّارًا

*for otherwise they will mislead your servants and beget only sinners and disbelievers.*

[Q 71:28]

رَبِّ اغْفِرْ لِي وَلِوَالِدَيَّ وَلِمَنْ دَخَلَ بَيْتِيَ مُؤْمِنًا وَلِلْمُؤْمِنِينَ وَالْمُؤْمِنَاتِ وَلَا تَزِدِ الظَّالِمِينَ إِلَّا تَبَارًا

*My Lord, forgive me, my parents and whoever enters my house as a believer, and all the believers, men and women alike; and do not increase the wrongdoers save in destruction."*

→ ($C_1$) Q 11:36–41,48:

[Q 11:36]

وَأُوحِيَ إِلَىٰ نُوحٍ أَنَّهُ لَنْ يُؤْمِنَ مِنْ قَوْمِكَ إِلَّا مَنْ قَدْ آمَنَ فَلَا تَبْتَئِسْ بِمَا كَانُوا يَفْعَلُونَ

*And it was revealed to Nūḥ: "None of your people will believe, except those who have already done so; hence do not be distressed by what they may do.*

[Q 11:37]

وَاصْنَعِ الْفُلْكَ بِأَعْيُنِنَا وَوَحْيِنَا وَلَا تُخَاطِبْنِي فِي الَّذِينَ ظَلَمُوا ۚ إِنَّهُمْ مُغْرَقُونَ

*Build the ark under our eyes and inspiration and do not plead with me concerning those who have wronged – for they shall be drowned!'"*

[Q 11:38]

وَيَصْنَعُ الْفُلْكَ وَكُلَّمَا مَرَّ عَلَيْهِ مَلَأٌ مِنْ قَوْمِهِ سَخِرُوا مِنْهُ ۚ قَالَ إِنْ تَسْخَرُوا مِنَّا فَإِنَّا نَسْخَرُ مِنْكُمْ كَمَا تَسْخَرُونَ

*So he built the ark, and whenever the leaders of his people passed by they mocked him. He said: "You may deride us now, but we will come to deride you in the same manner,*

[Q 11:39]

فَسَوْفَ تَعْلَمُونَ مَنْ يَأْتِيهِ عَذَابٌ يُخْزِيهِ وَيَحِلُّ عَلَيْهِ عَذَابٌ مُقِيمٌ

*and then you will find out who will get a humiliating punishment and upon whom a lasting suffering will alight."*

[Q 11:40]
حَتَّىٰ إِذَا جَاءَ أَمْرُنَا وَفَارَ التَّنُّورُ قُلْنَا احْمِلْ فِيهَا مِنْ كُلٍّ زَوْجَيْنِ اثْنَيْنِ وَأَهْلَكَ إِلَّا مَنْ سَبَقَ عَلَيْهِ الْقَوْلُ وَمَنْ آمَنَ ۚ وَمَا آمَنَ مَعَهُ إِلَّا قَلِيلٌ

*When our command came and the oven boiled, we said: "Load upon the ark two of every kind together with your own family – save those against whom the verdict has already been rendered – and those who have believed." But only a few had believed with him.*

[Q 11:41]
وَقَالَ ارْكَبُوا فِيهَا بِسْمِ اللَّهِ مَجْرَاهَا وَمُرْسَاهَا ۚ إِنَّ رَبِّي لَغَفُورٌ رَحِيمٌ

*He said: "Embark therein! In the name of God it shall sail and anchor – for surely my Lord is all-forgiving and merciful."*

[Q 11:48]
قِيلَ يَا نُوحُ اهْبِطْ بِسَلَامٍ مِنَّا وَبَرَكَاتٍ عَلَيْكَ وَعَلَىٰ أُمَمٍ مِمَّنْ مَعَكَ ۚ وَأُمَمٌ سَنُمَتِّعُهُمْ ثُمَّ يَمَسُّهُمْ مِنَّا عَذَابٌ أَلِيمٌ

*It was said: "Nūḥ, disembark in peace from us with blessings upon you and upon the nations that shall spring from those who are with you. To other nations we will grant enjoyment for a time; then a painful punishment from us will touch them."*

• Stage II (quranic Noah narrative IIIa's first reworking and expansion = Q 11:25–34,36–48):
→ ($A_2$) Q 11:25–34 (= $A_1$):

[Q 11:25]
وَلَقَدْ أَرْسَلْنَا نُوحًا إِلَىٰ قَوْمِهِ إِنِّي لَكُمْ نَذِيرٌ مُبِينٌ

*We sent Nūḥ to his people* [and he said to them]*: "I am to you a warner* [and I tell you]*:*

[Q 11:26]
أَنْ لَا تَعْبُدُوا إِلَّا اللَّهَ ۖ إِنِّي أَخَافُ عَلَيْكُمْ عَذَابَ يَوْمٍ أَلِيمٍ

*Worship no one but God – for* [otherwise] *I fear for you the punishment of a painful day!"*

[Q 11:27]
فَقَالَ الْمَلَأُ الَّذِينَ كَفَرُوا مِنْ قَوْمِهِ مَا نَرَاكَ إِلَّا بَشَرًا مِثْلَنَا وَمَا نَرَاكَ اتَّبَعَكَ إِلَّا الَّذِينَ هُمْ أَرَاذِلُنَا بَادِيَ الرَّأْيِ وَمَا نَرَىٰ لَكُمْ عَلَيْنَا مِنْ فَضْلٍ بَلْ نَظُنُّكُمْ كَاذِبِينَ

*But the leading disbelievers among his people said: "We do not see you but as a man like ourselves, and it is patent that only the vilest of us follow you; we do not see that you are any better than we are – in fact we think you are liars* [sic]*."*

[Q 11:28]
قَالَ يَا قَوْمِ أَرَأَيْتُمْ إِنْ كُنْتُ عَلَىٰ بَيِّنَةٍ مِنْ رَبِّي وَآتَانِي رَحْمَةً مِنْ عِنْدِهِ فَعُمِّيَتْ عَلَيْكُمْ أَنُلْزِمُكُمُوهَا وَأَنْتُمْ لَهَا كَارِهُونَ

*He said: "My people, think: suppose I do have with me a clear sign from my Lord, and that he has bestowed his mercy upon me, but that this has been obscured for you – could we force you to accept it against your will?*

[Q 11:29]

وَيَا قَوْمِ لَا أَسْأَلُكُمْ عَلَيْهِ مَالًا ۖ إِنْ أَجْرِيَ إِلَّا عَلَى اللَّهِ ۚ وَمَا أَنَا بِطَارِدِ الَّذِينَ آمَنُوا ۚ إِنَّهُمْ مُلَاقُو رَبِّهِمْ وَلَٰكِنِّي أَرَاكُمْ قَوْمًا تَجْهَلُونَ

*My people, I ask no reward from you for this – my reward falls upon God alone. I will not drive away the faithful – surely they shall meet their Lord; but I see you are an ignorant people.*

[Q 11:30]

وَيَا قَوْمِ مَنْ يَنْصُرُنِي مِنَ اللَّهِ إِنْ طَرَدْتُهُمْ ۚ أَفَلَا تَذَكَّرُونَ

*My people, who would help me against God if I were to drive them away? Will you not take heed?*

[Q 11:31]

وَلَا أَقُولُ لَكُمْ عِنْدِي خَزَائِنُ اللَّهِ وَلَا أَعْلَمُ الْغَيْبَ وَلَا أَقُولُ إِنِّي مَلَكٌ وَلَا أَقُولُ لِلَّذِينَ تَزْدَرِي أَعْيُنُكُمْ لَنْ يُؤْتِيَهُمُ اللَّهُ خَيْرًا ۖ اللَّهُ أَعْلَمُ بِمَا فِي أَنْفُسِهِمْ ۖ إِنِّي إِذًا لَمِنَ الظَّالِمِينَ

*I am not telling you that I hold God's treasures, or that I know what is hidden, or that I am an angel; nor do I say that God will grant no good to those who are despised in your eyes: God knows best what is in their souls! – Otherwise I would be among the wrongdoers."*

[Q 11:32]

قَالُوا يَا نُوحُ قَدْ جَادَلْتَنَا فَأَكْثَرْتَ جِدَالَنَا فَأْتِنَا بِمَا تَعِدُنَا إِنْ كُنْتَ مِنَ الصَّادِقِينَ

*They said: "Nūḥ, you have long argued with us. Bring down on us the punishment you have threaten us with if you are speaking the truth!"*

[Q 11:33]

قَالَ إِنَّمَا يَأْتِيكُمْ بِهِ اللَّهُ إِنْ شَاءَ وَمَا أَنْتُمْ بِمُعْجِزِينَ

*He said: "It is God who will bring it down if he wishes, and you will not be able to cause him to fail.*

[Q 11:34]

وَلَا يَنْفَعُكُمْ نُصْحِي إِنْ أَرَدْتُ أَنْ أَنْصَحَ لَكُمْ إِنْ كَانَ اللَّهُ يُرِيدُ أَنْ يُغْوِيَكُمْ ۚ هُوَ رَبُّكُمْ وَإِلَيْهِ تُرْجَعُونَ

*Although I do want to advise you, my advice will be of no use to you if he is willing to leave you in your delusions. He is your Lord and to him you shall be returned!"*

→ ($B_2$) Suppression of Q 71:5–28.
→ ($C_2$) Q 11:36–41,48 (= C1) + Q 11:42–7 introduced between its penultimate and concluding verses (i.e., between Q 11:41 and 48):

[Q 11:36]

وَأُوحِيَ إِلَىٰ نُوحٍ أَنَّهُ لَنْ يُؤْمِنَ مِنْ قَوْمِكَ إِلَّا مَنْ قَدْ آمَنَ فَلَا تَبْتَئِسْ بِمَا كَانُوا يَفْعَلُونَ

*And it was revealed to Nūḥ: "None of your people will believe, except those who have already done so; hence do not be distressed by what they may do.*

[Q 11:37]

وَاصْنَعِ الْفُلْكَ بِأَعْيُنِنَا وَوَحْيِنَا وَلَا تُخَاطِبْنِي فِي الَّذِينَ ظَلَمُوا ۚ إِنَّهُمْ مُغْرَقُونَ

*Build the ark under our eyes and inspiration and do not plead with me concerning those who have wronged – for they shall be drowned!'"*

[Q 11:38]

وَيَصْنَعُ الْفُلْكَ وَكُلَّمَا مَرَّ عَلَيْهِ مَلَأٌ مِنْ قَوْمِهِ سَخِرُوا مِنْهُ ۚ قَالَ إِنْ تَسْخَرُوا مِنَّا فَإِنَّا نَسْخَرُ مِنْكُمْ كَمَا تَسْخَرُونَ

*So he built the ark, and whenever the leaders of his people passed by they mocked him. He said: "You may deride us now, but we will come to deride you in the same manner,*

[Q 11:39]

فَسَوْفَ تَعْلَمُونَ مَنْ يَأْتِيهِ عَذَابٌ يُخْزِيهِ وَيَحِلُّ عَلَيْهِ عَذَابٌ مُقِيمٌ

*and then you will find out who will get a humiliating punishment and upon whom a lasting suffering will alight."*

[Q 11:40]

حَتَّىٰ إِذَا جَاءَ أَمْرُنَا وَفَارَ التَّنُّورُ قُلْنَا احْمِلْ فِيهَا مِنْ كُلٍّ زَوْجَيْنِ اثْنَيْنِ وَأَهْلَكَ إِلَّا مَنْ سَبَقَ عَلَيْهِ الْقَوْلُ وَمَنْ آمَنَ ۚ وَمَا آمَنَ مَعَهُ إِلَّا قَلِيلٌ

*When our command came and the oven boiled, we said: "Load upon the ark two of every kind together with your own family – save those against whom the verdict has already been rendered – and those who have believed." But only a few had believed with him.*

[Q 11:41]

وَقَالَ ارْكَبُوا فِيهَا بِسْمِ اللَّهِ مَجْرَاهَا وَمُرْسَاهَا ۚ إِنَّ رَبِّي لَغَفُورٌ رَحِيمٌ

*He said: "Embark therein! In the name of God it shall sail and anchor – for surely my Lord is all-forgiving and merciful."*

[Q 11:42]

وَهِيَ تَجْرِي بِهِمْ فِي مَوْجٍ كَالْجِبَالِ وَنَادَىٰ نُوحٌ ابْنَهُ وَكَانَ فِي مَعْزِلٍ يَا بُنَيَّ ارْكَبْ مَعَنَا وَلَا تَكُنْ مَعَ الْكَافِرِينَ

*It sailed with them amidst waves like mountains; and Nūḥ called to his son who stood apart* [from them]*: "My son, get on board with us and do not stay with the disbelievers!'"*

[Q 11:43]

قَالَ سَآوِي إِلَىٰ جَبَلٍ يَعْصِمُنِي مِنَ الْمَاءِ ۚ قَالَ لَا عَاصِمَ الْيَوْمَ مِنْ أَمْرِ اللَّهِ إِلَّا مَنْ رَحِمَ ۚ وَحَالَ بَيْنَهُمَا الْمَوْجُ فَكَانَ مِنَ الْمُغْرَقِينَ

*But he replied: "I will take refuge on a mountain to save me from the water!'"* [Nūḥ] *said: "There is no refuge today from God's command but for those on whom he has mercy!" The waves came between them and he was among the drowned.*

[Q 11:44]

وَقِيلَ يَا أَرْضُ ابْلَعِي مَاءَكِ وَيَا سَمَاءُ أَقْلِعِي وَغِيضَ الْمَاءُ وَقُضِيَ الْأَمْرُ وَاسْتَوَتْ عَلَى الْجُودِيِّ ۖ وَقِيلَ بُعْدًا لِلْقَوْمِ الظَّالِمِينَ

*Then it was said: "Earth, swallow your water!; and heaven, withhold* [your rain]*!" The waters subsided and the matter was accomplished. The ark settled on* [Mount] *al-Ǧūdiyy and it was said: "Gone are the wrongdoers!"*

[Q 11:45]

وَنَادَىٰ نُوحٌ رَبَّهُ فَقَالَ رَبِّ إِنَّ ابْنِي مِنْ أَهْلِي وَإِنَّ وَعْدَكَ الْحَقُّ وَأَنتَ أَحْكَمُ الْحَاكِمِينَ

*Nūḥ called out to his Lord and said: "My Lord, my son is from my family. So if your promise is true and you are indeed the most just of all judges –"*

[Q 11:46]

قَالَ يَا نُوحُ إِنَّهُ لَيْسَ مِنْ أَهْلِكَ ۖ إِنَّهُ عَمَلٌ غَيْرُ صَالِحٍ ۖ فَلَا تَسْأَلْنِ مَا لَيْسَ لَكَ بِهِ عِلْمٌ ۖ إِنِّي أَعِظُكَ أَن تَكُونَ مِنَ الْجَاهِلِينَ

*He said: "Nūḥ, he is not of your family; what he did was not right. But do not ask me things you know nothing about. I advise you, lest you be counted among the ignorant."*

[Q 11:47]

قَالَ رَبِّ إِنِّي أَعُوذُ بِكَ أَنْ أَسْأَلَكَ مَا لَيْسَ لِي بِهِ عِلْمٌ ۖ وَإِلَّا تَغْفِرْ لِي وَتَرْحَمْنِي أَكُن مِّنَ الْخَاسِرِينَ

*He said: "My Lord, I take refuge with you from asking that about which I have no knowledge! And unless you forgive me and have mercy on me I shall be among the losers!"*

[Q 11:48]

قِيلَ يَا نُوحُ اهْبِطْ بِسَلَامٍ مِّنَّا وَبَرَكَاتٍ عَلَيْكَ وَعَلَىٰ أُمَمٍ مِّمَّن مَّعَكَ ۚ وَأُمَمٌ سَنُمَتِّعُهُمْ ثُمَّ يَمَسُّهُم مِّنَّا عَذَابٌ أَلِيمٌ

*It was said: "Nūḥ, disembark in peace from us with blessings upon you and upon the nations that shall spring from those who are with you. To other nations we will grant enjoyment for a time; then a painful punishment from us will touch them."*

• Stage $III_1$ (setting apart and expanding quranic Noah narrative VIIa to produce quranic Noah narrative no. VII = Q 71):

→ ($D_1$) Addition of Q 71:1–4 to $B_1$ (i.e., to Q 71:5–28) to form a separate new narrative:

[Q 71:1]

إِنَّا أَرْسَلْنَا نُوحًا إِلَىٰ قَوْمِهِ أَنْ أَنذِرْ قَوْمَكَ مِن قَبْلِ أَن يَأْتِيَهُمْ عَذَابٌ أَلِيمٌ

*We sent Nūḥ to his people*[, saying]*: "Warn your people before a painful punishment comes to them!"*

[Q 71:2]

قَالَ يَا قَوْمِ إِنِّي لَكُمْ نَذِيرٌ مُّبِينٌ

*And so he said: "My people, I am to you a clear warner.*

[Q 71:3]

أَنِ اعْبُدُوا اللَّهَ وَاتَّقُوهُ وَأَطِيعُونِ

*Worship God, fear him and obey me!*

[Q 71:4]

يَغْفِرْ لَكُم مِّن ذُنُوبِكُمْ وَيُؤَخِّرْكُمْ إِلَىٰ أَجَلٍ مُّسَمًّى ۚ إِنَّ أَجَلَ اللَّهِ إِذَا جَاءَ لَا يُؤَخَّرُ ۖ لَوْ كُنتُمْ تَعْلَمُونَ

*He will forgive you your sins and spare you until the time he has appointed; then, when it arrives, it will not be delayed – if only you understood!"*

[Q 71:5]

قَالَ رَبِّ إِنِّي دَعَوْتُ قَوْمِي لَيْلًا وَنَهَارًا

*He said: "My Lord, I have called my people night and day;*

[Q 71:6]

فَلَمْ يَزِدْهُمْ دُعَائِي إِلَّا فِرَارًا

*yet my calling has only increased them in flight:*

[Q 71:7]

وَإِنِّي كُلَّمَا دَعَوْتُهُمْ لِتَغْفِرَ لَهُمْ جَعَلُوا أَصَابِعَهُمْ فِي آذَانِهِمْ وَاسْتَغْشَوْا ثِيَابَهُمْ وَأَصَرُّوا وَاسْتَكْبَرُوا اسْتِكْبَارًا

*every time I called them, so that you may forgive them, they put their fingers in their ears and covered themselves with their garments; they persisted* [in their rebellion] *and proved arrogant and defiant.*

[Q 71:8]

ثُمَّ إِنِّي دَعَوْتُهُمْ جِهَارًا

*I have called them openly;*

[Q 71:9]

ثُمَّ إِنِّي أَعْلَنْتُ لَهُمْ وَأَسْرَرْتُ لَهُمْ إِسْرَارًا

*I have preached to them in public and talked to them in private.*

[Q 71:10]

فَقُلْتُ اسْتَغْفِرُوا رَبَّكُمْ إِنَّهُ كَانَ غَفَّارًا

*I told them: 'Ask forgiveness of your Lord, for he is all-forgiving!*

[Q 71:11]

يُرْسِلِ السَّمَاءَ عَلَيْكُمْ مِدْرَارًا

*He will send down from above abundant* [rain] *for you,*

[Q 71:12]

وَيُمْدِدْكُمْ بِأَمْوَالٍ وَبَنِينَ وَيَجْعَلْ لَكُمْ جَنَّاتٍ وَيَجْعَلْ لَكُمْ أَنْهَارًا

*and give you wealth and sons, and provide you with gardens and rivers!*

[Q 71:13]

مَا لَكُمْ لَا تَرْجُونَ لِلَّهِ وَقَارًا

*What is the matter with you? Why do you not accept God's greatness,*

[Q 71:14]

وَقَدْ خَلَقَكُمْ أَطْوَارًا

*when it is stage by stage that he has created you?*

[Q 71:15]

أَلَمْ تَرَوْا كَيْفَ خَلَقَ اللَّهُ سَبْعَ سَمَاوَاتٍ طِبَاقًا

*Have you never wondered how God created seven heavens one upon another,*

[Q 71:16]

وَجَعَلَ الْقَمَرَ فِيهِنَّ نُورًا وَجَعَلَ الشَّمْسَ سِرَاجًا

*and placed the moon as a light and the sun as a lamp therein?*

[Q 71:17]

وَاللَّهُ أَنْبَتَكُمْ مِنَ الْأَرْضِ نَبَاتًا

*Or how he has made you grow out of the earth*

[Q 71:18]

ثُمَّ يُعِيدُكُمْ فِيهَا وَيُخْرِجُكُمْ إِخْرَاجًا

*and how he will return you into it and then bring you out again?*

[Q 71:19]

وَاللَّهُ جَعَلَ لَكُمُ الْأَرْضَ بِسَاطًا

*Or how he has laid the earth for you*

[Q 71:20]

لِتَسْلُكُوا مِنْهَا سُبُلًا فِجَاجًا

*so that you can walk along it?'"*

[Q 71:21]

قَالَ نُوحٌ رَبِّ إِنَّهُمْ عَصَوْنِي وَاتَّبَعُوا مَنْ لَمْ يَزِدْهُ مَالُهُ وَوَلَدُهُ إِلَّا خَسَارًا

*Then Nūḥ said: "My Lord, they have disobeyed me and followed those whose riches and children will increase but their ruin,*

[Q 71:22]

وَمَكَرُوا مَكْرًا كُبَّارًا

*who have laid a plot* [against me]

[Q 71:23]

وَقَالُوا لَا تَذَرُنَّ آلِهَتَكُمْ وَلَا تَذَرُنَّ وَدًّا وَلَا سُوَاعًا وَلَا يَغُوثَ وَيَعُوقَ وَنَسْرًا

*saying: 'Do not leave your gods! Do not leave Wadd, Suwā', Yagūṯ, Ya'ūq or Nasr!'*

[Q 71:24]

وَقَدْ أَضَلُّوا كَثِيرًا ۖ وَلَا تَزِدِ الظَّالِمِينَ إِلَّا ضَلَالًا

*They have already misled many.* [Therefore, my Lord,] *I ask you not to increase the wrongdoers save in error!"*

[Q 71:25]

مِمَّا خَطِيئَاتِهِمْ أُغْرِقُوا فَأُدْخِلُوا نَارًا فَلَمْ يَجِدُوا لَهُمْ مِنْ دُونِ اللَّهِ أَنْصَارًا

*Because of their sins they were drowned and thrown into the Fire, and they found no one to help them against God.*

[Q 71:26]

وَقَالَ نُوحٌ رَبِّ لَا تَذَرْ عَلَى الْأَرْضِ مِنَ الْكَافِرِينَ دَيَّارًا

*Nūḥ said: "My Lord, do not leave upon the earth even one of the disbelievers,*

[Q 71:27]

إِنَّكَ إِنْ تَذَرْهُمْ يُضِلُّوا عِبَادَكَ وَلَا يَلِدُوا إِلَّا فَاجِرًا كَفَّارًا

*for otherwise they will mislead your servants and beget only sinners and disbelievers.*

[Q 71:28]

رَبِّ اغْفِرْ لِي وَلِوَالِدَيَّ وَلِمَنْ دَخَلَ بَيْتِيَ مُؤْمِنًا وَلِلْمُؤْمِنِينَ وَالْمُؤْمِنَاتِ وَلَا تَزِدِ الظَّالِمِينَ إِلَّا تَبَارًا

*My Lord, forgive me, my parents and whoever enters my house as a believer, and all the believers, men and women alike; and do not increase the wrongdoers save in destruction."*

• Stage $III_{ii}$ (quranic Noah narrative IIIa's final reworking and expansion = Q 11:25–49):
→ ($E_1$) Addition of Q 11:35, 49 to {$A_2$ + $C_2$} (i.e., to Q 11:25–34,36–48) after its two concluding verses (Q 11:34 and 48, respectively):

[Q 11:25]

وَلَقَدْ أَرْسَلْنَا نُوحًا إِلَىٰ قَوْمِهِ إِنِّي لَكُمْ نَذِيرٌ مُبِينٌ

*We sent Nūḥ to his people* [and he said to them]*: "I am to you a warner* [and I tell you]*:*

[Q 11:26]

أَنْ لَا تَعْبُدُوا إِلَّا اللَّهَ ۖ إِنِّي أَخَافُ عَلَيْكُمْ عَذَابَ يَوْمٍ أَلِيمٍ

*Worship no one but God – for* [otherwise] *I fear for you the punishment of a painful day!"*

[Q 11:27]

فَقَالَ الْمَلَأُ الَّذِينَ كَفَرُوا مِنْ قَوْمِهِ مَا نَرَاكَ إِلَّا بَشَرًا مِثْلَنَا وَمَا نَرَاكَ اتَّبَعَكَ إِلَّا الَّذِينَ هُمْ أَرَاذِلُنَا بَادِيَ الرَّأْيِ وَمَا نَرَىٰ لَكُمْ عَلَيْنَا مِنْ
فَضْلٍ بَلْ نَظُنُّكُمْ كَاذِبِينَ

*But the leading disbelievers among his people said: "We do not see you but as a man like ourselves, and it is patent that only the vilest of us follow you; we do not see that you are any better than we are – in fact we think you are liars* [sic]."

[Q 11:28]

قَالَ يَا قَوْمِ أَرَأَيْتُمْ إِنْ كُنْتُ عَلَىٰ بَيِّنَةٍ مِنْ رَبِّي وَآتَانِي رَحْمَةً مِنْ عِنْدِهِ فَعُمِّيَتْ عَلَيْكُمْ أَنُلْزِمُكُمُوهَا وَأَنْتُمْ لَهَا كَارِهُونَ

*He said: "My people, think: suppose I do have with me a clear sign from my Lord, and that he has bestowed his mercy upon me, but that this has been obscured for you – could we force you to accept it against your will?*

[Q 11:29]

وَيَا قَوْمِ لَا أَسْأَلُكُمْ عَلَيْهِ مَالًا ۖ إِنْ أَجْرِيَ إِلَّا عَلَى اللَّهِ ۚ وَمَا أَنَا بِطَارِدِ الَّذِينَ آمَنُوا ۚ إِنَّهُمْ مُلَاقُو رَبِّهِمْ وَلَٰكِنِّي أَرَاكُمْ قَوْمًا تَجْهَلُونَ

*My people, I ask no reward from you for this – my reward falls upon God alone. I will not drive away the faithful – surely they shall meet their Lord; but I see you are an ignorant people.*

[Q 11:30]

وَيَا قَوْمِ مَنْ يَنْصُرُنِي مِنَ اللَّهِ إِنْ طَرَدْتُهُمْ ۚ أَفَلَا تَذَكَّرُونَ

*My people, who would help me against God if I were to drive them away? Will you not take heed?*

[Q 11:31]

وَلَا أَقُولُ لَكُمْ عِنْدِي خَزَائِنُ اللَّهِ وَلَا أَعْلَمُ الْغَيْبَ وَلَا أَقُولُ إِنِّي مَلَكٌ وَلَا أَقُولُ لِلَّذِينَ تَزْدَرِي أَعْيُنُكُمْ لَنْ يُؤْتِيَهُمُ اللَّهُ خَيْرًا ۖ اللَّهُ أَعْلَمُ
بِمَا فِي أَنْفُسِهِمْ ۖ إِنِّي إِذًا لَمِنَ الظَّالِمِينَ

*I am not telling you that I hold God's treasures, or that I know what is hidden, or that I am an angel; nor do I say that God will grant no good to those who are despised in your eyes: God knows best what is in their souls! – Otherwise I would be among the wrongdoers."*

[Q 11:32]

قَالُوا يَا نُوحُ قَدْ جَادَلْتَنَا فَأَكْثَرْتَ جِدَالَنَا فَأْتِنَا بِمَا تَعِدُنَا إِنْ كُنْتَ مِنَ الصَّادِقِينَ

*They said: "Nūḥ, you have long argued with us. Bring down on us the punishment you have threaten us with if you are speaking the truth!"*

[Q 11:33]

قَالَ إِنَّمَا يَأْتِيكُمْ بِهِ اللَّهُ إِنْ شَاءَ وَمَا أَنْتُمْ بِمُعْجِزِينَ

*He said: "It is God who will bring it down if he wishes, and you will not be able to cause him to fail.*

[Q 11:34]

وَلَا يَنْفَعُكُمْ نُصْحِي إِنْ أَرَدْتُ أَنْ أَنْصَحَ لَكُمْ إِنْ كَانَ اللَّهُ يُرِيدُ أَنْ يُغْوِيَكُمْ ۚ هُوَ رَبُّكُمْ وَإِلَيْهِ تُرْجَعُونَ

*Although I do want to advise you, my advice will be of no use to you if he is willing to leave you in your delusions. He is your Lord and to him you shall be returned!*

[Q 11:35 (first verse added)]

أَمْ يَقُولُونَ افْتَرَاهُ ۖ قُلْ إِنِ افْتَرَيْتُهُ فَعَلَيَّ إِجْرَامِي وَأَنَا بَرِيءٌ مِمَّا تُجْرِمُونَ

*If they say: 'He has forged it,' say: 'If I have forged it, then my sin falls upon me, but I am innocent of what you do."*

[Q 11:36]

وَأُوحِيَ إِلَىٰ نُوحٍ أَنَّهُ لَنْ يُؤْمِنَ مِنْ قَوْمِكَ إِلَّا مَنْ قَدْ آمَنَ فَلَا تَبْتَئِسْ بِمَا كَانُوا يَفْعَلُونَ

*And it was revealed to Nūḥ: "None of your people will believe, except those who have already done so; hence do not be distressed by what they may do.*

[Q 11:37]

وَاصْنَعِ الْفُلْكَ بِأَعْيُنِنَا وَوَحْيِنَا وَلَا تُخَاطِبْنِي فِي الَّذِينَ ظَلَمُوا ۚ إِنَّهُمْ مُغْرَقُونَ

*Build the ark under our eyes and inspiration and do not plead with me concerning those who have wronged – for they shall be drowned!"*

[Q 11:38]

وَيَصْنَعُ الْفُلْكَ وَكُلَّمَا مَرَّ عَلَيْهِ مَلَأٌ مِنْ قَوْمِهِ سَخِرُوا مِنْهُ ۚ قَالَ إِنْ تَسْخَرُوا مِنَّا فَإِنَّا نَسْخَرُ مِنْكُمْ كَمَا تَسْخَرُونَ

*So he built the ark, and whenever the leaders of his people passed by they mocked him. He said: "You may deride us now, but we will come to deride you in the same manner,*

[Q 11:39]

فَسَوْفَ تَعْلَمُونَ مَنْ يَأْتِيهِ عَذَابٌ يُخْزِيهِ وَيَحِلُّ عَلَيْهِ عَذَابٌ مُقِيمٌ

*and then you will find out who will get a humiliating punishment and upon whom a lasting suffering will alight."*

[Q 11:40]

حَتَّىٰ إِذَا جَاءَ أَمْرُنَا وَفَارَ التَّنُّورُ قُلْنَا احْمِلْ فِيهَا مِنْ كُلٍّ زَوْجَيْنِ اثْنَيْنِ وَأَهْلَكَ إِلَّا مَنْ سَبَقَ عَلَيْهِ الْقَوْلُ وَمَنْ آمَنَ ۚ وَمَا آمَنَ مَعَهُ إِلَّا قَلِيلٌ

*When our command came and the oven boiled, we said: "Load upon the ark two of every kind together with your own family – save those against whom the verdict has already been rendered – and those who have believed." But only a few had believed with him.*

[Q 11:41]

وَقَالَ ارْكَبُوا فِيهَا بِسْمِ اللَّهِ مَجْرَاهَا وَمُرْسَاهَا ۚ إِنَّ رَبِّي لَغَفُورٌ رَحِيمٌ

*He said: "Embark therein! In the name of God it shall sail and anchor – for surely my Lord is all-forgiving and merciful."*

[Q 11:42]

وَهِيَ تَجْرِي بِهِمْ فِي مَوْجٍ كَالْجِبَالِ وَنَادَىٰ نُوحٌ ابْنَهُ وَكَانَ فِي مَعْزِلٍ يَا بُنَيَّ ارْكَبْ مَعَنَا وَلَا تَكُنْ مَعَ الْكَافِرِينَ

*It sailed with them amidst waves like mountains; and Nūḥ called to his son who stood apart* [from them]*: "My son, get on board with us and do not stay with the disbelievers!'"*

[Q 11:43]

قَالَ سَآوِي إِلَىٰ جَبَلٍ يَعْصِمُنِي مِنَ الْمَاءِ ۚ قَالَ لَا عَاصِمَ الْيَوْمَ مِنْ أَمْرِ اللَّهِ إِلَّا مَنْ رَحِمَ ۚ وَحَالَ بَيْنَهُمَا الْمَوْجُ فَكَانَ مِنَ الْمُغْرَقِينَ

*But he replied: "I will take refuge on a mountain to save me from the water!'"* [Nūḥ] *said: "There is no refuge today from God's command but for those on whom he has mercy!" The waves came between them and he was among the drowned.*

[Q 11:44]
وَقِيلَ يَا أَرْضُ ابْلَعِي مَاءَكِ وَيَا سَمَاءُ أَقْلِعِي وَغِيضَ الْمَاءُ وَقُضِيَ الْأَمْرُ وَاسْتَوَتْ عَلَى الْجُودِيِّ ۖ وَقِيلَ بُعْدًا لِلْقَوْمِ الظَّالِمِينَ
*Then it was said: "Earth, swallow your water!; and heaven, withhold* [your rain]*!" The waters subsided and the matter was accomplished. The ark settled on* [Mount] *al-Ǧūdiyy and it was said: "Gone are the wrongdoers!"*

[Q 11:45]
وَنَادَىٰ نُوحٌ رَبَّهُ فَقَالَ رَبِّ إِنَّ ابْنِي مِنْ أَهْلِي وَإِنَّ وَعْدَكَ الْحَقُّ وَأَنْتَ أَحْكَمُ الْحَاكِمِينَ
*Nūḥ called out to his Lord and said: "My Lord, my son is from my family. So if your promise is true and you are indeed the most just of all judges –"*

[Q 11:46]
قَالَ يَا نُوحُ إِنَّهُ لَيْسَ مِنْ أَهْلِكَ ۖ إِنَّهُ عَمَلٌ غَيْرُ صَالِحٍ ۖ فَلَا تَسْأَلْنِ مَا لَيْسَ لَكَ بِهِ عِلْمٌ ۖ إِنِّي أَعِظُكَ أَنْ تَكُونَ مِنَ الْجَاهِلِينَ
*He said: "Nūḥ, he is not of your family; what he did was not right. But do not ask me things you know nothing about. I advise you, lest you be counted among the ignorant."*

[Q 11:47]
قَالَ رَبِّ إِنِّي أَعُوذُ بِكَ أَنْ أَسْأَلَكَ مَا لَيْسَ لِي بِهِ عِلْمٌ ۖ وَإِلَّا تَغْفِرْ لِي وَتَرْحَمْنِي أَكُنْ مِنَ الْخَاسِرِينَ
*He said: "My Lord, I take refuge with you from asking that about which I have no knowledge! And unless you forgive me and have mercy on me I shall be among the losers!"*

[Q 11:48]
قِيلَ يَا نُوحُ اهْبِطْ بِسَلَامٍ مِنَّا وَبَرَكَاتٍ عَلَيْكَ وَعَلَىٰ أُمَمٍ مِمَّنْ مَعَكَ ۚ وَأُمَمٌ سَنُمَتِّعُهُمْ ثُمَّ يَمَسُّهُمْ مِنَّا عَذَابٌ أَلِيمٌ
*It was said: "Nūḥ, disembark in peace from us with blessings upon you and upon the nations that shall spring from those who are with you. To other nations we will grant enjoyment for a time; then a painful punishment from us will touch them."*

[Q 11:49 (second verse added)]
تِلْكَ مِنْ أَنْبَاءِ الْغَيْبِ نُوحِيهَا إِلَيْكَ ۖ مَا كُنْتَ تَعْلَمُهَا أَنْتَ وَلَا قَوْمُكَ مِنْ قَبْلِ هَٰذَا ۖ فَاصْبِرْ ۖ إِنَّ الْعَاقِبَةَ لِلْمُتَّقِينَ
*That is from the news of the unseen which we reveal to you; neither you nor your people knew it before this; so be patient, for the* [best] *outcome belongs to the god-fearers.*

• Alternatively, Stage $\text{III}_{\text{ii}}$ might have preceded Stage $\text{III}_{\text{i}}$. Yet this would not affect the overall argument made here regarding the original story behind the Noah narratives in Q 11 and 71.

## *Excursus B.* Q 11:35,49 and the redactional scribal background of the Qur'ān

There is something intriguing in the consoling words addressed to the quranic prophet in Q 11:35,49. As observed by Dorothy Peters (2008: 134–5), a strikingly similar rhetorical pattern is found in 4QTanḥûmîm 9–13, a fragmentary Hebrew manuscript found in Qumran Cave 4 (see Høvenhagen 2011), in which – following Isaiah 54:7–10 – God's words of consolation to Noah in Genesis 8:21–2; 9:8–17 are used to comfort the writer/speaker against his own distress![8] Typological identification of the days of Noah with the end of time (cf. already 1Enoch 93:4),[9] and hence with the messianic era in which the coming of the Messiah, the Son of Man, is expected, is explicit in Matthew 24:37–9;[10] Luke 17:26,[11] and 2Peter 3:5–7,10–12,[12] and implicit in the identification of the Messiah with Noah himself (on which see chapter two above and chapter seven below). Yet among the Jewish and Christian parabiblical writings that predate the Qur'ān, 4QTanḥ is unique (*a*) in its identification of the writer/speaker with Noah and (*b*) in introducing the latter into God's speech – the two motifs that we find again in Q 11:49.

Now the apparent connection between Q 11:49, 4QTanḥûmîm 9–13, and Isaiah 54:7–10 may either be casual or not. If it is a coincidence, the author of Q 11:49 unpremeditatedly chose an earlier documented rhetorical pattern to highlight on their own the symbolic link between the days of Noah and the end of time. If it is not, then three contrasting hypotheses emerge:

(1) the author of Q 11:35,49, however deliberately drawing on Isaiah 54:7–10 and/or 7Tanḥûmîm 9–13 (or a similar document unknown to us), did not have the aforementioned New Testament passages in mind and merely intended to stress the idea that the quranic prophet was the herald of the eschaton;
(2) s/he had those New Testament passages in mind but simply wanted to stress the idea, once more, that the quranic prophet was the herald of the eschaton;
(3) against all quranic evidence to the contrary, s/he somehow viewed the quranic prophet himself as the Messiah and intended to subliminally underline that identification without making it flagrant.

None of these possibilities should be dismissed *a priori*, albeit the last one seems a little weak at best (but on this point, see the afterword to the present book). On the other hand, it is possible to infer from the composite nature of the quranic corpus and the fact that there might have been several quranic prophets rather than just one (on which see the introduction above and chapter seven below) that even if the quranic prophet alluded to in Q 11:35,49 may have been thought of as the Messiah by his followers, other quranic prophets may not. Lastly:

(4) one could alternatively read Q 11:35,49 as a later interpolation intended to project Muḥammad's own messiaship (on which see the afterword below) back onto the quranic prophet.

Bet that as it may, any of these altogether different hypotheses would provide additional evidence of the plausible scribal background of the quranic Noah narratives – and of the whole quranic corpus, for that matter.

# Chapter 6 / Reading Backwards: Sources and Precedents of the Quranic Noah

As examined above, the quranic Noah narratives integrate several themes, motifs, and literary *topoi*. A further distinction must now be made between these categories. A single abstract theme, such as the prophet's rejection, can be set out by recourse to several particular motifs, such as accusations of his talking nonsense or being possessed, which vary from one text to another. Usually all major themes (e.g., the prophet's divine commission, his self-legitimation before his opponents, or his vindication by God) additionally function as literary *topoi*. Conversely, a motif used to illustrate a given theme need not necessarily be envisaged as literary *topos*, though some may function as literary *topoi* in their own right, depending on whether they occur in other texts, as well. Thus Noah's intercession for his rebellious son in quranic Noah narrative no. III, which vaguely resembles Abraham's plea for Sodom in Genesis 18 and David's lament for Absalom in 2Samuel 18, and is used in the Qur'ān to illustrate the prophet's intimacy with God and his intercessory role, is to the best of my knowledge unrivalled in any other parabiblical writing, as no biblical prophet fits that image. Hence Noah's intercession for his rebellious son, albeit an important (if enigmatic) theme in quranic Noah narrative no. III, cannot be considered a literary *topos* proper. Nor is the accusation of Noah talking nonsense and being possessed strictly paralleled elsewhere in the Jewish and Christian literature predating the quranic Noah narratives. However, it should be recalled here that in Genesis 9:20–7 Noah is said to have become drunk and taken his clothes off after drinking wine produced by a vineyard that he himself had planted once out of the ark, i.e., after the flood. This motif indeed became quite prominent in rabbinic literature, probably in order to downplay Noah's righteousness and wisdom against claims to the contrary made by Enochic Jews and Christians alike, or by the Enochic Jews first and then by some Christians.[1] As Daniel Machiela writes, "[t]here are numerous indications that during the 3rd to the 2nd centuries BCE Noah enjoyed a flurry of interest among certain Jewish groups, perhaps because of his relevance for those who adopted an apocalyptic worldview and felt that they too lived amidst a hopelessly wicked generation" (2009: 101). According to Machiela, 1QapGen, with its "positive reading" of Noah's drunkenness, must be cited as the "primary example" for such an exalted view of Noah (101–2). I would go even further to argue that Noah, as a symbol of the righteous seed from which a new humanity would rise (as also perhaps as a semi-supernatural being modelled after certain Babylonian epic legends), might well have been the original key-figure in Jewish apocalypticism – a figure whose quasi-messianic role (a reminder perhaps of the messianic role attributed in the early Second Temple Period to the mourned king of Judah, whose temporal rule came to an abrupt end after the Babylonian exile together with the priestly rule of his most loyal supporters, arguably the Levites) was later partially transferred *inter alios* to Levi (in the Aramaic Levy Document from Qumran and later the Testaments of the Twelve Patriarchs), Enoch (in most of 1Enoch, where nonetheless Noah remains a crucial figure), Melchizedek (in 2Enoch), Jesus (in the New Testament), and Seth (in some Gnostic traits).[2] By the 4th century CE, discussions about Noah's drunkenness and its disputed meaning had become a literary *topos* in Jewish-Christian polemics, especially in Syria and Mesopotamia, as reflected in the works of both Aphrahat and Ephraem (Koltun-Fromm 1997; Van Rompay 1997; Brock 2005). Christian authors, for whom Noah and the Ark functioned as typological symbols for Christ and the Church (Benjamins 1998), claimed Noah's authority by reinterpreting his drunkenness as a transitory though divinely inspired state that granted him access to wisdom, whereas the rabbinic authors mocked him on account of his drunkenness. Very likely it is this same Jewish-Christian controversy that is reissued in the Qur'ān, which takes sides along the Christian view by reclaiming Noah as a divinely inspired man (though just a man, like Christ himself is) against those (read the rabbinic Jews) who accused him of talking nonsense and being possessed. One may find here an additional proof of the Christian setting to which the Qur'ān (or its *Grundschriften*) originally belonged. Moreover, as will be shown below, the *Sīra* literature uses a similar (or rather the same) *topos* in order to defend Muḥammad against the accusation of sorcery made by his opponents, thus (once more) modelling Muḥammad after Noah shortly after a passage that further stresses Muḥammad's quasi-messianic, Christ-like traits (see chapter seven below). In short, one should refrain from reading every motif as a literary *topos*, but at the same time be aware that concealed behind a seemingly unparalleled motif, some other motif or even a specific literary *topos* might be brought to light.

Likewise, it is necessary to distinguish between proper sources and mere precedents. It is one thing to explore possible textual dependences that may give us a glimpse into the redactional and editorial work undertaken in the Qur'ān and/or its *Grundschriften*, and quite another thing to acknowledge the materials thus collected and reworked as part and parcel of an ongoing winding trend of thought, even if both things point to a web of overlapping textual and ideological relations.

On the other hand, it should be stressed that alleged proximity in time and space, while being one of the soundest criteria upon which the historian should be asked to rely when searching for specific textual sources, is not in itself the sole criterion to which the latter is expected to appeal, especially when dealing with a context elusive enough to demand further and constant clarification. The study of Islamic origins has undergone such a profound revision in the past decades, and is still in need of so many new explorations, that it is hard to tell what is close and what is not in terms of geography, or what is distant and what is not it terms of chronology. In other words, distinguishing between textual sources and precedents might at times be much more difficult than initially thought. Nevertheless, one should assign various degrees of probability to those texts which indistinctly seem to fit either category and may thus be construed as either sources or precedents, depending on whether or not one considers them to belong to the religious/scribal scribal milieu out of which Islam sprung.

Needless to say, stories about the persecution (and later divine vindication) of the righteous one chosen by God are as old as the Bible and have always played a vital role in Jewish and Christian imagination and salvation history (Nickelsburg 2006). Yet the picture of a divinely inspired Noah preaching to his contemporaries and being rejected and mocked by them surely stands as a highly peculiar theme to the biblical reader. Nonetheless, it is not without precedent. Noah is given special knowledge and/or divine wisdom in the Genesis Apocryphon (1QapGen 6:9–22; 7:16–19:?; 12:19–15:21) and two other qumranic manuscripts (4Q534 1:4–8, 4Q536 frags. 2+3, lines 8–9); 1Enoch 68:1; *Pirqê de-Rabbî 'Elî'ezer* 8, and Apocryphon of John NHC II 29:2–3 / NHC III 37:19–21 / BG 8502 72:16–73:2; cf. the references to the Book(s) of Noah in Aramaic Levi Document 10:10; 1QapGen 5:29 and Jubilees 10:14, as well as Noah's ability to praise God right from the cradle in 1 Enoch 106:3. Moreover, in 4Q534 1:9 we read that opposition against him would rise among his contemporaries, whereas in Apocryphon of John NHC II 29:3–5 / NHC III 37:21–2 / BG 8502 73:2–3 and the Concept of Our Great Power 38:26–8 it is said that he was rejected by them. Likewise, in Theophilus of Antioch's *Ad Autolycum* 3:19 and Jacob of Serugh's homilies,[3] Noah preaches to the people and calls them to repent, while both in Ephraem's *Commentary on Genesis* 6.9 (cf. his *Hymns on Faith* 56:2)[4] and in Book 3, chs. 2 (*in fine*) and 4 (in its first opening lines), of the Struggle of Adam and Eve with Satan – a 5th-6th century Syriac text extant in Arabic and Ethiopic that draws heavily upon the Cave of Treasures, albeit not as regards this supplementary information about Noah, which is lacking in the latter – he warns them about the coming flood, but they do not repent and even mock him (!), a motif that is also found in Narsai's *Homily on the Flood* 249 and in a number of rabbinic texts, such as *Sanhedrin* 108a-b; *Pirqê de-Rabbî 'Elî'ezer* 22; *Genesis Rabbah* 30:7; *Leviticus Rabbah* 27:5; and the section on Noah in *Sefer ha-Yašar*. In all probability Ephraem, Narsai, and the anonymous author of the Struggle of Adam and Eve with Satan provided the model for the quranic Noah narratives that include such a motif, namely Noah being mocked by the people (i.e., nos. I, III, IV, and VI). Yet it is interesting to note that whereas in Q 11:38 those who mock Noah do so when they see him build the ark, as in Ephraem's *Com-*

*mentary on Genesis* and Narsai's *Homily on the Flood*,[5] in Q 7:60; 23:25 and 54:9 they accuse him of talking nonsense or being possessed, and thus laugh at him after listening to his preaching. This is found neither in Ephraem nor in Narsai but in the Struggle of Adam and Eve with Satan 3.2,4, where Noah is insulted by his opponents, who point to him as a "twaddling old man."[6] Therefore I take the latter to be the source of quranic Noah narratives nos. I, IV, and VI, with Ephraem and/or Narsai the sources of quranic Noah narrative no. III.[7] However, attention must also be paid to the expression "those who disbelieved (*kafarū*)" in Q 11:27 and 23:24, by which its author means Noah's opponents. There is a fascinating parallel to this expression in Apocryphon of John NHC III 37:21–2 and BG 8502 73:3, whose authors write: "they did not believe (*pisteúein/apisteîn*) him" (without any further qualification) when referring to Noah's opponents; the sole difference is that the Qur'ān counts them among his own people, whereas NHC II 29:5 (but neither NHC III nor BG 8502!) reads instead: "those who were strangers to him did not listen to him." Cross-fertilisation between the Manichean and Gnostic communities being nowadays a well-grounded hypothesis in ancient religious studies, as evidenced *inter alia* by the fact that "the religious terminology used in the Coptic Nag Hammadi texts and Manichaica for missionary purposes belongs to the same vocabulary" (Van Lindt 2002: 196), and given moreover the plausible connections of formative Islam to Manichaeism (Gil 1992), it is certainly possible to see in the Apocryphon of John an hypothetical source for quranic Noah narrative no. IV (cf. also Q 26:111 and the eloquent reference to Noah's opponents as unwilling to "listen to him" in Q 71:7).

For all other quranic innovations, the sources are rather unclear and the precedents too vague, or else such innovations can easily be deduced from the more general notion that Noah was granted special knowledge to warn his contemporaries and to instruct them on the fundamentals of the true religion. The depiction of Noah's opponents as idolaters in Q 71:23 (cf. 7:59; 11:26; 23:23) is vaguely reminiscent, for instance, of Tertulian's *De Idolatria* 24, where it is stated that there was no place in Noah's ark for any possible kind of idolatry. It could be that quranic Noah narratives nos. I, III, IV, and VII reflect Tertulian's text or else the view endorsed in it, which might have been shared by other Christians, even if their names are unknown to us. Still, this is too hazy a coincidence to encourage any elaborate analysis. Likewise, comparison of the days of Noah with the end of time is a theme common enough to early Jewish and Christian literature to substantiate any concrete claim as to how it might have entered the proto-Muslim imagination.

The fact that both Ephraem's *Commentary on Genesis* and the Struggle of Adam and Eve with Satan may be envisaged as sources of some of the very distinctive motifs found in the quranic Noah narratives obviously points to Syrian

Christianity as a possible background for them. However, the precise extent to which Syrian Christianity is behind many of the theological notions, religious legends, and even the grammar and the lexicon of the Qur'ān, and the latter indebted to the miaphysite (Jacobite) and dyophysite (Nestorian) worldviews, is far from being clear. Yet scholarly discussion over the past decades shows that some very close relationship must indeed be established between Syrian Christianity and formative Islam. As Sydney Griffith writes,

> It is something of a truism among scholars of Syriac to say that the more deeply one is familiar with the works of the major writers of the classical period, especially the composers of liturgically significant, homiletic texts such as those written by Ephraem the Syrian (c. 306–73), Narsai of Edessa and Nisibis (c. 399–502), or Jacob of Serugh (c. 451–521), the more one hears echoes of many of the standard themes and characteristic turns of phrase at various points in the discourse of the Arabic Qur'ān (2008: 109).

Likewise, it is not strange to find traces of possible oral Syriac traditions, or even subtexts, lying at the very core of certain quranic pericopes. To return to one of the examples examined above, the quranic Noah narratives reflect either Ephraem's writings or an oral tradition in which it is fair to suppose that Ephraem's writings had played an almost undisputed role from the 4th century onwards. Still, one must remain cautious when searching for possible quranic sources and careful not to overstate mere conjectures (on which see the excursus below).

## *Excursus*. A Syriac source behind the blessing of Noah in Q 37:78–81?

In his widely discussed essay on what he calls the Syro-Aramaic background to the language of the Qur'ān,[8] Christoph Luxenberg (2007: 157–60) proposes to identify a Syriacism in the quranic pericope on the blessing of Noah contained in *Sūrat aṣ-Ṣāffāt* (Q 37), more precisely in the final word of its second verse (Q 37:79); accordingly, he offers a new, challenging interpretation of vv. 78–80, which constitute but the first three segments of a four- or (if vv. 73–4 and 127–8 are also counted in it, on which see below) six-segment refrain repeatedly if not homogeneously displayed in vv. 78–81 (regarding Noah), 105 and 108–11 (Abraham), 119–22 (Moses and Aaron), and 129–32 (Elijah).

In what follows I will review Luxenburg's philological argument, which clearly needs to be nuanced.[9] Nonetheless, I will try to substantiate his overall hermeneutical argument by further examining the whole refrain and the verses preceding it, especially vv. 73–4 (and, more broadly, vv. 11–74). One thing of which Luxenberg seems unaware is that the association of Noah with the eschaton is rather fundamental in the Qur'ān – and recurrent for that matter – an additional argument that could back up his interpretation of vv. 78–80. But before reassessing Luxenberg's reading, let us first take a closer look at the text:

Q 37:78:

وَتَرَكْنَا عَلَيْهِ فِي الْآخِرِينَ

Q 37:79:

سَلَامٌ عَلَىٰ نُوحٍ فِي الْعَالَمِينَ

Q 37:80:

إِنَّا كَذَٰلِكَ نَجْزِي الْمُحْسِنِينَ

Q 37:81:

إِنَّهُ مِنْ عِبَادِنَا الْمُؤْمِنِينَ

Q 37:105:

قَدْ صَدَّقْتَ الرُّؤْيَا ۚ إِنَّا كَذَٰلِكَ نَجْزِي الْمُحْسِنِينَ

Q 37:108:

وَتَرَكْنَا عَلَيْهِ فِي الْآخِرِينَ

Q 37:109:

سَلَامٌ عَلَىٰ إِبْرَاهِيمَ

Q 37:110:

كَذَٰلِكَ نَجْزِي الْمُحْسِنِينَ

Q 37:111:

إِنَّهُ مِنْ عِبَادِنَا الْمُؤْمِنِينَ

Q 37:119:

وَتَرَكْنَا عَلَيْهِمَا فِي الْآخِرِينَ

Q 37:120:

سَلَامٌ عَلَىٰ مُوسَىٰ وَهَارُونَ

Q 37:121:

إِنَّا كَذَٰلِكَ نَجْزِي الْمُحْسِنِينَ

Q 37:122:

إِنَّهُمَا مِنْ عِبَادِنَا الْمُؤْمِنِينَ

Q 37:129:

وَتَرَكْنَا عَلَيْهِ فِي الْآخِرِينَ

Q 37:130:

سَلَامٌ عَلَىٰ إِلْ يَاسِينَ

Q 37:131:

إِنَّا كَذَٰلِكَ نَجْزِي الْمُحْسِنِينَ

Q 37:132:

إِنَّهُ مِنْ عِبَادِنَا الْمُؤْمِنِينَ

Note that the refrain in vv. 78–81 is reproduced almost verbatim (save the final period in v. 79) in vv. 108–111, 119–122, and 129–32, with minor adjustments made to fit the verbal number; and that v. 80 alone is reproduced in v. 105. It should also be stressed that the opening of v. 113, which does not form part of the refrain (. . . و بركنا عليه و على إسحاق 'We have blessed him [i.e. Ibrāhīm = Abraham] and Isḥāq [= Isaac]'; alternatively: 'We have bestowed our blessing upon him and upon

Isḥāq: *wa-bāraknā 'alayhi wa-'alà Isḥāq*), closely resembles that of vv. 78, 108, 119, and 129, although the verb changes in it.

Conforming to standard quranic orthography and vocalisation (against which the ancient quranic *rasm* or "consonantal skeleton" presents a much more ambiguous text, lacking as it does the diacritics that began to be used in the early 2nd/8th century to mark out similar consonants and fix their appropriate vocalisation), and guided by aṭ-Ṭabarī's hermeneutical insights (on which see Luxenberg 2007: 158), most translators render these verses as follows:

Q 37:78: *We have left him* (wa-taraknā 'alayhi) *among those of later times* (fī-l-aḫirīn).
Q 37:79: *Peace upon Nūḥ* (= Noah) *in the Universe* (or, *in the worlds*: fī-l-'ālamīn)*!*
Q 37:80: *Thus do we reward the righteous* (al-muḥsinīn).
Q 37:81: *For he is to be counted among our faithful servants* ('ibādinā-l-mu'minīn).

Q 37:105: *Thus do we reward the righteous* (al-muḥsinīn).

Q 37:108: *We have left him* (wa-taraknā 'alayhi) *among those of later times* (fī-l-aḫirīn).
Q 37:109: *Peace upon Ibrāhīm* (= Abraham)*!*
Q 37:110: *Thus do we reward the righteous* (al-muḥsinīn).
Q 37:111: *For he is to be counted among our faithful servants* ('ibādinā-l-mu'minīn).

Q 37:119: *We have left them* (wa-taraknā 'alayhimā) *among those of later times* (fī-l-aḫirīn).
Q 37:120: *Peace upon Mūsà* (= Moses) *and Hārūn* (=Aaron)*!*
Q 37:121: *Thus do we reward the righteous* (al-muḥsinīn).
Q 37:122: *For they are to be counted among our faithful servants* ('ibādinā-l-mu'minīn).

Q 37:129: *We have left him* (wa-taraknā 'alayhi) *among those of later times* (fī-l-aḫirīn).
Q 37:130: *Peace upon Ilyāsīn* (= Elijah)*!*
Q 37:131: *Thus do we reward the righteous* (al-muḥsinīn).
Q 37:132: *For he is to be counted our faithful servants* ('ibādinā-l-mu'minīn).

Yet this translation presents several philological problems, as regards (1) the verb in vv. 78, 108, 119, and 129; (2) the semantics of their concluding phrase (which is the same in all such verses); (3) the morphology of the final word in v. 79 as well as its meaning; and (4) the purpose of the whole refrain in light of its preceding verses (especially vv. 73–4). I shall deal with these matters successively:

(1) To begin with, it must be noted that vv. 78, 108, and 129 should rather be translated: "We have left *upon* [sic] him among those of later times;" likewise, vv. 119 should be translated "We have left *upon* [sic] them among those of later times," for otherwise the preposition على *'alà* ('upon') is omitted – and it should not be. Now, as weird as this may sound in English, so too it sounds odd in Arabic (cf. the insightful comments by Barth 1916: 124–5; Paret 1982: 371; Luxenberg 2007: 158; Stewart 2010: 244).[10] Conversely, the blessing action in v. 113 better matches the subsequent preposition على (which occurs twice in that very verse: "We have bestowed our blessing *upon* him and *upon* Isḥāq"). This led Jacob Barth in 1916, and more recently Luxenberg (and Stewart), to assume that the original verb in v. 78 (*taraknā*) should rather be the verb now (only) found in v. 113 (*bāraknā*), which was thus misread by transforming its initial *b* into a *t*. This is highly plausible. The *rasm* in vv. 78, 108, 113, 119, and 129 runs ىركنا , which can be read as either تركنا *taraknā* by adding two diacritics above the otherwise undefined first consonant (so vv. 78, 108, 119, 129) or بركنا *bāraknā* if only a single diacritic is added beneath it (v. 113). As I have just argued, this second reading would better fit the syntax in vv. 78, 108, 119, and 129, which could then be alternatively translated as follows (i.e., regardless of their concluding phrase: فى الأخرين , to which I shall return later):

| | |
|---|---|
| Q 37:78,108,129: | *We have bestowed our blessing upon him* (wa-bāraknā 'alayhi) . . . |
| Q 37:119: | *We have bestowed our blessing upon them* (wa-bāraknā 'alay-himā) . . . |

In my view, there is absolutely nothing to be objected to this emendation of the verb in v. 78.

(2) According to Luxenberg (2007: 158–9), however, the semantics of the second half of vv. 78, 108, 119, and 129 should likewise be revised. In short, he advocates that the expression فى الأخرين *fī-l-aḫirīn* is not so much intended to mean "those of later times" as "the last days," i.e., the eschaton. The plural noun phrase الأخرين is not uncommon in the Qur'ān: it occurs five times with the preposition فى *fī* ("in": Q 26:84; 37:78,108,119,129), four times with the preposition من *min* ("from," "among": Q 56:14,40,49; 77:17), and only once with the preposition ل *li-* ("for": Q 43:56). In the last case it denotes the idea of otherness, which is also inherent to the root *'.ḫ.r.* but which does not concern us here. Conversely, when preceded by the preposition من it always appears in opposition to الأوّلين *al-awwalīn* (cf. Q 56:13,39,49; 77:16) and ought to be translated, depending on the context, as "those of earlier times," "the ancient people," "the first ones," etc. Thus vv. 56:13–

14 read: "a number among those of earlier times / but (only) a few among the contemporaries (= those of later times)." One must therefore ask whether a similar meaning may correspond to the word الاخرين when it is displayed alone (i.e., without its antonym الأوّلين) and preceded by the preposition فى. To answer this question, it must first be noted that فى may legitimately be translated as "among" in certain quranic passages (see e.g. the comments made below apropos the final phrase in v. 79, which also includes the preposition فى), "for" likewise being a possible alternative translation in such cases. It must also be stressed, secondly, that reading vv. 26:84; 37:78,108,119,129 in light of vv. 56:14,40,49; 77:17 proves to be anything but a spurious option, for الاخرين could very well be intended to mean "those of later times" there as well. It goes without saying that if the author of Q 37:78,108,119, and 129 simply wanted to express the notion that Noah's, Abraham's, Moses's, Aaron's, and Elijah's blessing was bestowed upon them by God to have their memory preserved among those of later times, s/he could have used the preposition ل as in Q 43:56 (فَجَعَلْنَاهُمْ سَلَفًا وَمَثَلًا لِلْآخِرِينَ "We left them as a reminder and an example *for* other peoples"); but the fact that s/he instead used the preposition فى (as in 26.84) does not preclude that eventual meaning. Therefore vv. 78, 108, 119, and 129 may alternatively be translated as follows: "We have bestowed our blessing upon him/them in the last days," as Luxenberg proposes; or: "We have bestowed our blessing upon him/them for those of later times" (i.e., for the generations to come). The choice depends on whether one implicitly links v. 78 to vv. 73–4 or v. 79 (if فى العلمين is there intended to mean "among all men"), on which see below.[11]

(3) Luxenberg further suggests (2007: 159) that علمين i.e., the final Arabic word in v. 79 (which is usually read *'ālamīn* in the plural form), is a misreading of the Syriac noun ܥܠܡܝܢ (*ālmīn*), meaning "both worlds." There is no denying that the (arguably anti-Arian) expressions "both worlds"/"in both worlds" are quite frequent, for instance, in Ephraem's writings, where they denote the spiritual and material worlds (cf. e.g. his *Hymn on Virginity* 7.1, the response to his *Hymn on Paradise* 15 and his *Commentary on the Epistle to the Hebrews ad* 1:2). But on all grounds Luxenberg makes a mountain out of a molehill, as there simply is no dual form in Syriac! *'Ālmīn* is a regular Syriac plural noun that might (only might) take a dual meaning depending on the context (i.e., if "the worlds" in question prove to be "two" worlds instead of, say, three, four, etc., as happens in Ephraem's aforementioned passages). So, as Daniel King writes, "[o]ne cannot see how the Arabic dual could have been originally 'intended' here on the basis of a transcription" (2009: 54). Yet Luxenberg may not be completely wrong, for it is plain as a pikestaff that the quranic *rasm* (i.e., the undotted Arabic word) علمىں can be read either in the plural or the dual form: *'ālamīn*/*'ālamayn*.[12] In short, there is no need to take the final word in v. 79 as a plural noun *per se*. Even the dotted word

علمين as it nowadays figures in every single copy (*muṣḥaf*) of the Qur'ān may indistinctively be read as *'ālamīn* or *'ālamayn*; in fact, the latter might well have been the original quranic vocalisation, though Luxenberg does not seem to be aware of it. Yet this can surely be objected to as overly abstract reasoning, for upon closer examination the Qur'ān seems to support the plural reading quite clearly. The noun phrase العلمين occurs seventy-three times in the Qur'ān: forty-one times in genitive form following the noun ربّ *rabb* ("Lord") to denote God (ربّ العلمين : so Q 1:2; 2:131; 5:28; 6:45,71,162; 7:54,61,67,104,121; 10:10,37; 26:16,23,47,77,98,109, 127,145,164,180; 27:8,44; 28:30; 32:2; 37:87,182; 39:75; 40:64–6; 41:9; 43:46; 45:36; 56:80; 59:16; 69:43; 81:29; 83:6) and thirty-two times in several phrases following the prepositions ل *li-* ("for," fourteen times: Q 3:96,108; 6:90; 12:104; 21:71,91,107; 25:1; 29:10,15; 30:22; 38:87; 68:52; 81:27), على *'alà* ("over," "above," nine times: Q 2:47,122,251; 3:33,42; 6:86; 7:140; 44:32; 45:16), من *min* ("from," "among," five times: Q 5:20,115; 7:80; 26:165; 29:28), عن *'an* ("with respect to," "in front of," three times: Q 3:97; 15:70; 29:6), and only once following the preposition فى *fī* ("in," "among?": Q 37:79). Therefore the expression فى العلمين constitutes a *hapax legomenon* (i.e., an expression elsewhere unmatched) in the quranic lexicon. In all other cases (including those in which it is employed in genitive form together with the noun ربّ to form God's name ربّ العلمين , of which an illustration is provided in Q 37:87), العلمين it is to my mind rightly interpreted in the plural form, though it should probably be translated as "all men/women" instead of "the worlds." Thus in Q 3:33, Adam, Noah, and Abraham's family are chosen by God "over all (other) men" (cf. Israel's election in 2:47,122; 44:32; 45:16; Mary's in 3:42; and Ishmael's, Elijah's, Jonas's and Lot's in 6:86); in 3:97 and 29:6 God is declared to be rich "with respect to all men," i.e., in contrast to these; whereas in 29:10 God knows what "all men" conceal in their hearts. As to the composite divine name ربّ العلمين , it could certainly be read in the dual form, i.e., as *rabb al-'ālamayn*, "Lord of both worlds" (one of these worlds being the present life and the other being the hereafter), but it is commonly, and in my view correctly, interpreted in the plural form as *rabb al-'ālamīn*, a composite term that may be translated either as "Lord of the worlds" (and of every single creature found in them) or, more precisely perhaps, as "Lord of all men" (cf. de Prémare 2002: 437–8, n. 156). I personally think that فى العلمين in v. 37:79 likewise ought to be read in the plural instead of the dual form, as meaning "among all men"; nonetheless, it would also make sense to translate it with the English phrase "in all the worlds" in light of v. 37:87, where the "Universe" is clearly meant to be the referent (note the discussion about the stars and their earthly idols in vv. 83–6, 88–98). As to Luxenberg's translation, it cannot be entirely dismissed, given the eschatological tone of the refrain and its preceding verses, on which see the next paragraph. Besides, it is somewhat intriguing that, in contrast to vv. 109, 120, and 130, only v. 79 includes the phrase فى العلمين. Yet it is apparent that v. 120 originally lacked this phrase, since in the only pre- (or at least non-) "Uthmanic," partially extant quranic manuscript that we know of (which might simply be pre-Marwanid or pre-Abbasid),[13] i.e., the *scriptio inferior* in Codex Ṣan'ā' 1 (DAM 01–27.1 fol. 29B = Q 37:118–44, on which see the recent critical edition by Sadeghi and Goudarzi 2012: 104), v. 120 (l. 2) clearly ends after هرون Hārūn (whose و is almost illegible); nor does there seem to be room enough between the incomplete name السىں Ilyāsīn (of which only the initial ا is fully legible) and the likewise incomplete next word (كدلك ?) in l. 8 to suppose that v. 130 may have ended with the phrase "in both worlds"/"in the worlds," as v. 79 does according to the so-called Uthmanic vulgata. As to the section containing vv. 104–17, it is apparently missing from Codex Ṣan'ā' 1, so at first sight no definite conclusion can be reached with respect to v. 109. Yet judging from Ibn Abī Dāwūd's *Kitāb al-Maṣāḥif* and Jeffery's exhaustive compilation of the variants reported about the old quranic codices, neither Ibn Mas'ūd's nor Ubayy b. Ka'b's recensions seem to have differed from the so-called Uthmanic codex regarding vv. 109, 120, and 130. Inasmuch as the section containing vv. 69–81 is missing too from Codex Ṣan'ā' 1 (which in spite of some structural coincidences significantly differs from what we know of Ibn Mas'ūd's and Ubayy b. Ka'b's recensions), the phrase فى الأخرين may thus be said to be exclusive to v. 37.79, as it figures in so-called Uthmanic vulgata and, by omission, in both Ibn Mas'ūd's and Ubayy b. Ka'b's codices.

(4) In any event, i.e., regardless of his philological argument, I think Luxenberg is right to emphasise that vv. 78–80 should be acknowledged as having an eschatological flavour. Put differently: his overall hermeneutical argument is apparently correct. On my reading, v. 80 must in fact be linked, on the one hand, to vv. 75–7, in which Noah's earthly reward is expressly mentioned; but it must also be connected, on the other hand (as also v. 78 and less probably, but still possibly, v. 79), to vv. 11–74, which do put forward a series of unmistakable eschatological warnings (vv. 11–72) culminating in the statement contained in vv. 73–4:

Q 37:73:

فَانْظُرْ كَيْفَ كَانَ عَاقِبَةُ الْمُنْذَرِينَ

*Behold the end met by (all) those who were admonished –*

Q 37:74:

إِلَّا عِبَادَ اللهِ الْمُخْلَصِينَ

*save God's sincere servants* (illā 'ibād Allāh al-muḫlaṣīn)*!*

A further proof that v. 78 ought to be read in light of vv. 73–4 is in my view provided by Elijah's blessing in v. 129, as v. 74 is eloquently reproduced verbatim in vv. 127–8: فكذّبوه فإنّهم لمحضرون / إلّا عباد الله المخلصين "They denied him, but they shall be summoned – / save God's sincere servants"). Cf. also the implicit connection between vv. 75 and 127: v. 127 reports that Elijah (who is only mentioned three times in the Qur'ān: in vv. 37:123 [as Ilyās] and 130 [as Ilyāsīn], and [again as Ilyās] in v. 85 of *Sūrat al-An'ām* [Q 6]) was rejected by the people (a motif with which we are quite familiar as regards Noah, and that is both present in all quranic Noah narratives and fundamental to understanding them, as I have earlier argued), whereas in v. 75 we read that Noah invoked God (as he often does in the quranic Noah narratives after feeling rejected) – asking God to help him, one may safely deduce. Surely the reader will not need to be reminded, first, that this twofold motif (rejection/claim) is frequently followed in the quranic Noah narratives by God's words of consolation to Noah, and thereby to the quranic prophet; and, secondly, that in quranic Noah narrative no. III (11:49), God asks the quranic prophet (who is there explicitly modelled after Noah) to be patient and then comforts him by granting him a good afterlife. So it is in my view beyond question that at least the verses concerning Noah and Elijah in *Sūrat aṣ-Ṣāffāt* present some eschatological qualities. The eschatological atmosphere of the Elijah passage, and by implication the Noah passage and the refrain in Q 37, is moreover confirmed in my opinion by Ibn Mas'ūd's recension, in which Elijah is replaced in vv. 123 and 130 by Idrīs/Idrāsīn (Jeffery 1937:80), i.e., by Enoch – an eschatological figure very likely modelled after that of Noah in the Jewish literature of the Second Temple Period (see chapter two above). Both Elijah and Idrīs/Enoch (who is evoked in Q 19:56–7 and 21:85–6) must be seen as transhistorical numinous characters: both were raised by God and allowed immortal life (cf. Genesis 5:22,24; 2Kings 2:1,3,5,11; and Q 19:56–7); both are given angelic assistance (as is the quranic prophet) to instruct the righteous about the eschaton (cf. e.g. Enoch's heavenly journeys and visions in 1Enoch 12–36; 37–71; 79–80; 83–90, his instruction to the righteous in 1Enoch 81–2; 91–105: and Elijah's visions in the two Elijah apocalypses currently known as 1- and 2Elijah); both are equally granted a salient role in the end of time (cf. the well-known motif of Elijah's return in Malachi 3:1; 4:5–6; Matthew 11:10,14; 17:9–13: and the identification of Enoch with the Son of Man in 1Enoch 71:14, after which Enoch's angelic metamorphosis is imagined in 2Enoch 22 and 3Enoch 3–15); and both are reported to have had a heavenly encounter with Muḥammad in several Islamic traditions relative to Muḥammad's *mi'rāğ* or "heavenly ascent."[14] It cannot be coincidental, then, that Elijah (in the so-called Uthmanic vulgata – as also in Codex Ṣan'ā' 1 and Ubayy b. Ka'b's recension, for that matter) and Idrīs (in Ibn Mas'ūd's) figure in these verses in a fashion that is unparalleled in the Qur'ān in both content and length. Last but not least, the vocabulary in vv. 78–81 and 129–32 amounts to the evidence that they ought to be read in connection with vv. 73–4 and 127–8, respectively. Note the allusion to God's "sincere" and "faithful servants" (عباد الله المخلصين ، عبادنا المؤمنين) in vv. 74, 81 and 132, and also the parallel reference to the "righteous" (المحسنين) in vv. 80 and 131; in short, they are those to be saved, i.e., those who will rejoice in the hereafter – like Noah and Elijah/Idrīs, therefore. A similar – if not the very same – idea is later applied to Abraham (vv. 108–11), Moses, and Aaron (vv. 119–22), whose reward in the present life is also mentioned in vv. 107, 112–13, 114–18. It is nevertheless crucial to distinguish between their earthly reward and that granted to them – as also to Noah, Elijah, and the righteous – in the hereafter, for otherwise the whole refrain might be misinterpreted. Indeed, I dare say that the excessive importance conferred by most quranic commentators and translators on vv. 76–7, 107, 112–13, and 114–18 (together with their systematic but canonically sanctioned misreading of the verb in v. 78) has mislead them in their interpretation.

Thus no less than four slightly different translations of vv. 78–81 appear to be plausible. Considering the degree to which each one shows some kind of eschatological concern (+/–), or else lacks it (0), they may be ordered as follows:

| | | | |
|---|---|---|---|
| (A) | + | Q 37:78: | *We have bestowed our blessing upon him in the last days.* |
| | | Q 37:79: | *Peace upon Nūḥ in both worlds!* |
| | | Q 37:80: | *Thus do we reward the righteous.* |
| | | Q 37:81 | *For he is to be counted among our faithful servants.* |
| (B) | – | Q 37:78: | *We have bestowed our blessing upon him in the last days.* |
| | | Q 37:79: | *Peace upon Nūḥ among all men!* |
| | | Q 37:80: | *Thus do we reward the righteous.* |
| | | Q 37:81 | *For he is to be counted among our faithful servants.* |
| (C) | 0 | Q 37:78: | *We have bestowed our blessing upon him for those of later times.* |
| | | Q 37:79: | *Peace upon Nūḥ among all men!* |
| | | Q 37:80: | *Thus do we reward the righteous.* |
| | | Q 37:81 | *For he is to be counted among our faithful servants.* |
| (D) | 0 | Q 37:78: | *We have left him/had his memory preserved among/for those of later times.* |
| | | Q 37:79: | *Peace upon Nūḥ in the Universe!* |
| | | Q 37:80: | *Thus do we reward the righteous.* |
| | | Q 37:81: | *For he is to be counted among our faithful servants.* |

D stands for the habitual reading of Noah's "blessing" (which is thus overlooked) in Q 37; C corresponds to Barth's, Luxenberg's, and Stewart's re-reading of the verb in v. 78 (with which I fully agree); whereas A is Luxenberg's translation (which I regard as being as likely as C, though not on the basis of Luxenberg's analysis); and B, my own. In sum, the traditional interpretation of these verses takes for granted that they point to the preservation of Noah's, Abraham's, Moses's, Aaron's, and Elijah's memory among the later generations. On my reading, they should rather be interpreted as dealing with divine election, complaisance, blessing, and reward in both the present life and (above all perhaps) the hereafter. It may be that exemplary tales, of which the emergent *ḥadīṯ* literature offers a good many illustrations from the 8th century onwards, became at that time more and more relevant than specific eschatological concerns. Transition from a messianic community to a more or less standardised religious community would normalise the preeminence thus conferred on social and political values. If so, the reinterpretation of the Noah story as reflected in *Sūrat aṣ-Ṣāffāt* might be said to have played a small but noticeable role in that transformation – or else to be a witness to it.

I shall come back to this issue (namely, the reuse of the quranic Noah story at different stages in the development of the early Islamic community) in the next chapter. In the meantime, what should be stressed is that vv. 78–81 in *Sūrat aṣ-Ṣāffāt* do not necessarily betray an obliterated Syriac source – although such a connection cannot be entirely dismissed, as I have argued. Yet they doubtless prove that a kind of *de-eschatologised* re-reading, even re-writing, of the quranic Noah story was undertaken at some point.[15]

# Chapter 7 / Reading Forward: From the Quranic Noah to the Muhammadan *Evangelium*

Slashed as much from within as from without (by means of its multiple reworked narratives and encrypted subtexts), the Qur'ān surely resembles anything but a plain textual surface: its interwoven verses and fitful notions oscillate in the midst of multiple trajectories, both textual and ideological, that need to be explored afresh. This is undoubtedly a tough task for the historian, who must of necessity set forth new interpretative hypotheses in order to unravel the purpose of the different and originally independent narratives into which the quranic text divides. To be sure, to think of these as discrete 'prophetical logia' seems just as reasonable as to describe them as homiletic, liturgical, and/or exegetical adjustments/expansions/contractions of a number of earlier texts.

As I have already pointed out, to think of them as authored by a single prophet (or scribe), on the other hand, is but one option out of many, and not necessarily the fairest one, as there is no evidence to support either this or the opposite view. Yet the opposite view seems to me a more plausible option, given the heterogeneous nature of the materials thus collected and reworked.

In addition, a parallel problem is knowing whether they all equally refer to a single figure – the figure that I have named above by recourse to the expression the "quranic prophet;" i.e., whether each refers to a single figure, and, furthermore, whether the collection has that very purpose. It is upon this twofold premise that I have built the present essay, however. That is, I take the collection to refer to a single prophetic figure, and moreover, I believe that some of its particular narratives also do so. Originally perhaps some of them did not, but instead attempted to provide an explanation for several texts that were considered crucial by a community or different communities, or perhaps exhortation to the members of these communities. Yet even in that case, such narratives as we now have them – and that is the essential point after all! – present traces of some kind of personal allusion whose referent appears to be a single individual. In short, at a given point in the history of their complex development and/or rewriting, no matter how elliptically, they were (re)framed as narratives about someone – a prophet. Hence the hypothesis of a single quranic prophet need not be judged too naive.

To be sure, in the quranic Noah narratives this anonymous prophet is described as a biblical prophet. Only later was he fully construed, and explicitly introduced, as an "Arabian prophet" (Wansbrough 2004: 58, 83). This and no other is in fact the basic purpose of the *Sīra* literature, i.e., Muḥammad's 'biography' as set out by Ibn Isḥāq (d. c. 150/767) and his editor, Ibn Hišām (d. c. 216/831) – which Wansbrough audaciously proposed to call the "Muhammadan evangelium."[1] The point that I would wish to make in this chapter is that the quranic Noah offered them an outstanding typological framework with which to inscribe their construction. To substantiate this claim, I will divide my argument into seven parts.

(*i*) As argued above (see the preceding chapter), the motif of the people laughing at God's messengers must be understood to originate in a Noahic *topos*, which was later reused in the Qur'ān and applied there either to Noah himself or to various other figures, including Moses and the quranic prophet. The two quranic passages recounting the people's accusation that Noah was a *mağnūn* (Q 23:25; 54:9) or the fact that they mocked and laughed at him (7:60; 11:38) ought to be related, therefore, to those passages in which similar accusations are raised against all other prophets (51:52), Moses (51:39), or the quranic prophet himself (7:184: أَوَلَمْ يَتَفَكَّرُوا ۗ مَا بِصَاحِبِهِمْ مِنْ جِنَّةٍ ۚ إِنْ هُوَ إِلَّا نَذِيرٌ مُبِينٌ "Do they not give thought? There is no madness in him [lit. in their companion]. He is just a clear warner!"; 37:36: وَيَقُولُونَ أَئِنَّا لَتَارِكُو آلِهَتِنَا لِشَاعِرٍ مَجْنُونٍ "They said: Are we to forsake our gods for a possessed poet?"; 44:14: ثُمَّ تَوَلَّوْا عَنْهُ وَقَالُوا مُعَلَّمٌ مَجْنُونٌ "They turned away and said: 'He has been taught [what to say]! He is possessed!'"; 52:29 فَذَكِّرْ فَمَا أَنْتَ بِنِعْمَتِ رَبِّكَ بِكَاهِنٍ وَلَا مَجْنُونٍ "So remind: By your Lord's grace you are neither a soothsayer nor a possessed man!"; 68:51: وَإِنْ يَكَادُ الَّذِينَ كَفَرُوا لَيُزْلِقُونَكَ بِأَبْصَارِهِمْ لَمَّا سَمِعُوا الذِّكْرَ وَيَقُولُونَ إِنَّهُ لَمَجْنُونٌ "The disbelievers would strike you down with their glances when they hear the reminder. They say: 'Surely he is possessed!'"), and also to the passage in which the latter is told that all previous prophets were mocked, too (6:10).

*(ii)* Already applied to the quranic prophet in several passages of the Qur'ān (namely 6:10; 7:184; 37:36; 44:14; 52:29; 68:51, two of them thus belonging to the same sūra containing quranic Noah narrative no. I), such *topoi* (and especially the accusation of his being possessed) were later repeatedly employed by Ibn Isḥāq and Ibn Hišām to describe the ill-treatment that Muḥammad presumably received from his own people in Mecca (Sīra 171, 183, 186, 232–3, 262, ed. Wüstenfeld). In Sīra 171 we read that a number of the Qurayš came to al-Walīd b. al-Mugīra to discuss with him Muḥammad's trustworthiness, and that they initially called Muḥammad a كاهن *kāhin* (i.e., a diviner; cf. Q 52:29; 69:42), a مجنون *mağnūn*, a poet, and a sorcerer. These epithets occur again a little further on in the text, when Muḥammad is likewise accused by some Qurayshites of being a liar, a poet, a sorcerer, a diviner, and a *majnūn* (S 183). Cf. S 186, where 'Utba b. Rabī'a acknowledges that Muḥammad's words are neither poetry, spells, nor witchcraft; S 232–3, where it is said that the people mocked and laughed at Muḥammad; and S 262, where Q 6:10 (وَلَقَدِ اسْتُهْزِئَ بِرُسُلٍ مِنْ قَبْلِكَ فَحَاقَ بِالَّذِينَ سَخِرُوا مِنْهُمْ مَا كَانُوا بِهِ يَسْتَهْزِئُونَ "Other messengers have been mocked before you, but those who mocked them were overwhelmed by what they had mocked!") is fully quoted and explained. Cf. also the attacks on the poets and soothsayers in Q 26:221–7; 69:41–2 (and again in 37:36).

(*iii*) However, used in the Qur'ān for the sake of theological controversy regarding Jesus' human status in the context of intra-Christian polemics, and also to stress the status of the quranic prophet (cf. Q 3:144; 6:8–10; 7:188; 11:12; 16:103), the quranic view that Noah was not an angel but a man (11:27; 23:24) very likely draws on previous Noah traditions that go back to 1Enoch 106–7 and other related writings. The fact that such traditions were somehow employed to clarify not only Jesus' but also the quranic prophet's human status adds to the aforementioned evidence that the latter is partly modelled after Noah in the Qur'ān. It is most remarkable that in some well-documented Jewish Noah traditions, Noah is ambiguously depicted as an angel and then declared to be only a man; and that based upon those very same traditions, Jesus' portrayal in the New Testament and the New Testament apocrypha conversely ends up proclaiming his divine sonship![2] On my reading, the quranic presentation of Noah as no more than a man serves first to highlight Jesus' own human status (cf. the prophetic list in Q 33:7, which makes it crystal clear that Noah, Abraham, Moses, and Jesus belong to the same condition, i.e., that they all are human beings chosen by God to be his apostles). An additional proof of this can be found in Q 10:68–70. Albeit in need of close re-examination so as to determine their concrete setting and purpose, anti-trinitarian formulae reclaiming Jesus as God's apostle and Messiah but contesting his divine sonship are sufficiently documented in the Qur'ān to require further comment; but it is interesting to note that quranic Noah narrative no. II, where Noah is moreover introduced as a Muslim (i.e., as a man submitted to God's authority [10:72]), immediately follows one of such formulae, in which we read that God has no son and that those who claim the opposite lie and will be severely punished in the afterlife (Q 10:68–70). As an aside, even if in quranic Noah narratives nos. III and IV it is Noah's opponents who mock him for being only a man (that is, they laugh at his warning because no angel has been sent with him and he is just a man like them; cf. 11.27; 23:24), their words are never refuted; cf. 7:63, where Noah himself implicitly admits his purely human condition by declaring that he is a man from/like them; and 26:115, where he proclaims to be but a warner. Yet at the same time, clarification of Noah's human condition contributes to emphasising that of the quranic prophet (cf. Q 3:144; 6:8–10; 7:188; 11:12,27; 16:103; 23:24; and also the apparent typologies underlying quranic Noah narrative nos. II and V, on which see chapter five above).

(*iv*) Likewise, Muḥammad is portrayed in the Sīra as being only a man (S 100–2). Yet – and to my mind this has never been properly highlighted – he is simultaneously given certain Noahic and Christological traits (in S 101–2 and 171) that seem to make of him a new and rather ambiguous messianic figure, both in contrast to the mainstream Christian view of Jesus, and perhaps also as a substitute for the latter. Muḥammad's birth is narrated by Ibn Isḥāq and Ibn Hišām in the following terms:[3] ʻAbd Allāh b. ʻAbd al-Muṭṭalib (i.e., Muḥammad's father) was married to Wahb b. ʻAbd Manāf's daughter Āmina; he "consummated his marriage immediately and his wife conceived the apostle of God . . . [who] was the noblest of his people in birth and the greatest in honour, both on his father's and his mother's side" (100–1). Thus Muḥammad's conception counters Jesus': whereas the latter was miraculously conceived, the former was not, but was rather born of a man and a woman whose reputation is conveniently stressed. This notwithstanding, there are some peculiar facts about Muḥammad's birth that are worthy of note. First, a woman who ʻAbd Allāh b. ʻAbd al-Muṭṭalib had encountered prior to his marriage, and who had proposed to him upon that occasion, meets him again after Muḥammad is born; when he asks why she does not renew her previous proposal, she replies that "the light that was with him the day before had left him and that she no longer had need of him;" moreover, she adds that "her brother Waraqa b. Naufal, who had been a Christian and studied the scriptures," had told her that "a prophet would rise among [their] people" (S 101). Second, Āmina (i.e., Muḥammad's mother) is alleged to have often said that "when she was pregnant with God's apostle . . . a voice told her, 'You are pregnant with the lord [sic!] of this people, and when he is born say, "I put him in the care of the One from the evil of every envier; then call him Muḥammad"'" (S 102). Finally, while Āmina was pregnant "she saw a light come forth from her" (S 102). Therefore Muḥammad is announced to his mother by an angel; a light comes forth from her when she is pregnant; and a mysterious light also inhabits his father prior to his marriage, as though Muḥammad's miraculous seed were already in him, awaiting a womb in which to bear fruit. All of this recalls Noah's, Melchizedek's, and Jesus' luminous births in the pre-quranic texts mentioned in chapter two above, which I have also examined elsewhere (Segovia 2011). Further remarks in S 171 on Muḥammad as someone who would "separate a man from his father, or from his brother, or from his wife, or from his family" (cf. Matthew 10:34–6), or as "a palm-tree whose branches are fruitful" (a widespread Jewish metaphor alluding to the seed of the righteous), help to reinforce this overall impression (cf. Van Reeth 2011a). On the other hand, it is curious that of Noah's and Jesus's two salient messianic qualities, namely their luminous nature and their ability to speak from the cradle (or the midwife's arms), only the former is applied to Muḥammad, whereas – as argued above – the latter is applied to Jesus in both the Arabic Gospel of the Infancy and the Qur'ān. Nevertheless, such qualities constitute the two halves of a messianic symbol, which is thus reinterpreted and reused in the *Sīra* of Muḥammad and applied thereby to the Arabian prophet. It is then legitimate to ask whether Muḥammad is here introduced as a prophet or as the Messiah himself! Yet no clear answer can be elicited *apropos* this intriguing issue. Note, for instance, the subordination of Muḥammad to Jesus in S 106 and the way in which Jesus is explicitly downplayed in S 237 for being worshiped by his followers. In my opinion, therefore, Muḥammad's role is here quite ambiguous, but perhaps this is just normal. It may be that he is depicted in messianic terms because he is also thought of as the Paraclete (παράκλητος) announced in John 14:16,26; 15:26; 16:7 (cf. S 149–50).[4] Or it may be that a time came in which it was easier to rely upon a new charismatic figure deprived of the polemical traits commonly bestowed upon Jesus by his followers, or at least by most of these – certainly not by the Arab Christians from whom the community of the quranic prophet sprang, save that a late date for their anti-trinitarian controversy was to be acknowledged[5] – than to keep proclaiming Jesus's lordship (note the reference to Muḥammad as lord in S 101!). In this case, it would be appropriate to see either Ibn Isḥāq's work or, less probably, Ibn Hišām's recension (which date to the mid-2nd/8th and mid-3rd/9th centuries, respectively) as representing a transitory yet decisive step in the development of the Islamic community: a step that would mark – or rather, given the Marwanid foundations of the earliest Islamic community, re-inscribe and formally validate once the Abbasids had risen to power – the transition from an originally Christian milieu to a new religious setting. The transition from the quranic prophet as the herald of the eschaton to Muḥammad as the founder of a new messianic community (cf. Wansbrough 2006: 148–9) should probably be read, in turn, as its once tentative, though later abandoned, corollary (on which see the afterword to this book).[6]

(*v*) Furthermore, the prophetic model of Noah as inscribed in the Qur'ān helped to enhance the quranic prophet's, and thereby Muḥammad's, eschatological credentials. As I have argued, typological identification of the days of Noah with the end of time (cf. Q 11:49) is explicit in 1Enoch 93:4; Matthew 24:37–9; Luke 17:26; and 2Peter 3:5–7,10–12, for example, and implicit in the identification of Jesus (and the Messiah, more broadly) with Noah himself (see *iii* above). In turn, identification of the quranic prophet and later Muḥammad with Noah should be interpreted as a gesture attempting to enhance their eschatological credentials.

(*vi*) Finally, that very same model was meant to comfort the quranic prophet, and thereby Muḥammad, in his distress by granting him the promise of his future vindication – and also that of his community. The end of time being considered more or less imminent by the quranic prophet and his community (I follow here Casanova 1911–24), it is only natural to suppose that the comforting of the former in his distress was required in the quranic Noah narratives. Additionally, it served to strengthen the prophet's final vindication, thus once more earning him strong eschatological credentials. In the Muhammadan *evangelium*, a similar logic is set out to authenticate Muḥammad's mission.

(*vii*) In conclusión, keeping all of this in mind, I think it is important to note overall that in Muḥammad's Sīra the very first "facts" reported about his preaching are, first, the opposition that he presumably met with and, second, God's willingness to comfort him in his distress (S 155). This clearly echoes the life of the quranic prophet in the quranic Noah narratives. Shortly after learning about Muḥammad's divine commission and his earliest visions and revelations (S 150–5), the reader is reminded that prophecy is a "troublesome burden" that only resolute men can bear with God's assistance, and then told that Muḥammad carried to the Meccans the divine message thus entrusted to him "in spite of the opposition which he met with." Thereupon it is reported that Ḫadīja, Muḥammad's first wife, was also the first person to believe in him, and that it was "by her" that God comforted him, for "she strengthened him, lightened his burden, proclaimed his truth, and belittled men's opposition" (S 155). The aforementioned general pattern applied to Noah and the quranic prophet, commission + opposition + consolation (on which see elements a–d in chapter three above and their multiple developments as analysed in chapters four and five), therefore also underlies Muḥammad's presentation in the *Sīra* narrative.

To cut the matter short: If I am correct, Abraham and Moses (as well as, to a certain extent, Joseph and, which is doubtless more interesting, Jesus) should not be regarded as Muḥammad's sole prophetic models. For without Noah's very basic, adaptable, and far-reaching *exemplum*, of which the Qur'ān offers a good many hints, some essential traits of both the quranic prophet and Muḥammad would remain almost completely in the shadows – that is, one would be unable to properly understand their figures and some crucial aspects concerning the meaning and purpose of the quranic Noah narratives and the interpretative techniques put forth in the *Sīra* of Muḥammad after these. That such aspects, in turn, are vital to understanding the origins of Islam in all their complexity is thus evident.

## *Excursus A.* Ibn Isḥāq's original Noah narrative

As is well known, Ibn Hišām's *Sīra* consists of an abridged edition of Ibn Isḥāq's previous and largely fictional work on human "history" from Adam to the rise of Islam, which he wrote for the instruction of the young prince al-Mahdī upon the request of his father, the Abbasid caliph al-Manṣūr. Ibn Isḥāq's original work – which was known to Ibn Hišām through a recension made by al-Bakkā'ī, one of Ibn Isḥāq's disciples – was divided into three complementary sections: the Book of the Beginnings (*Kitāb al-Mubtada'*), the Book of Muḥammad's Advent (*Kitāb al-Mab'aṯ*), and the Book of Muḥammad's Military Campaigns (*Kitāb al-Maġāzī*), of which it must be noted that Ibn Hišām entirely omitted the first one and some portions of the second one, probably due to the fact that in his own time the biblical and rabbinic legends extensively used by Ibn Isḥāq were no longer in vogue for the Muslim elite (Newby 1989: 10–12). Yet Ibn Isḥāq's *Kitāb al-Mubtada'* was tentatively reconstructed in 1989 by Gordon Darnell Newby after the doxographic references contained in the works of various Muslim authors such as aṭ-Ṭabarī, aṯ-Ṯa'labī, al-Maqdisī, and al-Azraqī, who drew on a number of different sources, including the traditions transmitted by Ibn Isḥāq's closest pupil, Salama b. al-Faḍl, in addition to al-Bakkā'ī's and Ibn Bukayr's recensions.[7]

Judging from the references preserved in aṭ-Ṭabarī's *Tārīḫ ar-Rusul wa-l-Mulūk* and *Ǧāmi' al-Bayān fī Tafsīr al-Qur'ān*, al-Maqdisī's *Kitāb al-Bad' wa-l-Tārīḫ* and al-Azraqī's *Aḫbār Makka*, Ibn Isḥāq's original work included not just the earliest para-quranic narrative on Noah and the flood known to us, but also a lengthy account full of thoughtful insights, which is worth examining at this juncture, however briefly, since it sheds supplementary light on the overall purpose of Ibn Isḥāq *Heilgeschichte* ("salvation history") and the part played by Muḥammad therein.

Apparently, Ibn Isḥāq's original Noah narrative followed that of Adam and Eve, thus keeping with the biblical chronology in the Book of Genesis. Six consecutive themes can be recognised in it: (1) the rejection of Noah's warnings by his contemporaries; (2) Noah's own complaint addressed to God; (3) God's instructions and promise of salvation to Noah; (4) the flood story; (5) a seven-part chronology extending from the days of the Noah to the days of Muḥammad (i.e., from the flood to the dawn of Islam); and (6) a genealogy linking the Arabs to Noah's descendants.

As earlier mentioned (see chapters three–five above), elements 1) and 2) are also salient in the quranic Noah narratives, and Ibn Isḥāq indeed quotes Q 11:37–9 and 71:5–27 at some length. He further mentions Q 11:40 *apropos* God's promise of salvation to Noah; Q 54:11–12 in his description of the flood waters brought upon the earth by God: and Q 54:14 regarding Noah's salvation, whereas his flood story presents some noticeable rabbinic additions (Newby 1989: 44).

Especially noteworthy for our purpose here, however, is Ibn Isḥāq's chronology, which divides into seven major periods: (*a*) from Adam to Noah, (*b*) from Noah to Abraham, (*c*) from Abraham to Joseph, (*d*) from Joseph to Moses, (*e*) from Moses to Solomon, (*f*) from Solomon to Jesus, and (*g*) from Jesus to Muḥammad. Ibn Isḥāq's chronology is intended to provide, therefore, a biblical background for the rise of Islam by inscribing Muḥammad's sending as the corollary of all previous history (cf. Newby 1989: 44–5). Moreover, this is the ideological context in which Ibn Isḥāq mentions Muḥammad for the first time in his work. So here too, as in the Qur'ān, we find an essential if implicit connection between the figures of Noah and Muḥammad.

## *Excursus B.* Re-imagining ancient messianic roles: Prophets, messiahs and charismatic leaders in the literature of Second Temple Judaism and earliest Christianity

John Collins (2010: 4–20) rightly notes that pre-rabbinic Jewish messianism was an astonishingly complex phenomenon due to its multifarious and thus, to a certain extent, unstable and elusive character. And of course a similar point can be made about early Christian messianism, which only gradually became something of its own, i.e., different from its pre-rabbinic Jewish matrix; the earliest Christological developments within the Jesus movement prove eloquent in this respect (see Neusner, Green and Frerichs 1987; Charlesworth 1992; Yarbro Collins and Collins 2008: 101–203).

In short, pre-rabbinic Jewish messianism knew at least five overlapping subtypes whose specific contour lines, therefore, are not always easy to grasp. They may be succinctly described as follows:[8] (1) a sort of royal messianism centred on the figure of a "king-messiah," often of Davidic lineage, who was expected to restore Israel and to rule over it eternally; (2) a priestly messianism displayed around the contrasting figure of a "priest-messiah," likewise projected into the future; (3) a kind of prophetic/charismatic messianism whose main character was identified with a past or present "prophet" or "teacher of righteousness;" (4) an overtly super-human messianism endorsing the figure of an either divine or angelic, and hence "celestial messiah;" and (5) a somewhat indeterminate human messianism apparently resulting from the juxtaposition of subtypes 3) and 4), but with rather frequent overtones of subtypes 1) and 2).

Let's now take a closer look at them – and at their texts:

(1) *Royal/Davidic messianism.* Its sources must be sought in texts such as 2Samuel 7. Jacob's blessing in Genesis 49 and Balaam's oracle in Numbers 24:15–19 are also representative of this trend of thought, which one certainly finds again in Isaiah 11:1–9; Jeremiah 23:5–6; Amos 9:11; Micah 5:2–5; Zechariah 9:9–10; 11–13; and other later writings such as the Psalms of Solomon 17; the translation of Numbers 24:17 in the Septuagint and its interpretation in Philo's *De Praemiis et Poenis*; the Targumim (see e.g. *Targum Pseudo-Jonathan ad* Gen 49:11); and two post-70 CE apocalyptic writings, namely 4Ezra 12:32 and 2Baruch 72:2–73:1. Conversely, Isa 45:1 and Jer 27:6 speak instead of a foreign (i.e., non-Davidic) king-messiah. Lastly, several Dead Sea Scrolls such as CD; 1QM; 1QS; 1QSa; 1QSb; 4QpIsa; 4Q174–5; 4Q252; and 4Q285 must be mentioned as well, and it is moreover important to underline that in some of these scrolls the Messiah is addition-

ally called the "Prince of the Congregation" (so CD, 1QM, 1QSb, 4QpIsa, 4Q285). Cf. the New-Testament passages that explicitly speak of Jesus' Davidic lineage: Matthew 1:6; 2:1–6; 9:27; 12:22–3; 21:9,15; Mark 10:47–8; 11:1–10; 12:35–7; Luke 1:32–3,69; 2:4–5; 3:31; 19:38; John 7:42; 12:13; Acts 2:30; 13:16–41; 15:16; Romans 1:3–4; 2Timothy 2:8; Revelation 3:7; 5:5; 22:16.

(2) *Priestly messianism*. Although this particular subtype is especially well documented in the literature from Qumran, its roots go back to the Pentateuch (cf. Leviticus 4:3,5,16 and Numbers 24:15–19, where the "scepter" and the "star" are introduced to symbolise two different characters; cf. also the allusions to the priests as "luminaries" in Testament of Levi 14:3 and, albeit indirectly, 1Enoch 86:1,3; 90:21) and Zechariah 4:12; 6:11. To be sure, this priestly subtype also emerges in later works such as the Wisdom of Ben Sira (Sirach 45:6–22; 50:1), the Aramaic Levi Document (4:1–6:5; 10; frag. 5), the Book of Daniel (9:25–6), the Book of Jubilees (31:14–18), and the Testaments of the Twelve Patriarchs (so TLevi 18:2–5). A supplementary remark now about the literature from Qumran: Whereas in CD and 11Q19 the political and priestly leadership are manifestly distinguished, 1QS and 1QSa go even further in that they speak of two Messiahs: a royal Messiah and a priestly Messiah; likewise, 1QM, 1QSb, 4Q258 argue for the subordination of the former to the latter (cf. that of the Messiah to the priests in 4QpIsa). Lastly, certain texts allude to the priestly Messiah without further qualification (so 4Q540–1). Cf. the priestly Christology in Hebrews 3–10.

(3) *Prophetic/charismatic messianism*. This concrete subtype is also documented in the literature from Qumran. Thus CD, for instance, re-interprets the Ballam oracle by identifying the "scepter" with a Davidic Messiah and the "star" with an "Interpreter of the Law," who is further depicted in another passage of the same document as a sage of old. A similar characterisation is applied in CD to the "Teacher of Righteousness," who is additionally given priestly traits in 4pSal[a], while 4Q174 equates the "Interpreter of the Law" and the Davidic Messiah. If the titles "Teacher of Righteousness" (which, far from being legendary, alludes to a historical, i.e., real character, no matter whether multiple or unique, as has been often discussed) and "Interpreter of the Law" do indistinctly point to a single figure whose return was moreover expected at the end of time, then it would be possible to see in this a precedent of the Christian belief that Jesus, the Messiah, was a teacher as well. Cf. e.g. Matthew 5–7; 10; 13; Mark 4:38; 9:17,38; 10:17,20,35; 12:14,19,32; 13:1; Luke, 7:40; 8:24; 9:33,38; 10:25; 11:45; 12:13; 18:18; 19:39; 20:21, 28–9; 21:7; John 1:38,49; 3:2,26; 4:31; 6:25; 9:2; 11:8. In turn, 1QS alludes to a "prophet" together with the two Messiahs of Aaron and Israel, i.e., together with the priestly Messiah and the Davidic Messiah. Lastly, 1Q175 mentions (after Deuteronomy 18:18) a future "prophet" susceptible of being identified with the "Teacher or Righteousness," an identification that can also be deduced from 4Q521. Further-

more, this figure is introduced in 1QpHab as the interpreter of the words of the prophets of Israel and, therefore, as he through whom God shall speak (note the parallel with Moses in Numbers 12:6–8). Cf. the references to Jesus as a prophet in Matt 21:11; Luke 4:16–21,24; 7:16; 24:19; John 4:19; 9:17; Acts 2:17–18; 3:22; 7:37; 10:38, and his depiction as the Interpreter of the Law in Matt 5:17–19.

(4) *Divine/angelic messianism.* Daniel 7:9 mentions two "thrones," one for the "Ancient of Days," i.e. God, and another one that is not explicitly assigned to anyone in particular. Yet subsequently an enigmatic figure called "one like a son of man" is alluded to in the text. He appears over the clouds of heaven and is introduced to the Ancient of Days, and we are moreover told that at the end of time he shall rule over all nations on earth (vv. 13–14). A similar expression is used in Dan 8:15 and 9:21 to describe the angel Gabriel (cf. the human appearance of the "living ones" in Ezekiel 1:5), while in Dan 12 Michael is introduced as the Messiah himself. Thus the "one like a son of man" in Dan 7:13–14 should be taken to be an angelic messianic figure. Additionally, 4Q491 11 i, a fragment from Qumran, speaks about someone "to whom no one can be compared," and then adds that he has taken his seat on a "throne" and that, in spite of his many sufferings, he now dwells with the "gods" (אלים *'elîm*). Are we to think once more of an angel, then? Or must we rather presume that this character implicitly alludes to an exalted man like Enoch (cf. 1Enoch 104:2,4,6) or a priest like Levi in Aramaic Levi Document 6:5? It is difficult to tell, but the parallels between 4Q491 11 i and the hymns attributed to the "Teacher of Righteousness" are quite remarkable, even if these two figures cannot be simply equated. Yet Michael Wise (2000) has insightfully suggested that it would be possible to see the "Teacher of Righteousness" as the author of a number of the first-person hymns found in Qumran and also as he who is alluded to in the third person in 4Q491 11 i. On the other hand, 1QSa and 4Q174 describe God as the "father" of the Davidic Messiah, who is therefore called the "son of God" (cf. too 4Q246), whereas the author of 4Ezra 6–7 bestows on the Messiah the attributes of the "one like a son of man" in Daniel and calls him "son" and "servant." Note likewise the description of David as "god" (אלהים *'elohîm*) in Psalm 45:6 and the recurrent identification of the Messiah with the pre-existent Wisdom of God in the Septuagint and the Targumin (on which see Yarbro Collins and Collins 2008: 54–62; Boyarin 2004: 113–19). The New Testament description of Jesus as both the Son of God and Wisdom incarnated is too well known to require any further comment at this juncture. To conclude, mention must be made of 1Enoch 37–71, which combines in a single figure, alternatively called "son of man" (39:6; 40:5; 46:2–4; 48:2; 62:7,9,14; 63:11; 69:26–7; 70:1; 71:14,17), "messiah" or "anointed one" (48:10; 52.4), "chosen one" (49:2,4; 51:3,5; 52:6,9; 53:6; 55:4; 61:8,10; 62:1; 70:1), and "righteous one" (38:2; 53:6), the attributes of the Davidic Messiah, the "servant of YHWH" in Isa 42:1–9; 49:1–6;

50:4–9; 52:13–53:12, the pre-existent Wisdom of God in Proverbs 8:22–31, the "one like a son of man" in Dan 7:13–14, and the angel committed to restore the world in 1En 10:11–11:2. Cf. the references to Jesus as the "son of man" in Matthew 10:32–3; 24:26–7; 25:31–46; 26:64; 28:16; Mark 2:12; 8:31,38; 9:12,31; 10:33–5,45; 13:26; 14:62; Luke 12:8–9; 17:22–37; 18:1–8; 22:69; John 3:13–16; 5:25–9; 9:35–9; 12:23–41; 13:31; Acts 7:56; 1Corinthians 15:23–8; 1Thessalonians 1:10; 2:19–20; 3:13; 4:13–18; 5:1–11:17; Revelation 1:7; 3:3.

(5) *Human messianism.* As shown above (and in chapter two) both legendary and real characters (e.g., a future Davidic king, Enoch, Noah, Melchizedek, the Teacher of Righteousness, the anonymous exalted one from Qumran, and finally Jesus) were often identified with the Messiah in the literature of pre-rabbinic Judaism and early Christianity.

It is important to note, moreover, that some of these human messiahs were specifically assigned prophetic overtones. Therefore, the eventual identification of the Messiah with a "prophet" like the quranic prophet or Muḥammad himself – if such was the case among some of their early followers, that is – need not be judged as too innovative, as it goes back to a many-centuries-old, ongoing messianic tradition that is fairly well documented in a remarkable number of texts and fragments preserved for us, in which "prophet" and "messiah" need not be distinct categories.

# Afterword: Reading Otherwise, or Re-imagining Muḥammad as a New Messiah

To sum up: As it happens, in a broad first stage in the formation of the early Islamic community (roughly from the mid-1st/7th century to the time when Ibn Isḥāq had his work on the "history" of humankind, the sending of Muḥammad, and Muḥammad's own life and expeditions composed, or perhaps earlier) the quranic Noah story was used to instantiate a number of focal episodes in the life of the quranic prophet and to stress his eschatological credentials. Yet throughout the Qur'ān, the anonymous quranic prophet remained somewhat subordinated to Jesus, who, apparently, was still understood to be the Messiah.[1] Later on (around the mid-2nd/8th century), we find that Muḥammad is, on the one hand, fully identified with the quranic prophet and, on the other hand, simultaneously given a quasi-messianic status by Ibn Isḥāq. On my reading, this twofold, unprecedented event can be said to represent a landmark in the development of the early Islamic community, for unmistakable (albeit scarce) traces of Muḥammad's identification with the quranic prophet can be found as early as the late 1st/7th century in 'Abd al-Malik's official inscriptions, where Muḥammad is seemingly introduced as God's apostle, whereas no previous clear-cut, unambiguous record of his promotion to a quasi-messianic status is known to us. Formerly undistinguished from the Christian setting to which it belonged (even if it must be acknowledged that it constituted a particular, specific community within it),[2] a new messianic community that would thereafter increasingly gravitate around its alleged founding figure thus seems to have been well formed by the 2nd/8th century. In either case, eschatological concerns seem to have been essential for its members, notwithstanding the fact that in the aforementioned second phase, social and political interests that were not new but became more and more alluring started to exert an increasing pressure among them. In either case, the Noah story was also retold in contexts in which it never lost its eschatological flavour. But this picture either changed dramatically shortly afterwards, or was already on its way to change, as mundane concerns grew more and more prominent. For, as I have attempted to show in this book, the Noah story was then not only retold but pointedly rewritten from a very different perspective: as an exemplary tale. One could take this to represent either a symptom of a new phase in the development of the early Islamic community or an outcome of the preceding stage. Yet the messianic hopes of the earlier proto-Muslim and Muslim groups did not vanish in the face of the new concerns that helped to transform the early Islamic community into something different, although they were visibly downplayed and forced to migrate elsewhere—to its margins. In short, they became an interstitial phenomenon, on which a final word is due in order to put a provisional end to the present study.

Significant (albeit generally overlooked) surviving traces of the interpretation of Muḥammad as a new Messiah are found in a series of fascinating texts studied by Uri Rubin in 1975 in a paper entitled "Pre-Existence and Light: Aspects of the Concept of Nūr Muḥammad," to which, quite surprisingly, almost nobody has paid renewed attention in the past three decades. Rubin's basic purpose in that paper was to examine the heavenly representations of Muḥammad in medieval, especially Shiite, Muslim literature, so the writings he surveys are rather late indeed. Yet I would like now to refer to them, for they not only prove that Muḥammad was marginally thought of as a new Messiah in medieval times and beyond, but also hint at the possibility that he was seen in that fashion from very early on in the development of the Islamic community. Thus Abū Bakr al-Bayhaqī's reference to a tradition presumably going back to ʿUmar b. al-Ḫaṭṭāb (Rubin 1975: 105–6) suggests, whatever its accuracy, that representing Muḥammad as the Messiah (or, at least, providing him with several messianic features) might have actually been an early practice in the Muslim world. Indeed, al-Bayhaqī, who lived in the last decades of the 10th century and the first half of the 11th century, was a reputed *ḥadīṯ* scholar, as well as a Sunni traditionalist, for which reason one need not dismiss the information he gives in his *Dalāʾil an-Nubuwwa* as serving a pro-Shiite agenda.

Now, in addition to expanding the motifs of Muḥammad's miraculous seed and luminous body, the texts examined by Rubin endorse the view (*a*) that Muḥammad's light was pre-existent (i.e., created before God's throne, the heavens, the earth, and the sea) and (*b*) that Muḥammad's name was from the beginning ($b_1$) inscribed on God's throne (to which it would moreover provide stability), ($b_2$) written on Adam's shoulders (as also on the celestial veils, on the leaves of the trees of paradise, between the eyes of the angels, and upon the necks of the *huris*), and ($b_3$) known by the angels, the demons, the prophets, the inhabitants of paradise and hell, the continents, and the seas.[3]

Illustrations of *b* are found in al-Bayhaqī's *Dalāʾil an-Nubuwwa* ($b_1$); al-Ḥalabī's *as-Sīra al-Ḥalabiyya* ($b_1$, $b_2$); al-Ḫarkūšī's *Šaraf an-Nabiyy* ($b_1$, $b_2$); Ibn al-Ǧawzī's *al-Wafā bi-Aḥwāl al-Muṣṭafā* ($b_1$, $b_2$); al-ʿIṣāmī's *Simṭ an-Nuǧūm al-ʿAwālī* ($b_1$, $b_3$); as-Suyūṭī's *al-Laʾālī al-Maṣnūʿa fī-l-Aḥādīṯ al-Mawḍūʿa* ($b_1$, $b_2$); aṯ-Ṯaʿlabī's *Qiṣaṣ al-Anbiyāʾ* ($b_2$); and az-Zurqānī's *Šarḥ ʿalà al-Mawāhib al-Laduniyya li-l-Qasṭallānī* ($b_1$, $b_2$). Rubin correctly notes that these texts, of Shiite and Sunnite provenance alike, echo the depiction of the Messiah/Son of Man in 1Enoch 48:3, where we read that his name was named before the Lord of Spirits (i.e. God) even before the sun and the constellations were created and the stars of heaven made. It should be highlighted that a similar point is made in the preceding verse (1En 48:2) and in vv. 48:6 and 62:7, where it is furthermore claimed that the Son of Man was chosen and hidden in God's presence before the world was created and forever preserved in the presence of his might. In turn, these passages in the Enochic Book of Parables are reminiscent of the prophet's election "from the womb" in Isaiah 49:1, the creation of the angels on the first day in Jubilees 3:2–11, and the role conferred to Wisdom as the instrument of creation in Proverbs 8:22–31 and Sirach 24:1–3, whereas the notion that the hidden Messiah is to be revealed at the end of time is expressly mentioned in 4Ezra 13:26,52.[4]

For its part *a* divides into two specific sub-motifs that are well illustrated in the aforementioned works of al-Ḫarkūšī, Ibn al-Ǧawzī, al-ʿIṣāmī, as-Suyūṭī, aṯ-Ṯaʿlabī, az-Zurqānī, and in al-Masʿūdī's *Iṯbāt al-Waṣiyya li-l-Imām ʿAlī b. Abī Ṭalib*, respectively: according to the former sub-motif ($a_1$), Muḥammad's light was the only cause of the creation of humankind, the heavens, the earth, paradise, and hell; according to the latter ($a_2$), it was not just the cause but also the substance of God's creation. Interestingly enough, on the other hand, az-Zurqānī establishes a significant parallel between Jesus and Muḥammad in this respect (the two being the cause of God's creation).

Therefore it is difficult to hold that the Arabian prophet was initially conceived as just a prophet by all early Muslims. The most one can say is, first, that his identification as a new Messiah might have undergone a three-phase process that possibly started without him being thought of as a messianic figure and culminated in the more or less agreed refusal to assign to him any explicit messianic traits (which were either dismissed or reworked into something else) after a period in which he was tentatively envisaged as a new Messiah; and second, that if such a reading proves correct, some of Muḥammad's messianic/heavenly trimmings happened to survive in a number of medieval Muslim circles.

The identification of Jesus rather than the quranic prophet with the Messiah, on the other hand, is well attested in the Qurʾān, which seemingly predates Ibn Isḥāq, Ibn Hišām, and the texts studied by Rubin, whereas these and their alleged sources may be said to be either contemporary with or later than Ibn Isḥāq and Ibn Hišām. Yet neither Ibn Isḥāq nor Ibn Hišām, in spite of stressing Muḥammad's human status in their writings, as we have seen, overtly decline to identify him with the Messiah; surely the construction of Muḥammad as a new Messiah is more explicit in the texts examined by Rubin than is in these two authors, but it is nonetheless observable in them as well. Additionally, differing emphases may tell us of different, perhaps competing, traditions, or else point to the gradual accommodation of one tradition within another. Yet things might be more complex. For it may also be that the identification of Muḥammad with the Messiah ran parallel to its dismissal from the very beginning as characteristic of a specific early Muslim group, whereas the depiction of Muḥammad as just a prophet is a well-known key notion in later Muslim dogma.

Be that as it may, an intriguing Noahic background is perceptible behind Ibn Isḥāq's and/or Ibn Hišām's contributions to the early Muslim debate over Muḥammad's messianic status, although Rubin fails to notice that it is the aforementioned Noahic messianic symbol that ultimately underlies not only the story of the newborn Muḥammad in Ibn Isḥāq/Ibn Hišām's account, but also later developments to which he himself pays attention, such as the one found in al-Ḫarkūšī's *Šaraf al-Nabiyy*, Ibn Šahrāšūb's *Manāqib Āl Abī Ṭālib*, al-ʿIṣāmī's *Simṭ an-Nuǧūm al-ʿAwālī*, and al-Maǧlisī's *Biḥār al-Anwār* (Rubin 1975: 63): "When Ḥalīma (i.e., Muḥammad's nurse) took him in her arms he opened his eyes and they beamed;" cf. 1Enoch 106:2–3: "When he (Noah) opened his eyes the house shone like the sun. And he stood up from the hands of the midwife opening his mouth and praising the Lord."

The final refusal of the somewhat awkward view according to which Muḥammad was but a new Messiah may have a rather simple explanation, however. The making of a new community and the sealing of salvation history required the making of a new sacred book, given the religious and scriptural context in which Islam emerged, first as a coalition (whether spontaneous or imposed from above is another issue) of different religious groups and then as a new state with its own religion; and it may be surmised that the subsequent elaboration of an authoritative scriptural corpus proved more abiding and consistent than the tentative making of a new Messiah as a means to strengthen the new collective identity beyond the natural delay of the eschaton. Likewise, the substitution of eschatological claims with political concerns may well have played a prominent role in the final refusal to identify Muḥammad with the Messiah (just as they probably also did in downplaying the quranic Noah's eschatological status). Lastly, avoidance of an overt dispute with Jews and Christians once they were granted citizenship in the Islamic state may have additionally contributed to such a refusal.

Still, re-imagining Muḥammad as a new Messiah proves fully consistent in light of several early Muslim texts, the message of which is worth being studied afresh, beyond the explicit or tacit assumptions – I dare say constraints – commonly set forth in the traditional interpretation of Muḥammad as the last prophet[5] – to say nothing of his usual depiction as a political ruler deprived of strong, or at least imminent, eschatological concerns. Alternatively, it could be that the quranic prophet himself – or at least the quranic prophet referred to in Q 11:49, and hence in one of the two major quranic Noah narratives – was already thought of as a new Messiah (and a new Noah!) by his followers, in which case identification of Muḥammad with the latter should not be regarded as an innovation/disruption of previous pre-Islamic (i.e. pre-Muhammadan) beliefs. As stated above, no definite conclusion can be reached on this point, but such a possibility certainly remains tempting.

# Notes

## Notes to Chapter 1

1. Wansbrough was wrong in presuming that the quranic corpus did not achieve unitary form until the Abbasid period. I therefore do not follow his late dating of the Qur'ān. Conversely, Alphonse Mingana's hypothesis that the latter only became uniform in Marwanid times (Mingana 1916) has received renewed support in the studies carried on by the late Alfred-Louis de Prémare, on which see the discussion below. Even more conservative scholars like Angelika Neuwirth (2007) and Omar Hamdan (2011) seem willing to admit, at least partly, this non-traditional view.
2. See the well-known Preface to Foucault 1970.

## Notes to Chapter 2

1. I give henceforth George Nickelsburg's and James VanderKam's new translation of 1Enoch (2004: 164–7). The Ethiopic, Greek and Latin versions present several textual variants (Nickelsburg 2001: 536–7; Stuckenbruck 2007: 622–5) which, for the most part, are not relevant for the present discussion. This notwithstanding, the Ethiopic text of 1En 106:3b (ወተናገረ፡ለእግዚአ፡ጽድቅ፡ *wa-tanāgara la-'əgzi'a ṣədq* ['and spoke to/with the Lord of righteousness']) should be borne in mind in light of what will be further said about Qur'ān 3:46.
2. Of a quasi-divine origin, one should add, albeit Noah is depicted as only human: cf. 1En 106:4–7,10–12 (i.e. Lamech's doubts about his son's nature); 106:16–18; 107:2 (i.e. Enoch's answer to Methuselah); 14:20 (where the Glory of God is described as "whiter than much snow"); and 46:1 (where God's own head is said to be "like white wool"). Cf. also Dan 7:9.
3. Fitzmyer 2004: 79; Stone 1999: 134–49; Nickelsburg 2001: 541–2; Orlov 2004; and Stuckenbruck 2007: 627–9, have diversely commented on the similarities between the Noah story in 1Enoch and 1QapGen, the Melchizedek story in 2Enoch and the infancy narratives about Jesus in Matthew, Luke and the Protevangelium of James; as also on the Noahic depictions of Jacob, Yahoel and Jesus in Joseph and Aseneth, the Apocalypse of Abraham and the Book of Revelation.

## Notes to Chapter 3

1. Q 3:33; 4:163–5; 6:84–90; 7:59–64; 9:70; 10:71–4; 11:25–49; 14:9–15; 17:3,17; 19:58; 21:76–7; 22:42; 23:23–30; 25:37; 26:105–22; 29:14–15; 33:7; 37:75–82; 38:11; 40:5,31; 42:13; 50:12; 51:46; 53:52; 54:9–17; 57:26; 66:10; 71:1–28.
2. Q 9:70; 14:9; 17:3,17; 21:76–7; 22:42; 25:37; 29:14–15; 33:7; 38:11; 40:5,31; 50:12; 51:46; 53:52; 66:10.
3. Q 3:33; 6:87; 19:58; 42:13.
4. Q 4:163.
5. Q 6:84; 19:58.

6. Q 4:163; 6:90; 19:58; 33:7; 57:26.
7. Q 4:164; 9:70; 14:9; 25:37; 29:14; 57:26.
8. Q 6:88; 17:3; 37:81; 66:10.
9. Q 14:9–13.
10. Q 14:9; 22:42; 25:37; 38:11; 40:5; 50:12.
11. Q 4:163; 6:90; 22:42; 25:41; 33:7; 42:13. On the ambiguous identity of the quranic prophet, which I have already alluded to and to which I shall return below, see Wansbrough 2004:53–84. Albeit I will make some critical remarks on it, Wansbrough's distinction between the multiple "prophetical *logia*" collected in the Qur'ān's and the "Muhammadan *evangelium*" set out in the *Sīra* literature should be borne in mind in what follows.
12. Q 3; 4; 6; 9; 14; 17; 19; 21; 22; 25; 29; 33; 37; 38; 40; 42; 50; 51; 53; 57; 66.
13. Q 7:59–64 (*Sūrat al-A'rāf*) = quranic Noah narrative no. I; 10:71–4 (*Sūrat Yūnus*) = quranic Noah narrative no. II; 11:25–49 (*Sūrat Hūd*) = quranic Noah narrative no. III; 23:23–30 (*Sūrat al-Mu'minūn*) = quranic Noah narrative no. IV; 26:105–22 (*Sūrat aš-Šu'arā*) = quranic Noah narrative no. V; 54:9–17 (*Sūrat al-Qamar*) = quranic Noah narrative no. VI; 71:1–28 (*Sūrat Nūḥ*) = quranic Noah narrative no. VII.
14. Q 71 = *Sūrat Nūḥ* (Noah).
15. Cf. Wansbrough 2004: 21–5 on 7:85–93; 11:84–95; 26:176–90 (Šu'ayb). For the biblical parallels and variants of such pattern, see Westermann 1991: 169–98.
16. 'Ād and Ṯamūd (Thamud) name two ancient Arab peoples – and their eponyms.
17. This verse reads وَتَرَكْنَا عَلَيْهِ فِي الْآخِرِينَ in the so-called Uthmanic vulgata. See for discussion Chapter 6 below.
18. A discussion of this alternative reading is offered in Chapter 6, as well.
19. See once more Chapter 6.

## Notes to Chapter 4

1. Notice the inverted position of quranic Noah narratives nos. II, III, V and VII in columns A and B, as well as the place of quranic Noah narratives nos. I and VI, III and VII in the latter.
2. I.e. Mount Judi, Ar. and Syr. Qardû.
3. According to Muslim exegetes these names represent five pre-Islamic Arabian idols; but see Pettipiece 2009.

## Notes to Chapter 5

1. Cf. Dye 2015a, whose insightful remark (*contra* Cuypers 2012) that the Qur'ān should be studied both as a *composite* and *composed* text I unreservedly share.
2. Uri Rubin rightly notes that the sufferings of the previous prophets are *recounted* to comfort the quranic prophet in his own distress (2006: 245), though I am not quite sure that Rubin himself would have his own assessment stressed in this manner. Nor am I as sure as Rubin seems to be as to whether the quranic prophet should be identified with Muḥammad; but see Chapter 7 below.
3. Note the position of both narratives within the traditional chronology of the quranic suras (s. 54 [quranic Noah narrative no. VI], s. 7 [quranic Noah narrative I], s. 26 [quranic Noah

narrative no. V], s. 10 [quranic Noah narrative no. II], s. 11 [quranic Noah narrative no. III], s. 71 [quranic Noah narrative no. VII], s. 23 [quranic Noah narrative no. V] = all Meccan), as also inside Nöldeke's more detailed sequence (s. 54 [quranic Noah narrative no. VI], s. 71 [quranic Noah narrative no. VII], s. 26 [quranic Noah narrative no. V], s. 23 [quranic Noah narrative no. IV] = Meccan II; s. 10 [quranic Noah narrative no. II], s. 11 [quranic Noah narrative no. III], s. 7 [quranic Noah narrative no. I] = Meccan III). None of them seems to be justified in my view, as they largely rely upon the "data" endorsed by the Islamic tradition (so the traditional Islamic chronology and to a lesser extent Nöldeke) and certain formal and stylistic premises (Nöldeke) which ought to be at their best thoroughly re-examined. On the problems posed by such chronologies see further Reynolds 2011a.

4. On Mecca, the traditional unified theory of the rise of Islam as coined by the Islamic tradition, and 'Abd al-Malik's propaganda see Sharon 1988. See also Van Reeth 2011b for a new reading of the opposition to Muḥammad in Mecca which does not move entirely beyond the traditional account but subverts none the less some of its basic and more questionable premises. I am grateful to Guillaume Dye for drawing my attention to these investigations. See now too Micheau 2012: 75–102.
5. Cf. Martin 2010: 255, who argues for a possible late date considering that Noah's building of the ark and the God's disembarkation orders may be taken to be late and optional embellishments.
6. As also elsewhere in the Qur'ān between the latter and e.g. Abraham (who "apparaît comme une rétroprojection de Mahomet lui-même" [Lory 2007a: 12]; I wonder whether the opposite would be more exact!) or Joseph (according to al-Ṭabarī's typological reading of Q 12:22).
7. On the relationship between the Qur'ān and the *Sīra* literature see Berg 2006. On the sources of Jesus' Noahic traits in the Qur'ān and the canonical and apocryphal Gospels, see Chapter 2 above.
8. (Isa 54:7–10: "7 For a passing moment I forsook you, / but with tender affection I shall bring you home again. / 8 In an upsurge of anger I hid my face from you for a moment; / but now have I pitied you with never-failing love, / says the LORD, your Redeemer. / 9 For this to me is like the days of Noah; / as I swore that the waters of Noah's flood should never again pour over the earth, / so now I swear to you / never again be angry with you or rebuke you. / 10 Though the mountains may move and the hills shake, / my love will be immovable and never fail, / and my covenant promising peace will not be shaken, / says the LORD in his pity for you" (REB). 4QTanḥ 9–13: "9 [A] short [moment] I deserted you, but with great compassion I will take you back. In a fit of anger [I] h[id my face] 10 [fr]om you [for a moment,] but with everlasting tenderness I took pity of you, says your redeemer. As in (the) days of Noah will this be for me; as 11 [I swore that the waters of] Noah [would not] flo[od] the earth, so I sworn not to become angry with you ag[a]in or threaten you. 12 Should [even the mountain]s move or the hills wobble, my compassion will not move from you [. . .] 13 [. . . des]perate (?) until the words of comfort and great glory" (García Martínez and Tigchelaar 1997: 357–61).
9. 1En 93:4: "After me there will arise a second week, / in which deceit and violence will spring up, / and in it will be the *first end*, / and in it a man will be saved . . . " (Nickelsburg and VanderKam 2004: 140; my emphasis).
10. Matt 24:37–9: "37 As it was in the days of Noah, so will it be when the Son of Man comes. 38 In the days before the flood they ate and drank and married, until the day that Noah

went into the ark, 39 and they knew nothing until the flood came and swept them all away. That is how it will be when the Son of Man comes" (REB).

11. Luke 17:26: "As it was in the days of Noah, so will it be in the days of the Son of Man" (REB)
12. 2Peter 3:5–7,10–12: "5 In maintaining this they forget that there were heavens and earth long ago, created by God's word out of water and with water; 6 and that the first world was destroyed by water, the water of the flood. 7 By God's word the present heavens and earth are being reserved for burning; they are being kept until the day of judgement when the godless will be destroyed"; "But the day of the Lord will come like a thief. On that day the heavens will disappear with a great rushing sound, the elements will be dissolved in flames, and the earth with all that it is in it will be brought to judgement. 11 Since the whole universe is to dissolve in this way, think what sort of people you ought to be, what devout and dedicated lives you should live! 12 Look forward to the coming day of God, and work to hasten it on; that day will set the heavens ablaze until they fall apart, and will melt the elements in flames" (REB).

## Notes to Chapter 6

1. See e.g. *Pirqê de-Rabbî 'Elî'ezer* 23, where it is affirmed that Satan helped Noah to plant the vineyard. Controversial attitudes towards Noah are found as early as the Dead Sea Scrolls (on which see Peters 2008) and continued well into the early centuries CE, as I shall comment below. On Noah's drunkenness, see Cohen 1974. On the rabbinic view that Christian beliefs were deeply rooted in the Enochic tradition, see Heschel 2006: 349; the key-text here is *Genesis Rabbah* 25:1, whose author's dismissal of the Enochic views about Enoch seem to be tacitly directed against the Christians (a similar point was made by Daniel Boyarin in discussion with Rachel Elior at the 4th Enoch Seminar held in Naples in June 2009).
2. See Segovia 2011 and Chapter 2 above, as well as the historical survey provided in Segovia 2013, chs. 1–2. On Sethian Gnosticism see Turner 1986.
3. Bedjan 1905–10: 2.23–4. I am grateful to Gabriel Said Reynolds for pointing out this latter reference to me.
4. I should like to thank Tommaso Tesei for drawing my attention to Ephraem's *Commentary on Genesis*.
5. Ephraem writes: "Although Noah was an example to [his contemporaries] by his righteousness and had, in his uprightness announced to them the flood during one hundred years, they still did not repent. So Noah said to them: 'Some of all flesh will come to be saved with me in the ark.' But they mocked him [saying], 'How will all the beasts and birds that are scattered throughout every corner of the earth come from all those regions?'" (McVey 1994: 138–9). In turn, Narsai's *Homily on the Flood* 235–50 reads (it is Noah who speaks in vv. 235–40): ". . . 'Repent from iniquity, / for lo, in our fashioning is being proclaimed / repentance, if you wish.' / As a herald was the voice / of the production of the ark crying out, / 'Arise, shake off the burden of your debts / o sleepers who are sunk in sin.' / Superfluous to them were / the voices of the fashioning of the ark / for the burden of evil had stopped up / hearing with admits understanding. / Noah alone had heard / and was waiting for the end / while the impudent mocked him / for his fashioning was not given credence (Frishman 1992: 30–1).

6. As to the Struggle of Adam and Eve with Satan 3.2,4, the two passages in question read: "But when Noah went about among them and told them [about what was to come] they laughed at him . . . and said: 'That twaddling old man! Whence will ever the waters come, above the tops of high mountains? We never saw water rise above mountains, and this old man says, a flood is coming!'"; "But Noah preached repeatedly to the children of Cain, saying, 'The flood will come and destroy you, if we do not repent.' But they would not hearken to him; they only laughed at him" (Malan 1882: 144–6).
7. On Syrian Christianity as a background to the rise of Islam and the composition of the Qur'ān, see Andrae 1926; Mingana 1927; Bowman 1964–65; Luxenberg 2007; Gilliot 2008; Griffith 2008; Ohlig and Puin 2010; Witztum 2011a, 2011b; El-Badawi 2014. Cf. Rippin 2008. On Syriac as the possible language behind the quranic Noah pericope in Q 37, see Luxenberg 2007: 157–60 and my own review of Luxenberg's reading in the Excursus below.
8. On which see the excellent review by Daniel King (2009).
9. Cf. Stewart 2010: 244, who rightly observes that Luxenberg's argument is not entirely new regarding his collateral analysis of the verb ترك *taraka* in v. 78, which he himself subscribes, but does not further comment on Luxenberg's provocative proposal concerning v. 79; and especially King's brief but eloquent note (2009: 54).
10. Stewart e.g. writes: "[T]he use of the verb *taraka* "to leave" with *'alā* "on" is odd. . . . Where is the direct object?" (2010: 244).
11. Interestingly enough, on the other hand, in a lecture recently delivered at the Van Leer Jerusalem Institute ("Qur'ānic Aspects of Jewish Messianism: The Case of Q 17:103–104 and Q 7:159," July 13, 2014), Uri Rubin has suggested that *al-āḫira* in Q 17:103–4 should be read as an allusion to "the end of days." If so, Luxenberg's argument would thereby find some additional support.
12. In Arabic the dual number is formed by adding the suffix ين *-ayn* to the noun when the latter is found in a prepositional phrase.
13. As I have already commented (see Chapter1 above), I share de Prémare's doubts (2002: 296–7; 2010) as to whether the quranic canon may be actually traced back to the time of 'Uṯmān, and moreover agree with him that such view oversimplifies the data at our disposal and their often contradictory reports.
14. On these figures, their interpretation in Islamic scripture, culture and religion, and Moses's mysterious page in Q 18:60–82, see e.g Massignon 1963; Erder 1990; Aubaile-Sallenave 2002; Tesei 2013: 135–47.
15. Building *inter alia* on the work of James Bellamy (1993, 1996, 2001), Behnam Sadeghi (2013: 30) distinguishes four types of scribal error that might eventually contribute to explain the apparent differences occasionally existing between the current canonical text of the Qur'ān and its hypothetical original wording: "(1) changes due to assimilation of parallels, (2) changes due to assimilation of nearby terms, (3) failings of short-term memory that are not due to the last two mechanisms, and (4) 'errors of the hand.'" Keeping this view in mind, the scribal "error" on Noah's blessing in Q 37 would seem to simultaneously fall under types 1, 2 and 3, and would therefore point to a series of concomitant errors rather than to a single type. However, Sadeghi does not seem to be fully aware of their eventual interconnectedness. But the major problem with his proposal is that it leaves all possible ideological distortions of the original text, whether intended or not – for ideology often proves to be an unconscious phenomenon–, entirely out of focus.

## Notes to Chapter 7

1. On the biblical model(s) of Ibn Isḥāq's "Arabian prophet" see however Newby 1989.
2. See Chapter 2 above.
3. Hereinafter I follow Guillaume's translation.
4. On Muḥammad as the Paraclete, see Van Reeth 2012.
5. But see now Kropp 2011!
6. On the Marwanid foundations of the Islamic religion, state and community, see Robinson: 2005; Segovia 2016. See also Segovia 2015a and 2015c, where I contend that Jesus' messiahship became decreasingly relevant to Muḥammad's heirs from the 710s onwards, whereas prior to that date it seems to have been acknowledged by Muḥammad's followers.
7. On the *Sīra* literature see Kister 1983; Rubin 1998; Motzki 2000; Milby 2008; and Kudelin 2010. On Ibn Bukayr's recension, de Prémare 2002: 357, 363.
8. I basically follow hereinafter Collins's very useful overview, although he fails to mention the fifth subtype on the list below, which in my view is likewise relevant for the study of both Second Temple eschatology and early Christology.

## Notes to the Afterword

1. See however the comments on Q 11.49 in Chapter 5 above.
2. For it is on the one hand relatively easy to see in what it might have diverged from other communities belonging to that very same religious milieu, but on the other hand difficult to work out the range of that apparent divergence. See however Segovia 2015a, 2015c, and 2016, where I offer a new classification and a tentative chronology of the Christian, pro-Christian and anti-Christian formulas contained in the Qur'ān, and the hypothesis that the Sassanian subduing of the Christian kingdom of Ḥimyar in 565 and the power thereby regained by its opponents, the pagans and the Jews of South- and Western Arabia, on the one hand, as well as the subsequent Sassanian invasion of the Near East in 612, on the other hand, encouraged an Christian restoration programme in the Ḥiǧāz that was led *inter alios* by Muḥammad.
3. See also the traditions studied in Szilágyi 2009 that contend that Muḥammad, like Jesus, ascended to heaven after his death.
4. See for these supplementary references Nickelsburg and VanderKam 2012: 169–71. On the Son of Man as a name for Israel's Messiah modelled after the Davidic King/Messiah, the Servant of the Lord in the Deutero-Isaianic corpus and the heavenly "one like a son of man" in Daniel 7:13–14, see Nickelsburg and VanderKam 2012: 44–5. On his plausible divine status, Boyarin 2012. On the many adaptations of such figure in Jewish and Christian literature, the New Testament included, see Nickelsburg and VanderKam 2012: 69–76.
5. Although al-Ḫarkūšī curiously links the view that it is with Muḥammad that all things began and will come to an end to the notion that he is the seal of all prophets (Rubin 1975: 106). Cf. however Ibn Saba''s treatment of Muḥammad's "second coming" as the "seal of prophets" in Rubin 2014: 94.

# Bibliography


Adang, C. 1996. *Muslim Writers on Judaism and the Hebrew Bible: From Ibn Rabban to Ibn Hazm*. Leiden & Boston: Brill.

Addas, C. 2007a. "Idrîs," in *Dictionnaire du Coran*, edited by M. A. Amir-Moezzi, 410–13. Paris: Robert Laffont.

– 2007b. "Noé," in *Dictionnaire du Coran*, edited by M. A. Amir-Moezzi, 598–602. Paris: Robert Laffont.

Ahituv, Sh., and E. Oren, eds. 1998 *The Origin of Early Islam: Current Debate — Biblical, Historical and Archaeological Perspectives*. Beer-Sheva. Ben-Gurion University of the Negev Press.

Amir-Moezzi, M. A. 1992. *Le guide divin dans le shi'isme originel*. Lagrasse: Verdier.

Amir-Moezzi, M. A., ed. 2007. *Dictionnaire du Coran*. Paris: Laffont.

Andrae, T. 1926. *Der Ursprung des Islams und das Christentum*. Uppsala: Almqvist & Wiksells.

– 1932. *Mohammed: sein Leben und sein Glaube*. Göttingen: Vandenhoeck & Ruprecht.

Arnaldez, R. 1970. *Mahomet, ou la prédication prophétique*. Paris: Seghers.

Aubaile-Sallenave, F. 2002. "Al-Khidr, 'l'homme au manteau vert' en pays musulman: ses fonctions, ses caractères, sa diffusion." *RO* 14: 11–35.

Avni, G. 2014. *The Byzantine-Islamic Transition in Palestine: An Archaeological Approach*. Oxford & New York: Oxford University Press.

Azaiez, M. 2015. *Le contre-discours coranique*. SHCME. Berlin & New York: De Gruyter should be added between Avni, G. 2014 and al-Azmeh, A. 2013

al-Azmeh, A. 2013. "Implausibility and Probability in the Study of Qur'anic Origins." Paper presented to the International Qur'anic Studies Association Conference (Baltimore, MD; November 22, 2013).

– 2014. *The Emergence of Islam in Late Antiquity: Allāh and His People*. Cambridge & New York: Cambridge University Press.

El-Badawi, E. I. 2014. *The Qur'ān and the Aramaic Gospel Traditions*. London & New York: Routledge.

Barth, J. 1916. "Studien zur Kritik und Exegese des Qorans." *Der Islam* 6: 113–48.

Bashear, S. 1984. مقدمة في التريخ الاخر؛ نحو قراة جديدة الرواية الاسلامية [An Introduction to the Other History: Towards a New Reading of the Islamic tradition]. Jerusalem.

– 1997. *Arabs and Others in Early Islam*. Princeton, NJ: Darwin Press.

– 2004. *Studies in Early Islamic Tradition*. Jerusalem: The Max Schloessinger Memorial Foundation & the Hebrew University of Jerusalem.

Baxter, W. 2006. "Noachic Traditions and the *Book of Noah*." *JSP* 15.3: 179–94.

Beaucamp, J., F. Briquel-Chatonnet, and Ch. Robin. 2010. *Juifs et chrétiens en Arabie aux V^e^ et VI^e^ siècles: regards croisés sur les sources*. Paris: Association des amis du Centre d'histoire et civilisation de Byzance.

Bedjan, P. 1905–10. *Homiliæ selectæ Mar-Jacobi Sarugensis*. 5 vols. Paris: Harrassowitz. Reprinted in 6 vols. with additional material by S. P. Brock, Piscataway, NJ: Gorgias Press, 2006.

Bell, R. 1926. *The Origins of Islam in Its Christian Environment*. London: Macmillan.

– 1937–9. *The Qur'an. Translated, with a Critical Rearrangement of the Surahs*. 2 vols. Edinburgh: T & T Clark.

Bellamy, J. A. 1993. "Some Proposed Emendations to the Text of the Koran." *JAOS* 113.4: 562–73.

– 1996. “More Proposed Emendations to the Text of the Koran.” *JAOS* 116.2: 196–204.
– 2001. “Textual Criticism of the Koran.” *JAOS* 121.1: 1–6.

Benjamins, H. S. 1998. “Noah, the Ark, and the Flood in Early Christian Theology: The Ship of the Church in the Making,” in *Interpretations of the Flood*, edited by F. García Martínez and G. P. Luttikhuizen, 134–49. TBN 1. Leiden & Boston: Brill.

Berg, H. 2000. *The Development of Exegesis in Early Islam: The Authenticity of Muslim Literature from the Formative Period*. London: Curzon.
– 2006. “Context: Muḥammad,” in *The Blackwell Companion to the Qur’ān*, edited by A. Rippin, 187–204. Oxford: Blackwell.

Berg, H., ed. 2003. *Method and Theory in the Study of Islamic Origins*. Leiden & Boston: Brill.

Berkey, J. P. 2003 *The Formation of Islam: Religion and Society in the Near East, 600–1800*. Cambridge & New York: Cambridge University Press.

Berque, J. 1993. *Relire le Coran*. Paris: Albin Michel.

Blachère, R. 1947. *Introduction au Coran*. Paris: Maisonneuve.
– 1952. *Le problème de Mahomet*. Paris: PUF.
– 1957. *Le Coran, traduit de l’arabe* (1947–51). 2 vols. Paris: Maisonneuve. 2nd ed.

Blenkinsopp, J. 2006. *Opening the Sealed Book: Interpretations of the Book of Isaiah in Late Antiquity*. Grand Rapids, MI & Cambridge: Eerdmans.

Bonner, M. 2004. *Arab-Byzantine Relations in Early Islamic Times*. VCS. Aldershot: Ashgate.

Boullata, I. J., ed. 2000. *Literary Structures of Religious Meaning in the Qur’ān*. London: Curzon.

Bowersock, G. W. 2012. *Empires in Collision in Late Antiquity*. Waltham, MA: Brandeis University Press & Historical Society of Israel.
– 2013. *The Throne of Adulis: Red Sea Wars on the Eve of Islam*. Oxford & New York: Oxford University Press.

Bowman, J. 1964–65. “The Debt of Islam to Monophysite Syrian Christianity.” *NTT* 19:177–201.

Boyarin, D. 2004. *Border Lines: The Partition of Judaeo-Christianity*. DRLAR. Philadelphia: University of Pennsylvania Press.
– 2012. *The Jewish Gospels: The Story of the Jewish Christ*. New York: The New Press.

Brinner, W. M. 2003. “Noah.,” in *Encyclopaedia of the Qur’ān*, edited by J. D. McAuliffe, 3.54–3. Leiden & Boston: Brill.

Brock, S. 1989. *A Garland of Hymns from the Early Church*. Foreword by Fr. M. F. Wahba. Mclean, VA: St. Athanasius Coptic Publishing Center.
– 2005. “*Sobria Ebrietas* according to Some Syriac Texts.” *ARAM* 17: 181–95.

Brockopp, J. E., ed. 2010. *The Cambridge Companion to Muḥammad*. Cambridge & New York: Cambridge University Press.

Brown, B. A. 2007. *Noah’s Other Son: Bridging the Gap between the Bible and the Qur’an*. London: Continuum.

Buitelaar, M., and H. Motzki, eds. 1993. *De Koran: Ontstaan, interpretatie en praktijk*. Muiderberg: Coutinho.

Burton, J. 1977. *The Collection of the Qur’an*. Cambridge: Cambridge University Press.

Caetani, L. 1905–26. *Annali dell’Islam*. 10 vols. Milan: Hoepli.
– 1910. *Mahometto, profeta d’Arabia*. Rome: CEI.

Calder, N., J. Mojaddedi, and A. Rippin, eds. 2013. *Classical Islam: A Sourcebook of Religious Literature* (2003). London & New York: Routledge. 2nd ed.

Cameron, A., and R. H. Hoyland, eds. 2010. *Doctrine and Debate in the East Christian World, 300–1500*. VCS. Aldershot: Ashgate.

Casanova, P. 1911–24. *Mohammed et la fin du monde. Étude critique sur l'Islam primitif.* 2 vols. Paris: Geuthner.
Chabbi, J. 2008. *Le Coran décrypté. Figures Bibliques en Arabie*. Paris: Fayard.
Charles, R. H. 1893. *The Book of Enoch*. Oxford: Clarendon Press.
– 1902. *The Book of Jubilees or Little Genesis*. London: SPCK.
Charlesworth, J. H. 1992. *Messianic Developments in Earliest Judaism and Christianity*. Minneapolis: Fortress.
Clippinger, D. 2001. "Intertextuality," in *Encyclopaedia of Postmodernism*, edited by V. E. Taylor and C. E. Winquist, 190–1. London & New York: Routledge.
Cohen, H. H. 1974. *The Drunkenness of Noah*. JS 4. Toscaloosa, AL: University of Alabama Press.
Collins, J. J. 1998. *The Apocalyptic Imagination: An Introduction to Jewish Apocalyptic Literature* (1984).Grand Rapids, MI & Cambridge: Eerdmans. 2nd ed.
– 2010. *The Scepter and the Star: Messianism in Light of the Dead Sea Scrolls* (1995). Grand Rapids, MI & Cambridge: Eerdmans. 2nd ed.
Cook, D. 2002. *Studies in Muslim Apocalyptic*. Princeton, NJ: Darwin Press.
Cook, M. 1981. *Early Muslim Dogma: A Source-Critical Study*. Cambridge: Cambridge University Press.
– 1983. *Muhammad*. Oxford: Oxford University Press.
– 2004a. "The Stemma of the Regional Codices of the Koran." *Graeco-Arabica* 9–10: 89–104.
– 2004b. *Studies in the Origins of Islamic Culture and Tradition*. VCS. Aldershot: Ashgate.
Crone, P. 1980. *Slaves on Horses: The Evolution of the Islamic Polity*. Cambridge: Cambridge University Press.
– 1987a. *Meccan Trade and the Rise of Islam*. Princeton, NJ: Princeton University Press.
– 1987b. *Roman, Provincial, and Islamic Law: The Origins of the Islamic Patronate*. Cambridge: Cambridge University Press.
Crone, P., and M. Cook. 1977. *Hagarism: The Making of the Islamic World*. Cambridge: Cambridge University Press.
Crone, P., and M. Hinds. 1986. *God's Caliph: Religious Authority in the First Centuries of Islam*. Cambridge: Cambridge University Press.
Cuypers, M. 2012. "L'analyse rhétorique face à la critique historique de John Wansbrough et de G. Lüling,' in *The Coming of the Comforter: When, Where, and to Whom? Studies on the Rise of Islam and Various Other Topics in Memory of John Wansbrough*, edited by C. A. Segovia and B. Lourié, 343–69. OJC 3. Piscataway, NJ: Gorgias Press.
Cuypers, M., and G. Gobillot. 2007. *Le Coran*. Paris: Le Cavalier Bleu.
Dabashi, H. 1989. *Authority in Islam: From the Rise of Muhammad to the Establishment of the Umayyads*. New Brunswick: Transition.
Dakake, M. M. 2007. *The Charismatic Community: Shi'ite Identity in Early Islam*. Albany, NY: State University of New York Press.
Déroche, F., 2009. *La transmission écrite du Coran dans les débuts de l'islam. Le codex Parisino-petropolitanus*. Leiden & Boston: Brill.
– 2014. *Qur'āns of the Umayyads*. LSIS 1. Leiden & Boston: Brill.
Déroche, F., and S. Noja Noseda. 1998–2001. *Sources de la transmission manuscrite du text coranique, I. Les manuscrits de style ḥiǧāzī*. 2 vols. Lesa: Fondazione Ferni Noja Noseda.
Dijkstra, J. H. F., and G. Fisher, eds. *Inside and Out: Interactions between Rome and the Peoples on the Arabian and Egyptian Frontiers in Late Antiquity*. LAHR 8. Leuven: Peeters.
Dillmann, A. 1853. *Das Buch Henoch übersetz und erklärt*. Leipzig: Vogel.

Dimant, D. 2006. "Two 'Scientific' Fictions: The So-Called Book of Noah and the Alleged Quotation of Jubilees in CD 16:3–4,' in *Studies in the Hebrew Bible, Qumran and the Septuagint Presented to Eugen Ulrich*, edited by P. Flint, E. Tov and J. C. VanderKam, 230–49. SVT 101. Leiden & Boston: Brill.
Donner, F. M. 1981. *The Early Islamic Conquests*. Princeton, NJ: Princeton University Press.
– 1998. *Narratives of Islamic Origins: The Beginnings of Islamic Historical Writing*. Princeton, NJ: Darwin Press.
– 2010. *Muhammad and the Believers: At the Origins of Islam*. Cambridge, MA: Harvard University Press.
Dye, G. 2012. "Lieux saintes communs, partagés ou confisqués: aux sources de quelques péricopes coraniques (Q 19:16–33)," in *Partage du sacré. Transferts, dévotions mixtes, rivalités interconfessionnelles*, edited by I. Dépret and G. Dye, 55–121. Brussels: EME.
– 2015a. "Approches historico-critiques et analyse rhétorique : quelques réflexions méthodologiques sur les études coraniques," in *Controverses sur les écritures canoniques de l'islam*, edited by D. de Smet and M. Ali Amir-Moezzi. Paris: Éditions du Cerf (forthcoming).
– 2015b. "Pourquoi et comment se fait un texte canonique. Quelques réflexions sur l'histoire du Coran" (forthcoming).
Dye, G., and F. Nobilio, eds. 2012. *Figures bibliques en islam*. Brussels: EME.
Eger, A. A. 2014. *The Islamic-Byzantine Frontier: Interaction and Exchange among Muslim and Christian Communities*. London: IB Tauris.
Erder, Y. 1990. "The Origin of the Name Idrīs in the Qur'ān: A Study on the Influence of Qumran Literature on Early Islam." *JNES* 49.4: 339–50.
Firestone, R. 1990. *Journeys in Holy Lands: The Evolution of the Abraham-Ishmael Legends in Islamic Exegesis*. New York: State University of New York Press.
– 1999. *Jihad: The Origin of Holy War in Islam*. Oxford & New York: Oxford University Press.
Fisher, G. 2011. *Between Empires: Arabs, Romans, and Sassanians in Late Antiquity*. Oxford & New York: Oxford University Press.
Fitzmyer, J. A. 2004. *The Genesis Apocryphon of Qumran Cave 1 [1Q20]: A Commentary* (1971). BO 18A. Rome: Biblical-Institute. 3rd ed.
Flügel, G. 1834. *Corani Textus Arabicus*. Leipzig: Tauchnitz.
– 1842. *Concordantiae Corani arabicae*. Leipzig: Tauchnitz.
Foucault, M. 1970. *The Order of Things: An Archaeology of Human Sciences*. Translated by A. M. Sheridan. New York: Random House.
Fowden, G. 1993. *Empire to Commonwealth: Consequences of Monotheism in Late Antiquity*. Princeton, NJ: Princeton University Press.
– 2014. *Before and After Muhammad: The First Millennium Refocused*. Princeton, NJ: Princeton University Press.
Frishman, J. 1992. "The Ways and Means of the Divine Economy: An Edition, Translation and Study of Six Biblical Homilies by Narsai." PhD dissertation, University of Leiden.
Gajda, I. 2009. *Le royaume de Ḥimyar à l'époque monothéiste. L'histoire de l'Arabie du Sud ancienne de la fin du Ive siècle de l'ère chrétienne jusqu'à l'avènement de l'islam*. MAIBL 40. Paris: Académie des Inscriptions et des Belles-Lettres & De Boccard.
Gallez, É.-M. 2005. *Le messie et son prophète. Aux origines de l'islam*. 2 vols. Paris: Versailles.
García Martínez, F. 1981. "4QMes ar y el Libro de Noé." *Salmanticensis* 28: 195–232.
– 1992. *Qumran and Apocalyptic: Studies on the Aramaic Texts from Qumran*. STDJ 9. Leiden & Boston: Brill.

– 1999. "Interpretations of the Flood in the Dead See Scrolls," in *Interpretations of the Flood*, edited by F. García Martínez and G. P. Luttikhuizen, 86–108. TBN 1. Leiden & Boston: Brill.

García Martínez, F., and E. J. C. Tigchelaar. 1997–1998. *The Dead Sea Scrolls Study Edition*. 2 vols. Leiden & Boston: Brill.

Gätjie, H. 1971. *Koran und Koranexegese*. Zurich: Artemis.

Geiger, A. 1833. *Was hat Mohammed aus dem Judenthume aufgenommen?* Bonn: Baaden.

Gil, M. 1992. "The Creed of Abū 'Āmir." *IOS* 12: 9–47.

Gilliot, C. 1990. *Exégèse, langue et théologie en islam. L'éxègese coranique de Tabari*. EM 32. Paris: Vrin.

– 2006. "Creation of a Fixed Text," in *The Cambridge Companion to the Qur'ān*, edited by J. D. McAuliffe, 41–57. Cambridge & New York: Cambridge University Press.

– 2008. "Reconsidering the Authorship of the Qur'ān: Is the Qur'ān Partly the Fruit of a Progressive and Collective Work," in *The Qur'ān in Its Historical Context*, edited by S. G. Reynolds, 88–108. RSQ. London & New York: Routledge.

Goerke, A., and Schoeler, G. 2008. *Die ältesten Berichte über das Leben Muhammads*. Princeton: Darwin Press.

Goiten, S. D. 1955. *Jews and Arabs: Their Contact through the Ages*. New York: Schocken.

Goldschmidt, L. 1916. *Der Koran*. Berlin: Brandus.

Goldziher, I. 1889–90. *Muhammedanische Studien*. 2 vols. Halle: Niemeyer.

– 1920. *Die Richtungen der islamischen Koranauslegung*. Leiden: Brill.

González Ferrín, E. 2013. *La angustia de Abraham: los orígenes culturales del islam*. Cordova: Almuzara.

Griffith, S. H. 2008. "Christian Lore and the Arabic Qur'ān: The 'Companions of the Cave' in *Sūrat al-Kahf* and in Syriac Christian Tradition," in *The Qur'ān in Its Historical Context*, edited by S. G. Reynolds, 109–37. RSQ. London & New York: Routledge.

– 2012. *The Church in the Shadow of the Mosque: Christians and Muslims in the World of Islam*. Princeton, NJ: Princeton University Press.

– 2013. *The Bible in Arabic: The Scriptures of the 'People of the Book' in the Language of Islam*. Princeton, NJ: Princeton University Press.

Grypeou, E., M. N. Swanson, and D. Thomas, eds. 2006. *The Encounter of Eastern Christianity with Early Islam*. Leiden & Boston: Brill.

Guillaume, A. 1924. *The Traditions of Islam: An Introduction to the Study of the Hadith Literature*. Oxford: Oxford University Press.

– 1955. *The Life of Muhammad: A Translation of Isḥāq's* Sīrat Rasūl Allāh *with Introduction and Notes*. Oxford & New York: Oxford University Press.

Haider, N. 2011 *The Origins of the Shī'a: Identity, Ritual, and Sacred Space in Eighth-Century Kūfa*. Cambridge & New York: Cambridge University Press.

Hamdan, O. 2011. "The Second Maṣāḥif Project: A Step Towards the Canonisation of the Qur'an Text," in *The Qur'ān in Context: Historical and Literary Investigations into the Qur'ānic Milieu*, edited by in A. Neuwirth, M. Marx, and N. Sinai, 795–835. TSQ 6. Leiden & Boston: Brill.

Hannah, D. D. 2007. "The Book of Noah, the Death of Herod the Great, and the Date of the Parables of Enoch," in *Enoch and the Messiah Son of Man: Revisiting the Book of Parables*, edited by G. Boccaccini, 469–77. Grand Rapids, MI & Cambridge: Eerdmans.

Hanson, P. D. 1979. *The Dawn of Apocalyptic: The Historical and Sociological Roots of Jewish Apocalyptic Eschatology* (1975). Philadelphia: Fortress. 2nd ed.

Hawting, G. R. 1999. *The Idea of Idolatry and the Emergence of Islam: From Polemic to History.* Cambridge & New York: Cambridge University Press.
– 2000. *The First Dynasty of Islam: The Umayyad Caliphate AD 661–750* (1986). London & New York: Routledge. 2nd ed.
– 2004. *The Development of Islamic Ritual.* VCS. Aldershot: Ashgate.
Heschel, A. J. 2006. *Heavenly Torah: As Refracted through the Generations.* Edited and translated by G. Tucker with L. Levin. Foreword by S. Heschel. New York: Continuum.
Hirschberg, H. Z. 1939. *Jüdische und christliche Lehren im vor- und frühislamische Arabien.* Krakow: Polska Akademia.
Hirschfeld, H. 1878. *Jüdische Elemente im Korân: ein Beitrag zur Korânforschung.* Berlin: self-published by the author.
– 1886. *Beiträge zur Erklärung des Korân.* Leipzig: Schulze.
– 1902. *New Researches into the Composition and the Exegesis of the Qoran.* London: Royal Asiatic Society.
Horovitz, J. 1926. *Koranische Untersuchungen.* Berlin: De Gruyter.
Høvenhagen, J. 2011. "4QTanḥumim (4Q176): Between Exegesis and Treatise?," in *The Mermaid and the Partridge: Essays from the Cpenhagen Conference on Revising Texts from Cave 4,* edited by G. J. Brooke & J. Høvenhagen, 151–68. Leiden & Boston: Brill.
Hoyland, R. G. 1997. *Seeing Islam as Others Saw It: A Survey and Evaluation of Christian, Jewish and Zoroastrian Writings on Early Islam.* Princeton, NJ: Darwin Press.
– 2001. *Arabia and the Arabs: From the Bronze Age to the Coming of Islam.* London & New York: Routledge.
– 2015. In God's Path: *The Arab Conquests and the Creation of an Islamic Empire.* Oxford & New York: Oxford University Press.
Hughes, A. W. 2012. *Theorizing Islam: Disciplinary Deconstruction and Reconstruction.* Sheffield & Bristol, CT: Equinox.
Izutsu, T. 1959. *The Structure of Ethical Terms in the Qu'an: A Study in Semantics.* Tokyo: The Keyo Institute of Philological Studies.
Jeffery, A. 1937. *Materials for the History of the Text of the Qur'ān: The Old Codices.* Leiden & Boston: Brill.
– 2007. *The Foreign Vocabulary of the Qur'ān* (1938). New ed. by G. Böwering and J. D. McAuliffe. Leiden: Brill.
Jomier, J. 1959. *Bible et Coran.* Paris: Cerf.
de Jonge, M. and J. Tromp. 1997. *Life of Adam and Eve and Related Literature.* Sheffield, UK: Sheffield Academic Press.
Juynboll, G. H. A. 1983. *Muslim Tradition: Studies in Chronology, Provenance, and Authorship of Early Ḥadīth.* Cambridge: Cambridge University Press.
– 1996. *Studies on the Origins and Uses of Islamic Ḥadīth.* VCS. Aldershot: Ashgate.
Katsch, A. I. 1954. *Judaism in Islam: Biblical and Talmudic Backgrounds of the Koran and Its Commentaries.* New York: New York University Press.
King, D. 2009. "A Christian Qur'ān? A Study in the Syrian Background to the Language of the Qur'ān as Presented in the Work of Christoph Luxenburg." *JLARC* 3: 44–71.
Kister, M. J. 1980. *Studies in Jāhiliyya and Early Islam.* VCS. Aldershot: Ashgate.
– 1983. "The Sīrah Literature," in *Arabic Literature to the End of the Umayyad Period*, edited by A.F.L. Beeston, T. M. Johnstone, R.B. Serjeant & G. R. Smith, 352–67. Cambridge & New York: Cambridge University Press.
– 1990. *Society and Religion from Jāhiliyya to Islam.* VCS. Aldershot: Ashgate.

Koltun-Fromm, N. 1997. "Aphrahat and the Rabbis on Noah's Righteousness in Light of the Jewish-Christian Polemic," in *The Book of Genesis in Jewish and Oriental Christian Interpretation*, edited by J. Frishman and L. Van Rompay, 57–71. TEG 5. Leuven: Peeters.

Kropp, M. 2011. "Tripartite, but Anti-Trinitarian Formulas in the Qur'ānic Corpus, Possibly Pre-Qur'ānic," in *New Perspectives on the Qur'ān: The Qur'ān in Its Historical Context 2*, edited by S. G. Reynolds, 247–64. RSQ. London & New York: Routledge.

Kropp, M., ed. 2007. *Results of Contemporary Research on the Qur'ān: The Question of a Historio-Critical Text of the Qur'ān*. BTS 100. Beirut & Wurzburg: Orient-Institut Beirut & Ergon Verlag.

Kudelin, A. B. 2010 "*Al-Sīra al-Nabawiyya* by Ibn Iṣḥāq – Ibn Hišām: The History of the Texts and the Problem of Authorship." *MO* 16.1: 6–11.

Lammens, H. 1912. *Fatima et les filles de Mahomet*. Rome: Biblical Institute.

– 1914. *Le berceau de l'Islam. L'Arabie occidentale à la veille de l'hégire*. Rome: Biblical Institute.

– 1924. *La Mecque à la veille de l'hégire*. Beirut: Imprimerie Catholique.

– 1928. *L'Arabie occidentale avant l'hégire*. Beirut: Imprimerie Catholique.

Lecker, M. 1998. *Jews and Arabs in Pre- and Early Islamic Arabia*. VCS. Aldershot: Ashgate.

Levy-Rubin, M. 2011. *Non-Muslims in the Early Islamic Empire: From Surrender to Coexistence*. Cambridge & New York: Cambridge University Press.

Lings, M. 1983. *Muhammad: His Life Based on the Earliest Sources*. London: Allen & Unwin; New York: Inner Traditions International.

Lory, P. 2007a. "Abraham," in *Dictionnaire du Coran*, edited by M. A. Amir-Moezzi, 9–14. Paris: Robert Laffont.

– 2007b. "Élie," in *Dictionnaire du Coran*, edited by M. A. Amir-Moezzi, 244–6. Paris: Robert Laffont.

Lüling, G. 1974. *Über den Ur-Qur'ān: Ansätze zur Rekonstruktion vorislamischer christlicher Strophenlieder im Qur'ān*. Erlangen: H. Lüling.

Luxenberg, Ch. 2007. *The Syro-Aramaic Reading of the Koran: A Contribution to the Decoding of the Language of the Koran* (2000). English translation by the author after the 3rd German ed. (2007). Berlin: Schiler.

Machiela, D. A. 2009. *The Dead Sea Genesis Apocryphon: A New Text and Translation with Introduction and Special Treatment of Columns 13–17*. STDJ 79. Leiden & Boston: Brill.

Madelung, W. 1997. *The Succession to Muhammad: A Study of the Early Caliphate*. Cambridge & New York: Cambridge University Press.

Madigan, D. A. 2006. *The Qur'ān Self-Image: Writing and Authority in Islam's Scripture*. Princeton, NJ: Princeton University Press.

Magness, J. 2003. *The Archaeology of the Early Islamic Settlement in Palestine*. Winona Lake, IN: Eisenbrauns.

Malan, S. C. 1882. *The Book of Adam and Eve, also Called The Conflict of Adam and Eve with Satan: A Book of the Early Eastern Church, Translated from the Ethiopic with Notes from the Kufale, Talmud, Midrashim, and Other Eastern Works*. London: Williams and Norgate.

Margoliouth, D. S. 1905. *Mohammed and the Rise of Islam*. New York: Putnam.

– 1914. *The Early Development of Mohammedanism*. London: Williams & Norgate.

– 1924. *The Relations between Arabs and Israelites prior to the Rise of Islam*. London: Oxford University Press.

Marshall, D. 1999. *God, Muhammad and the Unbelievers: A Qur'ānic Study*. London: Curzon.

Marsham, A. 2009. *Rituals of Islamic Monarchy: Accession and Succession in the First Muslim Empire*. Edinburgh: Edinburgh University Press.

Martin, E. 2010. "The Literary Presentation of Noah in the Qur'ān," in *Noah and his Book(s)*, edited by M. E. Stone, A. Amihay, and V. Hillel, 253–75. EJL. Atlanta, GA: Society of Biblical Literature.
Massignon, L. 1963. "Élie et son rôle transhistorique, Khadiriyya, en Islam," in idem, *Opera Minora* 1, 142–61. Beirut: Dar al-Maaref.
Masson, D. 1958. *Le Coran et la révélation judéo-chrétienne*. 2 vols. Paris: Maisonneuve.
McAuliffe, J. D. 1991. *Qur'ānic Christians: An Analysis of Classical and Modern Exegesis*. Cambridge & New York: Cambridge University Press.
McVey, K., ed. 1994. *The Fathers of the Church: St Ephrem the Syrian – Selected Prose Works*. Washington: Catholic University of America.
McAuliffe, J. D., ed. 2001–6. *Encyclopaedia of the Qur'ān*. 6 vols. Leiden & Boston: Brill.
– 2006. *The Cambridge Companion to the Qur'ān*. Cambridge & New York: Cambridge University Press.
Micheau, F. 2012. *Les débuts de l'Islam. Jalons pour une nouvelle histoire*. ID. Paris: Téraèdre.
Milby, K. A. 2008. "The Making of an Image: The Narrative Form of Ibn Ishaq's *Sirat Rasul Allah*." M.A. thesis. Georgia State University.
Milik, J. T. 1976. *The Books of Enoch: Aramaic Fragments of Qumran Cave 4*. Oxford: Clarendon Press.
Mingana, A. 1916. "The Transmission of the Ḳur'ān." *JMEOS* 5: 25–47.
– 1927. "Syriac Influence on the Style of the Ḳur'ān." *Bulletin of the John Rylands Library Manchester* 11: 77–98.
– 1933–9. *Catalogue of the Mingana Collection of Manuscripts*. Cambridge: Heffer.
Motzki, H. 1991. *Die Anfänge der islamischen Jurisprudenz*. Stuttgart: Steiner.
Motzki, H., ed. 2000. *The Biography of Muḥammad: The Issue of the Sources*. Leiden & Boston: Brill.
Moubarac, Y. 1958. *Abraham dans le Coran*. Paris: Vrin.
Muir, W. 1896. *The Coran: Its Composition and Teaching, and the Testimony It Bears to the Holy Scriptures* (1878). London: SPCK. 2nd ed.
– 1912. *The Life of Mahomet from Original Sources* (1858–94). New revised ed. by Th. H. Weir. Edinburgh: Grant.
Nesner, J., W. S. Green, and E. S. Frerichs, eds. 1987 *Judaisms and Their Messiahs at the Turn of the Christian Era*. Cambridge & New York: Cambridge University Press.
Newby, G. D. 1989. *The Making of the Last Prophet: A Reconstruction of the Earliest Biography of Muhammad*. Columbia: University of South Carolina Press.
Neuwirth, A. 2007. *Studien zur Komposition der Mekkanische Suren: Die literarische Form des Koran – ein Zeugnis einer Historizitat?* (1981). Berlin & New York: de Gruyter. 2nd ed.
– 2010. *Der Koran als Text der Späatantike: Ein europäaischer Zugang*. Berlin: Verlag der Weltreligionen.
– 2011. *Der Koran: Frühmekkanischen Suren: Poetische Prophetie Handkommentar mit Übersetzung*. Berlin: Verlag der Weltreligionen.
– 2015. *Der Koran: Mittelmekkanischen Suren: Ein neues Gottesvolk Handkommentar mit Übersetzung*. Berlin: Verlag der Weltreligionen.
Neuwirth, A., M. Marx, and N. Sinai, eds. 2011. *The Qur'ān in Context: Historical and Literary Investigations into the Qur'ānic Milieu*. TSQ 6. Leiden & Boston: Brill.
Neuwirth, A., and N. Sinai. 2011. "Introduction," in *The Qur'ān in Context: Historical and Literary Investigations into the Qur'ānic Milieu*, edited by A. Neuwirth, M. Marx, and N. Sinai, 1–24. TSQ. Leiden & Boston: Brill.

Nevo, Y. D., and J. Koren. 2000. *Crossroads to Islam: The Origins of the Arab Religion and the Arab State*. Armherst, NY: Prometheus Books.

Nickelsburg, G. W. E. 2001. *1 Enoch 1: A Commentary on the Book of Enoch, Chapters 1–36; 81–108*. Edited by K. Baltzer. Hermeneia. Minneapolis: Fortress.

– 2005. *Jewish Literature between the Bible and the Mishnah: A Historical and Literary Introduction* (1981). Minneapolis: Fortress. 2nd ed.

– 2006. *Resurrection, Immortality, and Eternal Life in Intertestamental Judaism and Early Christianity* (1972). HTS 56. Cambridge, MA: Harvard University Press. 2nd edition.

Nickelsburg, G. W. E., and J. C. VanderKam. 2004. *1 Enoch: A New Translation*. Minneapolis: Fortress.

— 2012. *1 Enoch 2: A Commentary on the Book of Enoch, Chapters 37–82*. Edited by K. Baltzer. Hermeneia. Minneapolis: Fortress.

Noja Noseda, S. 1974. *Mahometto, profeta dell'Islam*. Fossano: Esperienze.

Nöldeke, Th. 1863. *Das Leben Muhammeds*. Hanover: Rümpler.

Nöldeke, Th., F. Schwally, G. Bergsträsser, and O. Pretzl. 2013. *The History of the Qur'ān*. Translated by W. H. Behn. Leiden & Boston: Brill.

Noth, A. 1973. "Quellenkritische Studien zu Themen, Formen und Tendenzen frühislamischer Geschichtsüberlieferung." PhD dissertation, University of Bonn.

Ohlig, K.-H., and G. R. Puin, eds. 2010. *The Hidden Origins of Islam: New Research into Its Early History*. Amherst, NY: Prometheus Books.

Orlov, A. A. 2004. "Noah's Younger Brother Revisited: Anti-Noachic Polemics and the Date of 2 (Slavonic) Enoch." *Henoch* 26: 1–15.

O'Shaughnessy, Th. J. 1948. *The Koranic Concept of the Word of God*. Rome: Biblical Institute.

– 1969. *Muhammad's Thoughts on Death: A Thematic Study on the Qur'anic Data*. Leiden: Brill.

– 1985. *Creation and the Teaching of the Qur'an*. Rome: Biblical Institute.

Paret, R. 1982. *Der Koran: Übersetzung*. Stuttgart: Kohlhammer. 2nd edition.

Penn, M. Ph. 2015a. *Envisioning Islam: Syriac Christianity and the Early Muslim World*. DRLAR. Philadelphia: University of Pennsylvania Press.

– 2015b. *When Christians First Met Muslims: A Sourcebook of the Earliest Syriac Writings on Islam*. Berkeley: University of California Press.

Peters, D. M. 2008. *Noah Traditions in the Dead Sea Scrolls: Conversations and Controversies of Antiquity*. EJL 26. Atlanta, GA: Society of Biblical Literature.

Peters, F. E. 1994. *Muhammad and the Origins of Islam*. Albany, NY: State University of New York Press.

Pettipiece, T. 2009. *Pentadic Redaction in the Manichaean Kephalaia*. NHMS. Leiden & Boston: Brill.

Pohlmann, K.-F. 2013. *Die Entstehung des Korans: Neue Erkenntnisse aus Sicht der historisch-kritischen Bibelwissenschaft* (2012). Darmstadt: Wissenschaftliche Buchgesellschaft. 2nd ed.

Porter, P. A. 1983. *Metaphors and Monsters: A Literary-Critical Study of Daniel 7 and 8*. BOT 20. Lund: Gleerup.

Powers, David S. 2011. *Muḥammd Is Not the Father of Any of Your Men: The Making of the Last Prophet*. DRLAR. Philadelphia: University of Pennsylvania Press.

– 2014. *Zayd*. DRLAR. Philadelphia: University of Pennsylvania Press.

de Prémare, A.-L.

2002. *Les fondations de l'islam. Entre écriture et histoire*. Paris: Seuil.

2004. *Aux origines du Coran. Questions d'hier, approaches d'aujourd'hui*. ID. Paris: Téraèdre.

2010. "'Abd al-Malik b. Marwān and the Process of the Qur'ān's Composition," in *The Hidden Origins of Islam: New research into Its Early History*, edited by K.-H. Ohlig and G. R. Puin, 189–221. Armherst, NY: Prometheus Books.

Rahman, F. 2009. *Major Themes in the Qur'ān* (1980). Chicago: University of Chicago Press. 2nd ed.

Räisänen, H. 1971. *Das koranische Jesusbild: ein Beitrag zur Theologie des Korans*. Helsinki: Finnische Gesellschaft für Missiologie und Ökumenik.

Reeves, J. C. 1993. "Utnapishtim in the Book of Giants?" *JBL* 112: 110–5.

Reeves, J. C., ed. 2003. *Bible and Quran: Essays in Scriptural Intertextuality*. Atlanta, GA: Society of Biblical Literature.

Retsö, J. 2003. *The Arabs in Antiquity: Their History from the Assyrians to the Umayyads*. London & New York: RoutledgeCurzon.

Reynolds, G. S. 2010. *The Qur'ān in Its Biblical Subtext*. RSQ. London & New York: Routledge.

– 2011a. "Le problème de la chronologie du Coran." *Arabica* 58: 477–502.

Reynolds, G. S., ed. 2008. *The Qur'ān in Its Historical Context*. RSQ. London & New York: Routledge.

– 2011b. *New Perspectives on the Qur'ān: The Qur'ān in Its Historical Context 2*. RSQ. London & New York: Routledge.

Rippin, A. 1988. *Approaches to the History of the Interpretation of the Qur'ān*. Oxford: Clarendon.

– 1999. *The Qur'ān: Style and Contents*. VCS. Aldershot: Ashgate.

– 2001. *The Qur'ān and Its Interpretative Tradition*. VCS. Aldershot: Ashgate.

– 2008. "Syriac in the Qur'ān: Classical Muslim Theories," in *The Qur'ān in Its Historical Context*, edited by S. G. Reynolds, 249–61. RSQ. London: Routledge.

Rippin, A., ed. 1999. *The Qur'ān: Formative Interpretation*. VCS. Aldershot: Ashgate.

– 2006. *The Blackwell Companion to the Qur'ān*. Oxford: Blackwell.

Robinson, Ch. F. 2003. *Islamic Historiography*. Cambridge & New York: Cambridge University Press.

– 2004. *Empire and Elites after the Muslim Conquest: The Transformation of Northern Mesopotamia*. Cambridge & New York: Cambridge University Press.

– 2005. *'Abd al-Malik*. MMW. Oxford: OneWorld.

Robinson, N. 1996. *Discovering the Qur'an: A Contemporary Approach to a Veiled Text*. London: SCM.

Rodinson, M. 1961. *Mahomet*. Paris: Seuil.

Roggema, B. 2009. *The Legend of Sergius Baḥīrā: Eastern Christian Apologetics and Apocalyptic in Response to Islam*. Leiden & Boston: Brill.

Rubin, U. 1975. "Pre-Existence and Light: Aspects of the Concept of Nūr Muḥammad." *IOS* 5: 62–119. Reprinted in idem, *Muhammad the Prophet and Arabia* (VCS; Aldershot: Ashgate, 2011), No. IV.

– 1995. *The Eye of the Beholder: The Life of Muhammad as Viewed by the Early Muslims*. Princeton, NJ: Darwin Press.

– 1998. *The Life of Muḥammad*. VCS. Aldershot: Ashgate.

– 1999. *Between Bible and Qur'ān: The Children of Israel and the Islamic Self-Image*. Princeton, NJ: Darwin Press.

– 2006. "Prophets and Prophethood," in *The Blackwell Companion to the Qur'ān*, edited by A. Rippin, 234–47. Oxford: Blackwell.

– 2014. "The Seal of the Prophets and the Finality of Prophecy: On the Interpretation of the Qur'ānic Sūrat al-Aḥzāb (33)." *Zeitschrift der Deutschen Morgenländischen Gesellschaft* 164.1: 65–96.
Rubin, U., ed. 1998. *The Life of Muḥammad*. The Formation of the Classical Islamic World. VCS. Aldershot: Ashgate.
Rudolph, W. 1922. *Die Anhängigkeit des Korans von Judentum und Christentum*. Stuttgart: Kohlhammer.
Sacchi, P. 1990. *L'apocalittica giudaica e la sua storia*. BCR. Brescia: Paideia.
Sadeghi, B. 2013. "Criteria for Emending the Text of the Qur'ān," in *Law and Tradition in Classical Islamic Thought*, edited by. M. Cook, N. Haider, I. Rabb, and A. Sayeed, 21–41. PSITLH. New York: Palgrave Macmillan.
Sadeghi, B., and M. Goudarzi. 2012 "Ṣan'ā' 1 and the Origins of the Qur'ān." *Der Islam* 87: 1–129.
Said, E. W. 1978. *Orientalism: Western Conceptions of the Orient*. London & New York: Routledge–Kegan Paul & Vintage Books.
Schacht, J. 1950. *The Origins of Muhammadan Jurisprudence*. Oxford: Clarendon.
– 1964. *Introduction to Islamic Law*. Oxford: Clarendon.
Schapiro, I. 1907. *Die aggadische Elemente im Erzählender Teil des Korans*. Leipzig: Fock.
Schöller, M. 1998. *Exegetisches Denken un Prophetenbiographie: eine quellenkritische Analyse der Sira-Überlieferung zu Muhammads Konflikt mit den Juden*. Wiesbaden: Harrassowitz.
Segovia, C. A. 2011. "Noah as Eschatological Mediator Transposed: From 2 Enoch 71–72 to the Christological Echoes of 1 Enoch 106:3 in the Qur'ān." *Henoch* 33.1: 130–45.
– 2012. "Thematic and Structural Affinities between 1 Enoch and the Qur'ān: A Contribution to the Study of the Judaeo-Christian Apocalyptic Setting of the Early Islamic Faith," in *The Coming of the Comforter: When, Where, and to Whom? Studies on the Rise of Islam and Various Other Topics in Memory of John Wansbrough*, edited by C. A. Segovia and B. Lourié, 231–67. OJC 3. Piscataway, NJ: Gorgias Press.
– 2013. *Por una interpretación no cristiana de Pablo de Tarso: El redescubrimiento contemporáneo de un judío mesiánico*. Foreword by A. Piñero. Self-published by the author on iTunes Store.
– 2014. "Discussing/subverting Paul: Polemical Re-readings and Competitive Supersessionist Misreadings of Pauline Inclusivism in Late Antiquity: A Case Study on the Apocalypse of Abraham, Justin Martyr, and the Qur'ān." Paper presented to the 3rd Nangeroni Meeting of the Enoch Seminar: "Re-reading Paul as a Second-Temple Jewish Author" (Rome; June 22–6, 2014). To be published in *Paul the Jew: A Conversation between Pauline and Second Temple Scholars*, edited by C. A. Segovia and G. Boccaccini. Minneapolis: Fortress, 2015.
– 2015a. "A Messianic Controversy behind the Making of Muḥammad as the Last Prophet?" Paper presented to the 4th Nangeroni Meeting of the Enoch Seminar / 1st Nangeroni Meeting of the Early Islamic Studies Seminar: "Early Islam: The Sectarian Milieu of Late Antiquity?" (Milan; June 15–19, 2015).
– 2015b. "'Those on the Right' and 'Those on the Left': Rereading Qur'ān 56.1–56 (and the Founding Myth of Islam) in Light of Apocalypse of Abraham 21–2." *Studia Islamica*. (Forthcoming.)
– 2015c. "En torno a Mahoma como mesías: una nueva mirada a las raíces cristianas del islam." *Erebea* 5 (Forthcoming.)
– 2016. "Identity Politics and Scholarship in the Study of Islamic Origins: The Inscriptions of the Dome of the Rock as a Test Case," in *Identity, Politics, and Scholarship: The Study of*

*Islam and the Study of Religions*, edited by M. Sheddy. CE. Sheffield, UK, and Bristol, CT. Equinox. (Forthcoming.)

Segovia, C. A., and B. Lourié, eds. 2012. *The Coming of the Comforter: When, Where, and to Whom? Studies on the Rise of Islam and Various Other Topics in Memory of John Wansbrough*. OJC 3. Piscataway, NJ: Gorgias Press.

Sfar, M. 2000. *Le Coran est-il authentique?* Paris: self-published by the author.

Shahid, Irfan. 1984a. *Rome and the Arabs: A Prolegomenon to the Study of Byzantium and the Arabs*. Washington, DC: Dumbarton Oaks.

– 1984b. *Byzantium and the Arabs in the Fourth Century*. Washington, DC: Dumbarton Oaks.

– 1989. *Byzantium and the Arabs in the Fifth Century*. Washington, DC: Dumbarton Oaks.

– 1995. *Byzantium and the Arabs in the Sixth Century*. Washington, DC: Dumbarton Oaks.

Sharon, M. 1988. "The Birth of Islam in the Holy Land," in *The Holy Land in History and Thought*, edited by M. Sharon, 225–35. Leiden & Boston: Brill.

Shoemaker, Stephen J. 2012. *The Death of a Prophet: The End of Muhammd's Life and the Beginnings of Islam*. DRLAR. Philadelphia: University of Pennsylvania Press.

Shoshan, B. 2004. *Poetics of Islamic Historiography: Deconstructing Ṭabarī's History*. Leiden & Boston: Brill.

Sidersky, D. 1933. *Les origines des légendes musulmanes dans le Coran et dans les vies des prophètes*. Paris: Geuthner.

Sinai, M. 2009. *Fortschreibung un Auslegung: Studien zur frühen Koraninterpretation*. Wiesbaden: Harrassovitz.

– 2014. "When did the consonantal skeleton of the Quran reach closure? Part I." *BSOAS* 77.2: 273–92.

De Smet, M. D., G. Callatay, and J. M. F. van Reeth, eds. 2004. *Al-Kitāb: La sacralité du text dans le monde de l'islam*. Leuven: Belgian Society of Oriental Studies.

De Smet, M. D., and M.-A. Amir-Moezzi 2014. *Controverses sur les écritures canoniques de l'islam*. Paris: Cerf.

Speyer, H. 1931. *Die biblischen Erzählungen im Qoran*. Gräfenheinichen: Schulze.

Spitaler, A. 1935. Die Verszählung des Koran im islamischer Überlieferung. Munich: Bayerischen Akademie der Wissenschaften.

Sprenger, A. 1869. *Das Leben un die Lehre des Mohammad* (1861–5). 3 vols. Berlin: Nicolai. 2nd ed.

St Clair Tisdall, W. 1905. *The Original Sources of the Qur'ān*. London: SPCK.

Stewart, D. J. 2010. "Notes on Medieval and Modern Emendations of the Qur'ān," in *The Qur'ān in Its Historical Context*, edited by S. G. Reynolds, 225–48. RSQ. London & New York: Routledge.

Stone, M. E. 1999. "The Axis of History at Qumran," in *Pseudepigraphic Perspectives: The Apocrypha and Pseudepigrapha in Light of the Dead Sea Scrolls*, edited by E. G. Chazon and M. E. Stone, 134–49. STDJ 31. Leiden & Boston: Brill.

Stuckenbruck, L. T. 1997. *The Book of Giants from Qumran: Texts, Translations and Commentary*. Tübingen: Mohr Siebeck.

– 2004. "The Origins of Evil in Jewish Apocalyptic Tradition: The Interpretation of Gen 6:1–4 in the Second and Third Centuries B.C.E.," in *The Fall of the Angels*, edited by C. Auffarth and L. T. Stuckenbruck, 87–118. Leiden & Boston: Brill.

– 2007. *1 Enoch 91–108*. CEJL. Berlin & New York: De Gruyter.

Szilágyi, K. 2009. "A Prophet like Jesus: Christians and Muslims Debating Muḥammad's Death," *JSAI* 36: 131–71.

Tesei, T. 2013. "Deux légendes d'Alexandre le Grand dans le Coran. Une étude sur les origines du texte sacré arabe et sur ses liens avec les littératures chrétiennes et juives de l'Antiquité Tardive." PhD dissertation, Sapienza University of Rome/INALCO.
Talgam, R. 2014. *Mosaics of Faith: Floors of Pagans, Jews, Samaritans, Christians, and Muslims in the Holy Land*. Jerusalem & University Park, PA: Yad Ben-Zvi Institute & Pennsylvania State University Press.
Tamer, G. 2008. *Zeit und Gott: Hellenistische Zeitvorstellungen in der altarabischen Dichtung und im Koran*. Berlin & New York: De Gruyter.
Thomas, D. 1992. *Anti-Christian Polemic in Early Islam: 'Isā al-Warrāq's "Against the Trinity."* COP 45. Cambridge & New York: Cambridge University Press.
Thomas, D., ed. 2001. *Syrian Christians Under Islam: The First Thousand Years*. Leiden & Boston: Brill.
Tiller, P. A. 1993. *A Commentary on the Animal Apocalypse of 1 Enoch*. EJL. Atlanta: Society of Biblical Literature.
Torrey, Ch. C. 1892. *The Commercial-Theological Terms in the Koran*. Leiden: Brill.
Tottoli, R. 1999. *I profeti biblici nella tradizione islamica*. Brescia: Paideia.
– 2002. *Biblical Prophets in the Qur'ān and Muslim Literature*. Translated by M. Robertson. RSQ. London & New York: Routledge.
Tucker, W. F. 2008. *Mahdis and Millenarians: Shī'ite Extremists in Early Muslim Iraq*. Cambridge & New York: Cambridge University Press.
Turner, J. D. 1986. "Sethian Gnosticism: A Literary History," in *Nag Hammadi, Gnosticism and Early Christianity*, edited by C. W. Hendrik and R. Hodgson Jr., 55–86. Peabody, MA: Hendrickson.
Van Bladel, K. 2008. "The Alexander Legend in the Qur'ān 18:83–102," in *The Qur'ān in Its Historical* Context, edited by G. S. Reynolds, 175–2013. RSQ. London & New York: Routledge.
Van Lindt, P. 2002. "The Religious Terminology in the Nag Hammadi Texts and in Manichaean Literature," in *The Nag Hammadi Texts in the History of Religions*, edited by S. Giversen, T. Petersen and J. P. Sørensen, 191–7. HFS 26. Copenhagen: The Royal Danish Academy of Sciences and Letters.
Van Reeth, J. M. F. 2011a. "La typologie tu prophète selon le Coran: le cas de Jésus," in *Figures bibliques en Islam*, edited by G. Dye and F. Nobilio, 81–105. Fernelmont, BE: EME.
– 2011b. "Ville céleste, ville sainte, ville idéale dans la tradition musulmane." *Acta Orientalia Belgica* 24: 121–31.
– 2012. "Who Is the 'Other' Paraclete?," in *The Coming of the Comforter: When, Where, and to Whom? Studies on the Rise of Islam and Various Other Topics in Memory of John Wansbrough*, edited by C. A. Segovia and B. Lourié, 423–52. OJC 3. Piscataway, NJ: Gorgias Press.
Van Rompay, L. 1997. "Antiochene Biblical Interpretation: Greek and Syriac," in *The Book of Genesis in Jewish and Oriental Christian Interpretation*, edited by J. Frishman and L. Van Rompay, 103–23. TEG 5. Leuven: Peeters.
Versteegh, C. H. M. 1993. *Arabic Grammar and Qur'ānic Exegesis in Early Islam*. Leiden & Boston: Brill.
Vollers, K. 1906. *Volkssprache und Schriftsprache im alten Arabien*. Strasbourg: Tübner.
Waldstein, M., and F. Wisse. 1995. *The Apocryphon of John: Synopsis of Nag Hammadi Codices II,1; III,1; and IV,1 with BG 8502,2*. NHMS. Leiden & Boston: Brill.
Wansbrough, J. 2004. *Quranic Studies: Sources and Methods of Scriptural Interpretation* (1977). Foreword, translation, and expanded notes by A. Rippin. Amherst, NY: Prometheus Books.

– 2006. *The Sectarian Milieu: Contents and Composition of Islamic Salvation History* (1978). Foreword, translation, and expanded notes by G. Hawting. Amherst, NY: Prometheus Books.

Ward, W. D. 2014. *Mirage of the Saracen: Christians and Nomads in the Sinai Peninsula in Late Antiquity*. Berkeley: University of California Press.

Wasserstrom, S. M. 1995. *Between Muslim and Jew: The Problem of Symbiosis in Early Islam*. Princeton, NJ: Princeton University Press.

Watt, W. M. 1953. *Muhammad at Mecca*. Oxford: Clarendon.

– 1956. *Muhammad at Medina*. Oxford: Clarendon.

– 1961. Muhammad: Prophet and Statesman. Oxford: Oxford University Press.

– 1973. *The Formative Period of Islamic Thought*. Edinburgh: Edinburgh University Press.

Weil, Gustav. 1843. *Mohammed der Prophet: sein Leben un seine Lehre*. Stuttgart: Metzler.

– 1845. *Biblische Legenden der Muselmänner*. Frankfurt a. M.: Rütten.

– 1878. *Historisch-Kritische Einleitung in den Koran* (1844). Bielefeld-Leipzig: Velhagen & Klasing. 2nd ed.

Welch, A. T. 2000. "Formulaic Features of the Punishment Stories," in *Literary Structures of Religious Meaning in the Qur'an*, edited by I. J. Boullata, 77–116. CSQ. Richmond, UK: Curzon.

Wensinck, A. J. 1927. *A Handbook of Early Muhammadan Tradition*. Leiden: Brill.

– 1928. *Mohammed en de Joden te Medina* (1908). Leiden: Brill. 2nd ed.

– 1932. *The Muslim Creed: Its Genesis and Historical Development*. Cambridge: Cambridge University Press.

Westermann, C. 1991. *Basic Forms of Prophetic Speech*. Translated by H. C. White. Foreword by G. M. Tucker. Cambridge and Louisville, KY: The Lutterworth Press and Westminster/John Knox Press.

Wheeler, B. M. 2002. *Prophets in the Quran: An Introduction to the Qur'an and Muslim Exegesis*. London: Continuum.

2006. "Nuh," in *The Qur'an: An Encyclopedia*, edited by O. Leaman, 463–4. London: Routledge.

Wild, S., ed. 1996. *The Qur'ān as Text*. IPTSTS 27. Leiden & Boston: Brill.

Wise, M. 2000. "A Study of 4Q491c, 4Q471b, 4Q427 7 and 1QH[a] 25:35–26:10." *DSD* 7: 173–219.

Witztum, J. 2011a. "Joseph among the Ishmaelites: Q 12 in Light of Syriac Sources," in *New Perspectives on the Qur'ān: The Qur'ān in Its Historical Context 2*, edited by G. S. Reynolds, 425–48. RSQ. London & New York: Routledge.

– 2011b. "The Syriac Milieu of the Qur'*ān: The Recasting of Biblical Narratives*." PhD dissertation, Princeton University.

Wüstenfeld, F. 1858–60. كتاب سيرة رسول الله *: Das Leben Muhammeds nach Muhammed Ibn Ishâk bearbeitet von Abd el-Malik Ibn Hischâm*. 3 vols. Göttingen: Dieterich.

Yarbro Collins, A., and J. J. Collins. 2008. *King and Messiah as Son of God: Divine, Human, and Angelic Messianic Figures in Biblical and Related Literature*. Grand Rapids, MI & Cambridge: Eerdmans.

Zeitlin, I. M. 2007. *The Historical Muhammad*. Cambridge, MA: Polity Press.

Zellentin, M. H. 2013. The Qur'ān's Legal Culture: *The Didascalia Apostolorum as a Point of Departure*. Tübingen: Mohr Siebeck.

Zwemer, S. M. 1912. *The Moslem Christ: An Essay on the Life, Character, and Teachings of Jesus Christ according to the Koran and Orthodox Tradition*. Edinburgh: Oliphand, Anderson & Ferrier; New York: American Tract Society.

# Index of Ancient Writings

## Hebrew Bible

Genesis, 28, 85, 87, 99, 110
5:22, 99
5:24, 99
6:8–9:28, 28
8:21–2, 85
9:8–17, 85
9:20–7, 87
18, 87
49, 110

Leviticus, 111
4:3, 111
4:5, 111
4:16, 111

Numbers, 110–12
12:6–8, 112
24:15–19, 110–11
24:17, 110

Deuteronomy, 111
18:18, 111

2Samuel, 87, 110
7, 110
18, 87

2Kings, 99
2:1, 99
2:3, 99
2:5, 99
2:11, 99

Isaiah, 110, 112–13, 116
11:1–9, 110
42:1–9, 112
45:1, 110
49:1–6, 112
49:1, 116
50:4–9, 113
52:13–53:12, 113
54:7–10, 113
Jeremiah, 110
23:5–6, 110
27:6, 110

Ezekiel, 112
1:5, 112

Amos, 110
9:11, 110

Micah, 110
5:2–5, 110

Malachi, 99
3:1, 99
4:5–6, 99

Zechariah, 110–11
4:12, 111
6:11, 111
9:9–10, 110
11–13, 110

Psalms, 112
45:6, 112

Proverbs, 113
8:22–31, 113

Daniel, 111–12, 123
7:9, 112
7:13–14, 123
8:15, 112
9:21, 112
9:25–6, 111
12, 112

## Septuagint


Numbers, 110
24:17, 110


## New Testament


Matthew, 21, 85, 99, 105–6, 111–13, 118, 120
1:6, 111
1:18–19, 24
1:20, 24
2:1–6, 111
5–7, 111
5:17–19, 112
9:27, 111
10, 111
10:32–3, 113
10:34–6, 105
11:10, 99
11:14, 99
12:22–3, 111
13, 111
17:9–13, 99
21:9, 111
21:11, 112
21:15, 111
24:26–7, 113
24:37–9, 85, 106, 120
25:31–46, 113
26:64, 113
28:16, 113

Mark, 111, 113
2:12, 113
4:38, 111
8:31, 113
8:38, 113
9:12, 113
9:17, 111
9:31, 113
9:38, 111
10:17, 111
10:20, 111
10:33–5, 113
10:35, 111
10:45, 113
10:47–8, 111
11:1–10, 111
12:14, 111
12:19, 111
12:32, 111
12:35–7, 111
13:1, 111
13:26, 113
14:62, 113

Luke, XV, 22, 24, 85, 106, 111–13, 118 121
1–2, 24
1:32–3, 111
2:4–5, 111
3:31, 112
4:16–21, 111
4:24, 112
7:16, 112
7:40, 111
8:24, 111
9:33, 111
9:38, 111
10:25, 111
11:45, 111
12:8–9, 113
12:13, 111
17:22–37, 113
17:26, 22, 85, 106, 121
18:1–8, 113
18:18, 111
19:38, 111
19:39, 111
20:21, 111
20:28–9, 111
21:7, 111
22:69, 113
24:19, 112

John, 106, 111–13
1:38, 111
1:49, 111

3:2, 111
3:13–16, 113
3:26, 111
4:19, 112
4:31, 111
5:25–9, 00
6:25, 111
7:42, 00
9:2, 111
9:17, 112
9:35–9, 113
11:8, 111
12:13, 111
12:23–41, 113
13:31, 113
14:16, 106
14:26, 106
15:26, 106
16:7, 106

Acts, XV, 111–13
2:17–18, 112
2:30, 111
3:22, 112
7:37, 112
7:56, 113
10:38, 112
13:16–41, 111
15:16 111

Romans, 111
1:3–4, 111

1Corinthians, 111
15:23–8, 111

1Thessalonians, 111
1:10, 111
2:19–20, 111
3:13, 111
4:13–18, 111
5:1–11:17, 111

2Timothy, 111
2:8, 111

Hebrews, 111
3–10, 111

2Peter, 85, 106, 121
3:5–7, 85, 106, 121
3:10–12, 85, 106, 121

Revelation, 24, 111, 113, 118
1:7, 113
1:14, 24
3:3, 113
3:7, 111
5:5, 111
22:16, 111

## Apocrypha and Pseudepigrapha

Apocalypse of Abraham, 15, 24, 118
11:2, 24
21–2, 15
21:7, 15
22:1, 15
22:3–5, 15

Apocalypse of Noah, 23, 26–7

2Baruch, 110
72:2–73:1, 110

1Elijah, 99

2Elijah, 99

1Enoch, 15, 21–4, 26–7, 85, 88–9, 99, 104, 106, 111–13, 115, 117, 118
1–36 (= Book of the Watchers), 15, 22
1–5, 15
2:1–5:4, 15
6–11, 23, 26–7
10, 21
10:1–3, 22, 27
10:3, 22
10:11–11:2, 113
12–36, 99

14:20, 118
37–71 (= Book of Parables; or, the Similitudes of Enoch), 26, 99, 112
38:2, 112
39:6, 112
40:5, 112
46, 21
46:1, 118
46:2–4, 112
48–51, 21
48:2, 112
48:3, 115
48:6, 115
48:10, 112
49:2, 112
49:4, 112
51:3, 112
51:5, 112
52:6, 112
52:9, 112
53:6, 112
55:4, 112
60:1–10, 22–3, 27
60:23–5, 22–3, 27
60:23, 23
60:24–5, 23
61–2, 21
61:8, 112
61:10, 112
62:1, 112
62:7, 112, 115
62:9, 112
62:14, 112
63:11, 112
65:1–69:1, 22, 27
65:1, 22
65:2, 23
65:3, 22
65:4–5, 22
65:6–8, 22
65:9, 22
65:10–12, 22
65:11, 22
65:12, 23
67:1–3, 23
67:4–69:1, 23
68:1, 89
69:26–7, 112
70:1–2, 23
70:1, 23, 112
71:14, 23, 112
71:17, 23, 112
79–80, 99
81–2, 99
83–90 (= Book of Dreams; or, Enoch's Dream Visions), 99
83–4, 23, 27
83, 23
84, 23
86:1, 111
86:3, 111
89:1–8, 23, 27
89:1, 23
90:21, 111
91–105 (= Epistle of Enoch), 99
93:4–5, 23–4, 27
93:4, 22–3, 85, 106, 120
93:5, 22
93:8–10, 24
93:8, 23, 27
104:2, 112
104:4, 112
104:6, 112
106–7 (= Birth of Noah), 21–3, 26–7, 104
106:1–3, 22
106:2–3, 22, 117
106:2, 22, 24
106:3, 22, 24–5, 89, 118
106:4–7, 118
106:4, 22, 24
106:8–12, 22
106:10–12, 118
106:10–11, 22
106:13–107:2, 22
106:16–18, 118
106:18, 24
107:2, 22, 24, 118
107:3, 22

2Enoch, 23, 88, 99, 118
21:2–22:10, 23
22, 99
71–2, 23

71:18, 24
72:6, 24

3Enoch, 99
3–15, 99

4Ezra, 110, 112, 116
6–7, 112
12:32, 110
13:26, 116
13:52, 116

Joseph and Aseneth, 24, 118
22:7, 24

Jubilees, 89, 111
3:2–11, 116
10:14, 89
31:14–18, 111

Psalms of Solomon, 110
17, 110

Sirach, 111, 116
24:1–3, 116
45:6–22, 111
50:1, 111

Testaments of the Twelve Patriarchs, 88, 111
Testament of Levi, 111
14:3, 111
18:2–5, 111

## Dead Sea Scrolls

Aramaic Levi Document, 89, 111–12
4:1–6:5, 111
6:5, 112
10, 111
10:10, 89
frag. 5, 111

Commentary on Habakuk (4QpHab), 112

Commentary on Isaiah (4QpIsa), 110–11

Damascus Document (CD), 110–11

Genesis Apocryphon (1QapGen), 22–4, 27, 87, 89, 118
1–18, 27
1–17, 27
1–5, 23
1–5:25, 23
2, 24
5–18, 23
5–17, 23
5:29, 89
6:9–22, 89
7:16–19, 89
12:19–15:21, 89

Rule of the Community, 100–12
1QS, 110–11
1QSa, 110–12
1QSb, 110–11

War Scroll (1QM), 110–11

1Q19–19bis, 22–3, 27, 111

4Q174, 110–12

4Q175, 111

4QTanḥûmîm (4QTanḥ), 83, 120
9–13, 85, 120

4Q206, 26

4Q246, 112

4Q252, 110

4Q258, 111

4Q285, 110–11

4Q491, 112

4Q191 11 i, 112

4Q521, 111

4Q534, 22–3, 27, 89
1:4–8, 89
1:9–10, 27
1:9, 89

4Q536, 22–3, 27, 89
frags. 2+3 l.8–9, 89

4Q540, 111

4Q541, 111

6Q8, 27

11Q19, 111

## Targumim

*Targum Pseudo-Jonathan*, 110
*ad* Genesis 49:11, 110

## Rabbinic Literature

Mishnah and Talmudim

*Sanhedrin*, 89
108a-b, 89

Midrashim

*Genesis Rabbah*, 89, 121
25:1, 121
30:7, 89

*Leviticus Rabbah*, 89
27:5, 89

*Pirqê de-Rabbî ’Elî‘ezer*, 89, 121
8, 89
22, 89
23, 121

*Sefer ha-Yašar*, 89

## Other Early Jewish Texts

Philo
*De praemiis et poenis*, 110
*ad* Numbers 24:17, 110

## Early Christian Literature

NT Apocrypha

Arabic Gospel of the Infancy, 14, 24, 105
1:2, 14, 24

Protoevangelium of James, 24, 118
19:2, 24

Patristic Literature

Ephraem
*Commentary on Genesis*, 89–90, 121
6.9, 89
*Commentary on Hebrews*, 96
*ad* 1:2, 96

*Hymns on Faith*, 89
56:2, 89
*Hymns on Paradise*, 96
15, 96
*Hymns on Virginity*, 96
7:1, 96

Jacob of Serugh
*Homilies*, 00

Narsai
*Homily on the Flood*, 89–90, 121
235–50, 121
235–40, 121
249, 89

Tertulian
*De Idolatria*, 90
24, 90

Theophilus of Antioch
*Ad Autolycum*, 89
3:19, 89

Gnostic Texts

Apocryphon of John, 89–90
NHC II, 89–90
29:2–3, 89
29:3–5, 89
29:5, 90
NHC III, 89–90
37:19–21, 89
37:21–2, 89–90
BG 8502, 89–90
72:16–73.2, 89
73:2–3, 89
73:3, 90

Concept of Our Great Power, 89
38:26–8, 89

Other Early Christian Texts

Cave of Treasures, 89

Struggle of Adam and Eve with Satan, 89–90, 122
3.2, 90, 122
3.4, 90, 122

## Muslim Literature

Qur'ān

Uthmanic recension
1:2, 97
2:47, 97
2:122, 97
2:131, 00
2:251, 97
3, 119
3:7, 12, 111
3:33, 31, 49, 97, 118
3:42, 97
3:46, 14–15, 24–5, 118
3:96, 97
3:97, 97
3:108, 97
3:144, 16, 58, 60, 104
4, 119
4:163–5, 118
4:163, 29, 31, 49, 118–19
4:164, 31, 119
5:20, 97
5:28, 97
5:115, 97
6, 119
6:8–10, 58, 104
6:8, 60
6:9, 60
6:10, 58, 60, 103
6:45, 97
6:71, 97
6:84–90, 118
6:84, 31, 49, 118
6:85, 99
6:86, 97
6:87, 31, 118

6:88, 31, 119
6:90, 97
6:162, 97
7, 119
7:26–58, 56
7:36, 15
7:54, 97
7:59–64 [= QNN I], 30, 35–48, 55–6, 61–3, 118–19
7:59–63, 56
7:59–60, 63
7:59, 30, 31, 35, 40, 55–6, 61, 64, 90
7:60, 30–1, 35, 40, 55, 58, 60–1, 90, 103
7:61–3, 30, 55–6, 63–4
7:61–2, 66
7:61, 31, 35, 41, 56, 61, 97
7:62, 31, 36, 41, 61
7:63, 31, 36, 42, 61, 104
7:64, 31, 36, 42, 55–6, 61, 63–4
7:65–93, 56
7:67, 97
7:80, 97
7:85–93, 119
7:94–102, 56
7:104, 97
7:121, 97
7:140, 97
7:182–8, 56–7, 59
7:184, 58, 60, 103
7:188, 58, 60, 104
9, 119
9:70, 31, 49, 118–19
10, 120
10:6, 15
10:10, 97
10:37, 12, 97
10:68–70, 104
10:71–4 [= QNN II], 30, 35–48, 56, 61–2, 65, 118–19
10:71–2, 30, 65
10:71, 31, 35, 40, 56–7, 60–1, 66
10:72, 29–31, 35, 40, 104
10:73–4, 30, 65
10:73, 30, 31, 35, 41, 61
10:74, 36, 41, 61
10:94–109, 56–7, 59
11, 70, 74, 120
11:12–24, 56–7
11:12, 58, 60, 104
11:13, 60
11:25–49 [= QNN III], 19, 30, 35–48, 57, 61–2, 67, 81, 118–19
11:25–34, 57, 67, 70, 75, 81
11:25–6, 30
11:25, 30–1, 35, 40, 61, 67, 70, 75, 81
11:26, 30–1, 35, 40, 57, 61, 70, 75, 81, 90
11:27, 30–1, 35, 41, 57–8, 60–1, 70, 75, 81, 90, 104
11:28–31, 30, 57
11:28, 30–1, 36, 41, 61, 70, 75, 82
11:29, 31, 36, 42, 61, 71, 76, 82
11:30, 31, 36, 42, 61, 71, 76, 82
11:31, 31, 36, 43, 61, 71, 76, 82
11:32, 31–1, 37, 43, 57, 61, 71, 76, 82
11:33–4, 30, 57
11:33, 31–1, 37, 43, 61, 71, 76, 82
11:34, 68, 75, 81
11:35–9, 71
11:35–7, 57
11:35, 67–8, 70
11:36–48, 30, 57, 67, 75, 81
11:36–41, 67, 70, 74, 76
11:36–7, 67, 70
11:36, 31, 37, 44, 61, 68, 74, 76, 83
11:37–9, 00
11:37, 67
11:38–48, 67
11:38–41, 70
11:38–9, 57
11:38, 37, 44, 58, 60–1, 74, 77, 83, 89, 103
11:39, 37, 44, 61, 74, 77, 83
11:40–8, 57
11:.40, 38, 45, 61, 67, 75, 77, 83, 108
11:41, 38, 45, 57, 61, 75–7, 83
11:42–7, 67–8, 70, 76
11:42, 31, 38, 45, 57, 61, 76–7, 83
11:43, 30–1, 38, 46, 57, 61, 77, 83
11:44, 38, 46, 57, 61, 77, 84
11:45–7, 30, 57, 59
11:45, 31, 38, 46, 57, 61, 78, 84, 111
11:46, 39, 47, 57, 61, 67, 78, 84
11:47, 31, 39, 47, 57, 61, 78, 84
11:48, 39, 47, 57, 61, 74–6, 78, 81, 84

11:49, 29–30, 39, 47, 57, 59–60, 62, 67–8, 70, 81, 84–5, 99, 106, 117
11:84–95, 119
12:22, 120
12:104, 97
14, 119
14:9–15, 118
14:9–13, 119
14:9, 31, 49, 118–19
14:10, 31
14:11, 00
14:12, 31
14:13, 31
14:15, 31
15:70, 97
16:81, 15
16:103, 58, 60, 104
17, 119
17:3, 31, 49, 118–19
17:17, 50, 118
18:60–82, 122
18:83–102, 14
19, 119
19:29–30, 14–15, 24–5
19:56–7, 99
19:58, 32, 50, 118–19
21, 119
21:71, 97
21:76–7, 118
21:76, 32, 50, 118
21:77, 50
21:85–6, 99
21:91, 97
21:107, 97
22, 119
22:42, 29, 32, 50, 118–19
23, 120
23:23–30 [= QNN IV], 30, 35–48, 57, 61–2, 65, 118, 119
23:23–6, 65
23:23–5, 58
23:23, 30, 32, 35, 40, 57, 61, 65, 90
23:24–5, 57
23:24, 30, 32, 35, 40, 58, 60–1, 90, 104
23:25, 32, 35, 41, 56–7, 60–1, 90, 103
23:26–9, 58
23:26, 30, 32, 36, 41, 57, 61
23:27–9, 30, 57
23:27, 30, 36, 42, 61, 65
23:28, 36, 42, 62
23:29, 36, 43, 61
23:30, 30, 37, 43, 61
24:41, 15
24:44, 15
24:46, 15
25, 119
25:1, 97
25:4–6, 12
25:37, 32, 50, 118–19
25:41, 29, 32, 119
26, 119–20
26:16, 97
26:23, 97
26:47, 97
26:77, 97
26:84, 00
26:98, 97
26:105–22 [= QNN V], 30, 35–48, 58, 61–2, 66, 118–19
26:105, 32, 35, 40, 61, 66
26:106–10, 58, 66
26:106, 32, 35, 40, 61
26:107, 32, 35, 41, 62
26:108, 32, 36, 41, 61, 66
26:109, 32, 35, 41, 61
26:110, 32, 36, 42, 61, 66
26:111, 30, 32, 36, 43, 58, 61, 66, 90
26:112–15, 66
26:112, 30, 32, 37, 43, 58, 61
26:113, 32, 37, 43, 61
26:114, 32, 37, 43, 61
26:115, 32, 37, 44, 61, 104
26:116, 30, 32, 37, 44, 58, 61, 66
26:117–18, 30, 58, 66
26:117, 32, 37, 44, 61
26:118, 32, 37, 44, 61
26:119–20, 30, 58, 66
26:119, 37, 44, 61
26:120, 38, 45, 61
26:121–2, 30, 58, 66
26:121, 38, 45, 61

26:122, 38, 45, 61
26:125–6, 66
26:127, 97
26:131, 66
26:143–4, 66
26:145, 97
26:150, 66
26:162–3, 66
26:164, 97
26:165, 97
26:176–90, 119
26:178–9, 66
26:180, 97
26:221–7, 103
27:8, 97
27:44, 97
28:30, 97
29, 119
29:6, 97
29:10, 97
29:14–15, 118
29:14, 32, 50, 119
29:15, 32, 50, 97
29:28, 97
30:22, 97
32:2, 97
33, 119
33:7, 29, 32, 51, 104, 118–19
37, 119
37:11–74, 92, 98
37:11–72, 98
37:36, 58, 60, 103
37:69–81, 98
37:73–4, 92, 95–6, 98–9
37:73, 98
37:74, 98
37:75–82, 118
37:75–7, 98
37:75, 32, 51
37:76–7, 100
37:76, 51
37:77, 51
37:78–81, 92–3, 99–101
37:78–80, 92–8
37:78, 51, 92, 94–6, 98, 100–1, 122
37:79, 51, 92–4, 96–8, 100, 122
37:80, 51, 92–4, 98, 100
37:81, 32, 51, 92, 94, 100, 119
37:82, 51
37:83–6, 97
37:87, 97
37:88–98, 97
37:104–17, 98
37:105, 92–4
37:107, 100
37:108–11, 92–3, 100
37:108, 94–6
37:109, 93, 94, 97–9
37:110, 93–4
37:111, 93–4
37:112–13, 100
37:113, 93, 95
37:114–18, 100
37:118–44, 98
37:119–22, 92, 100
37:119, 93–6
37:120, 93–4, 97–8
37:121, 93–4
37:122, 93–4
37:123, 99
37:127–8, 92, 99
37:127, 99
37:129–32, 92–3, 99
37:129, 93, 94–6, 98
37:130, 93–4, 97–9
37:131, 93–3, 100
37:132, 93–4, 99
37:182, 97
38, 119
38:11, 32, 118–19
38:87, 97
39:75, 97
40, 119
40:5, 32, 52, 112, 118–19
40:30, 52
40:31, 52
40:64–6, 97
41:2–3, 12
41:3, 12
41:9, 97
42, 119
42:13, 29, 32, 52, 118–19
43:3–4, 12
43:46, 97

43:56, 95–6
44:14, 58, 60, 103
44:32, 97
45:16, 97
45:36, 97
50, 119
50:12, 32, 52, 118–19
51, 119
51:39, 58, 103
51:46, 52, 118–19
51:52, 58, 103
52:29, 58, 60, 103
53, 119
53:52, 52, 118–19
53:56, 12
54, 119
54:1–8, 64
54:9–17 [= QNN VI], 30, 35–48, 58, 61–2, 64, 118–19
54:9, 30, 33, 35, 40, 56, 58, 60–1, 64, 90, 103
54:10, 30, 35, 40, 58, 61
54:11–14, 30, 58, 64
54:11–12, 108
54:11, 30, 35, 41, 61
54:12, 36, 41, 61
54:13, 36, 42, 61
54:14, 36, 42, 61, 109
54:15–17, 30, 58, 64
54:15, 36, 43, 61
54:16–17, 52
54:16, 37, 43, 61
54:17, 37, 43, 61
54:21–2, 58
54:30, 58
54:32, 58
54:39–40, 58
54:43–55, 58
54:51, 58
56:1–56, 15
56:13–14, 95–6
56:13, 95
56:14, 95–6
56:39, 95
56:40, 95–6
56:49, 95–6
56:78, 12
56:80, 97
57, 119
57:26, 33, 52, 118–19
57:27, 33
59:16, 97
66, 119
66:10, 33, 53, 61, 118–19
68:51, 58, 60, 103
68:52, 97
69:41–2, 103
69:42, 103
69:43, 97
71 [= QNN VII], 59, 68, 70, 84, 119–20
71:1–28 [= QNN VII], 30, 35–48, 61–2, 118–19
71:1–4, 78
71:1, 30, 33, 35, 40, 59, 61, 78
71:2–22, 54
71:2–4, 30, 59
71:2, 33, 35, 40, 61, 78
71:3, 33, 35, 41, 61, 66, 78
71:4, 30, 33, 36, 41, 59, 61, 78
71:5–28, 30, 59, 67–8, 70–1, 76, 78
71:5–27, 108
71:5, 33, 36, 42, 61, 71, 79
71:6, 33, 36, 42, 61, 71, 79
71:7, 33, 36, 43, 59, 61, 72, 79, 90
71:8, 33, 37, 43, 61, 72, 79
71:9, 33, 37, 43, 61, 72, 79
71:10–23, 59
71:10–20, 30, 59
71:10, 33, 37, 43, 61, 72, 79
71:11, 33, 37, 44, 61, 72, 79
71:12, 33, 37, 44, 61, 72, 79
71:13, 33, 37, 44, 61, 72, 79
71:14, 33, 37, 44, 61, 72, 80
71:15, 33, 37, 44, 61, 72, 80
71:16, 33, 38, 45, 61, 73, 80
71:17, 33, 38, 45, 61, 73, 80
71:18, 33, 38, 45, 61, 73, 80
71:19, 33, 38, 46, 61, 73, 80
71:20, 33, 38, 46, 61, 73, 80
71:21–3, 30, 59
71:21, 33, 38, 46, 61, 73, 80
71:22, 33, 39, 47, 61, 73, 80
71:23, 33, 39, 47, 61, 73, 80, 90
71:24, 33, 39, 47, 61, 73, 81

71:25, 30, 33, 39, 47, 59, 61–2, 74, 81
71:26–8, 59
71:26, 33, 39, 48, 62, 74, 81
71:27, 33, 39, 48, 62, 74, 81
71:28, 33, 39, 48, 62, 74, 81
75:17–18, 12
77:16, 95
77:17, 95–6
81:27, 97
81:29, 97
83:6, 97
85:22, 12

Codex Ṣan'ā' 1 (DAM 01–27.1), 98–9
fol. 29B [= Q 37:118–44], 98
l. 2 [= 37:120], 98
l. 8 [= 37:130], 98

Ibn Mas'ūd, 98–9
[37:109], 98
[37:120], 98
[37:123], 99
[37:130], 98

Ubayy b. Ka'b, 98–9
[37:109], 98
[37:120], 98
[37:130], 98

Other Muslim Texts

al-Azraqī
*Aḫbār Makka*, 108

al-Bayhaqī
*Dalā'il an-Nubuwwa*, 115

al-Ḥalabī
*al-Sīra al-Ḥalabiyya*, 115

al-Ḫarkūšī
*Šaraf an-Nabiyy*, 115, 117

Ibn Abī Dāwūd
*Kitāb al-Maṣāḥif*, 98

Ibn al-Ǧawzī
*al-Wafā bi-Aḥwāl al-Muṣṭafā*, 115

Ibn Hišām
*Sīra* (ed. Wüstenfeld), 8, 14, 16, 18, 69, 88, 102–8, 119
100–2, 104
100–1, 105
101–2, 104
101, 105–6
102, 105
106, 105
149–50, 106
150–5, 107
155, 107
171, 104
183, 103
186, 103
232–3, 103
237, 106
262, 103

Ibn Isḥāq
*Kitāb al-Mubtada'*, 108
*Kitāb al-Mab'aṯ*, 108
*Kitāb al-Maġāzī*, 108

Ibn Šahrāšūb
*Manāqib Āl Abī Ṭālib*, 117

al-'Iṣāmī
*Simṭ an-Nuǧūm al-'Awālī*, 115, 117

al-Maǧlisī
*Biḥār al-Anwār*, 117

al-Maqdisī
*Kitāb al-Bad' wa-t-Tārīḫ*, 108

al-Mas'ūdī
*Iṯbāt al-Waṣiyya li-l-Imām 'Alī b. Abī Ṭalib*, 116

as-Suyūṭī
*al-La'ālī al-Maṣnū'a fī-l-Aḥādīṯ al-Mawḍū'a*, 115

aṭ-Ṭabarī
*Ǧāmiʿ al-Bayān fī Tafsīr al-Qurʾān*, 67, 108, 120
*ad* 12:22, 120
*Tārīḫ ar-Rusul wa-l-Mulūk*, 108

aṯ-Ṯaʿlabī
*Qiṣaṣ al-Anbiyāʾ*, 115

az-Zurqānī
*Šarḥ ʿalā al-Mawāhib al-Laduniyya li-l-Qasṭallānī*, 115

# Index of Ancient and Modern Authors


Adang, Camila, 4
Addas, Claude, 54
Ahituv, Shmuel, 4
Amir-Moezzi, Mohammad Ali, 4, 6–7
Andrae, Tor, 3, 122
Aphrahat, 88
Arnaldez, Roger, 4
Aubaile-Sallenave, Françoise, 122
Avni, Gideon, 8
Azaiez, Mehdi, 7
al-Azmeh, Aziz, 6, 11
al-Azraqī, Abū-l-Walīd, 108

El-Badawi, Emran Iqbal, 6, 9, 122
al-Bakkā'ī, Ziyād, 108
Barth, Jacob, 95, 100
Bashear, Suliman, 4–7
Baur, Ferdinand-Christian, 3
Baxter, Wayne, 23
al-Bayhaqī, Abū Bakr, 115
Beaucamp, Joëlle, 8
Becker, Carl Heinrich, 2
Bedjan, Paul, 121
Bell, Richard, 3
Bellamy, James A., 122
Benjamins, Hendrik S., 88
Berg, Herbert, 7, 16, 120
Bergsträsser, Gotthelf, 2
Berkey, Jonathan P., 7
Berque, Jacques, 4
Blachère, Régis, 3
Black, Matthew, 26
Blenkinsopp, Joseph, 27
Bonner, Michael, 6
Boullata, Issa J., 6
Bowersock, Glen W., 8
Bowman, John, 122
Boyarin, Daniel, 112, 121, 123
Briquel-Chatonnet, Françoise, 8
Brinner, William M., 54
Brock, Sebastian, 88
Brockopp, Jonathan E., 6
Brodeur, Patrice, XVI
Brown, Brian A., 54
Buitelaar, Marjo, 4
Burton, John, 4

Caetani, Leone, 3
Calder, Norman, 6
Callatay, Godefroid, 7
Cameron, Averil, 8
Casanova, Paul, 106
Chabbi, Jacqueline, 54
Charles, Robert Henry, 21
Charlesworth, James H., 110
Clippinger, David, 11
Cohen, H. Hirsch, 121
Collins, John J., 123
Cook, David B., 7
Cook, Michael, 4–6, 10
Crone, Patricia, 4–6
Cuypers, Michel, 7, 119

Dabashi, Hamid, 4
Dakake, Maria Massi, 6
Denis, Albert-Marie, 26
Déroche, François, 4, 6, 10
Dijkstra Jetse H. F., 8
Dillmann, Christian Friedrich August, 23, 26
Dimant, Devorah, 26–7
Doehnert, Albrecht, XVI
Donner, Fred M., 1, 4–6
Dye, Guillaume, XVI, 7, 13–14, 119–20

Eger, A. Asa, 7
Ephraem, 88–91, 96, 121
Erder, Yoram, 122
Ewald, Georg Heinrich August, 3

Firestone, Reuven, 4
Fisher, Greg, 8
Fitzmyer, Joseph A., 118
Flügel, Gustav, 2
Foucault, Michel, 12
Fowden, Garth, 4, 6
Fraenkel, Carlos, XVI
Frerichs, Ernest, 110

Frishman, Judith, 121
Gallez, Édouard-Marie, 7
Gajda, Iwona, 8
García Martínez, Florentino, 23, 26–7, 54, 120
Gätjie, Helmut, 4
Geiger, Abraham, 9
Gil, Moshe, 90
Gilliot, Claude, 4, 28, 122
Gobillot, Geneviève, 7
Goerke, Andreas, 6
Goiten, Solomon D., 3
Goldschmidt, Lazarus, 3
Goldziher, Ignaz, 2–4
González Ferrín, Emilio, 7
Goudarzi, Mohsen, 98
Green, William S., 110
Griffith, Sidney H., 6, 8, 91, 122
Grypeou, Emmanouela, 6
Guillaume, Alfred, 3, 123

Haider, Najam, 6
al-Ḫalabī, Nūr al-Dīn, 115
Hamdan, Omar, 10, 118
Hannah, Darrel D., 26
Hanson, Paul D., 27
al-Ḫarkūšī, Abū Sa'd, 115–17, 123
Hawting, Gerald R., 1, 4–6
Heschel, Abraham Joshua, 121
Hinds, Martin, 4
Hirschberg, Haim Zeel (Joachim Wilhelm), 3
Hirschfeld, Hartwig, 3
Horovitz, Josef, 3
Høvenhagen, Jesper, 85
Hoyland, Robert G., 4
Hughes, Aaron W., 7

Ibn Abī Dāwūd, 'Abd Allāh, 98
Ibn Bukayr, Yūnus, 108, 123
Ibn al-Faḍl, Salama, 108
Ibn Hišām, Abū Muḥammad, 16, 18–19, 102–4, 106, 108, 116–17
Ibn Isḥāq, Muḥammad, 18–19, 102–4, 106, 108–9, 114, 116–17, 123
Ibn al-Ǧawzī, Abū-l-Farāǧ, 115–16
Ibn Ka'b, Ubayy, 98–9
Ibn Mas'ūd, 'Abd Allāh, 98–9
Ibn Saba', 'Abd Allāh, 123
Ibn Sa'd, Muḥammad, 10
Ibn Ṯābit, Zayd, 13
Ibn Šahrāšūb, Muḥammad b. 'Alī, 117
Isaac, Ephraim, 26
al-'Iṣāmī, 'Abd al-Malik, 115–17
Izutsu, Toshihiko, 4

Jacob of Serugh, 89, 91
Jeffery, Arthur, 3, 98–9
Jomier, Jacques, 4
Jones Nelson, Alissa, XVI
Juynboll, Gautier H. A., 4

Katsch, Abraham I., 3
Kattan, Assaad Elias, XVI
King, Daniel, 96, 122
Kister, Meir J., 4, 123
Koltun-Fromm, Naomi, 88
Koren, Judith, 7
Kropp, Manfred, 1, 7, 28, 123
Kudelin, Alexander B., 123

Lammens, Henri, 3
Lecker, Michael, 4
Levy-Rubin, Milka, 6
Lings, Martin, 4
Lory, Pierre, 120
Lourié, Basil, 7, 15
Lüling, Günter, 4, 6
Luxenberg, Christoph, 7, 92, 94–8, 100–1, 122

Machiela, Daniel A., 87
Madelung, Wilferd F., 4
Madigan, Daniel A., 6
Magness, Jodi, 8
al-Maǧlisī, Muḥammad Bāqir, 117
Malan, Solomon C., 122
al-Maqdisī, Abū Muḥammad, 108
Margoliouth, David Samuel, 3
Marshall, David, 4
Marsham, Andrew, 6
Martin, Erica, 54, 59, 67–8, 120
Martin, François, 26
Marx, Michael, 5–6
Massignon, Louis, 122

Masson, Denise, 3
al-Mas'ūdī, Abū-l-Ḥasan, 116
McAuliffe, Jane Damen, 4, 6, 10
McVey, Kathleen, 121
Micheau, Françoise, 7, 120
Milby, Katherine A., 123
Milik, Józef Tadeusz, 23
Mingana, Alphonse, 3, 118, 122
Mojaddedi, Jawid, 6
Motzki, Harald, 4–6, 123
Moubarac, Youakim, 4
Muir, William, 2

Narsai of Edessa, 89–91
Neusner, Jacob, 110
Neuwirth, Angelika, 5–6, 9–10, 13, 118
Nevo, Yehuda D., 1, 7
Newby, Gordon Darnell, 4, 108–9, 123
Nickelsburg, George W. E., 23, 26–7, 89, 118, 120, 123
Nobilio, Fabien, 7
Noja Noseda, Sergio, 4
Nöldeke, Theodor, 2–3, 120
Noth, Albrecht, 4

Ohlig, Karl-Heinz, 7
Oren, Eliezer, 4
Orlov, Andrei A., 118
O'Shaughnessy, Thomas J., 3–4

Paret, Rudi, 95
Penn, Michael Philip, 6
Peters, Dorothy M., 21, 26–7, 85, 121
Peters, Francis E., 4
Pettipiece, Timothy, 119
Philo of Alexandria, 110
Pohlmann, Karl-Friedrich, 7, 28
Porter, Paul A., 23
Powers, David S., 7, 16
de Prémare, Alfred-Louis R., 7, 10, 28, 97, 118, 122–3
Pretzl, Otto, 2
Puin, Gerd R., 1, 7, 122

Rahman, Fazlur, 4
Räisänen, Heikki, 4
Reeves, John C., 6, 9, 27
Retsö, Jan, 8
Reynolds, Gabriel Said, XVI, 7, 9, 28, 120–1
Rippin, Andrew, 4–6, 122
Robin, Christian, 8
Robinson, Chase F., 6, 10, 123
Robinson, Neal, 4
Rodinson, Maxime, 4
Roggema, Barbara, 6
Rubin, Uri, 1, 4–6, 115–17, 119, 122–3
Rudolph, Wilhelm, 3

Sacchi, Paolo, 23
de Sacy, Antoine Issac Silvestre, 2
Sadeghi, Behnam, 98, 122
Said, Edward W., 10
Schacht, Joseph, 3
Schapiro, Israel, 3
Schoeler, Georg, 6
Schöller, Marco, 4
Schwally, Friedrich, 2
Segovia, Carlos A., 1, 7, 13–15, 105, 121, 123
Sfar, Mondher, 7
Shahid, Irfan, 8
Sharon, Moshe, 120
Shoemaker, Stephen J., 2, 7, 15
Shoshan, Boaz, 7
Sidersky, David, 3
Sinai, Nicolai, 5, 6, 9, 13
De Smet, M. Daniel, 7
Smith, Henry Preserved, 2
Speyer, Heinrich, 3
Spitaler, Anton, 3
Sprenger, Aloys, 2
St Clair Tisdall, William, 3
Stewart, Devin J., 95, 100, 122
Stone, Michael E., 27, 118
Stuckenbruck, Loren T., 27, 118
as-Suyūṭī, Ǧalāl al-Dīn, 115–16
Swanson, Mark N., 6
Szilágyi, Kristina, 123

aṭ-Ṭabarī, Abū Ǧa'far, 67, 94, 108
aṯ-Ṯa'labī, Abū Isḥāq, 108, 115–16
Talgam, Rina, 8
Tamer, Georges, XVI, 7
Tertulian, 90

Tesei, Tommaso, XVI, 121–2
Theophilus of Antioch, 89
Thomas, David R., 4, 6
Tigchelaar, Eibert J. C., 120
Tiller, Patrick A., 23
Torrey, Charles Cutler, 3
Tottoli, Roberto, 4, 6, 9, 15, 54
Tucker, William F., 6
Turner, John D., 121

Uhlig, Siegbert, 26

Valéry, Paul, 11
Van Bladel, Kevin, 14
Van Lindt, Paul, 90
Van Reeth, Jan M. F., 1, 7, 105, 120, 123
Van Rompay, Lucas, 88
VanderKam, James C., 118, 120, 123
Versteegh, Cornelis, 4
Vollers, Karl, 3

Wansbrough, John, 1, 4–6, 9, 15, 28, 69, 102, 106, 118–19
Ward, Walter D., 8
Wasserstrom, Steven M., 4
Watt, William Montgomery, 3–4
Weil, Gustav, 9, 2
Welch, Alford T., 54
Wensinck, Arent Jan, 3
Westermann, Claus, 119
Wheeler, Brian M., 54
Wild, Stefan, 4, 9, 14
Wise, Michael, 112
Witztum, Joseph, 122
Wüstenfeld, Ferdinand, 103

Yarbro Collins, Adela, 110, 112

Zeitlin, Irving M., 6
Zellentin, Holger M., 7
az-Zurqānī, Muḥammad, 115–16
Zwemer, Samuel Marinus, 3

www.ingramcontent.com/pod-product-compliance
Lightning Source LLC
Chambersburg PA
CBHW020412230426
43664CB00009B/1265